FRANCE

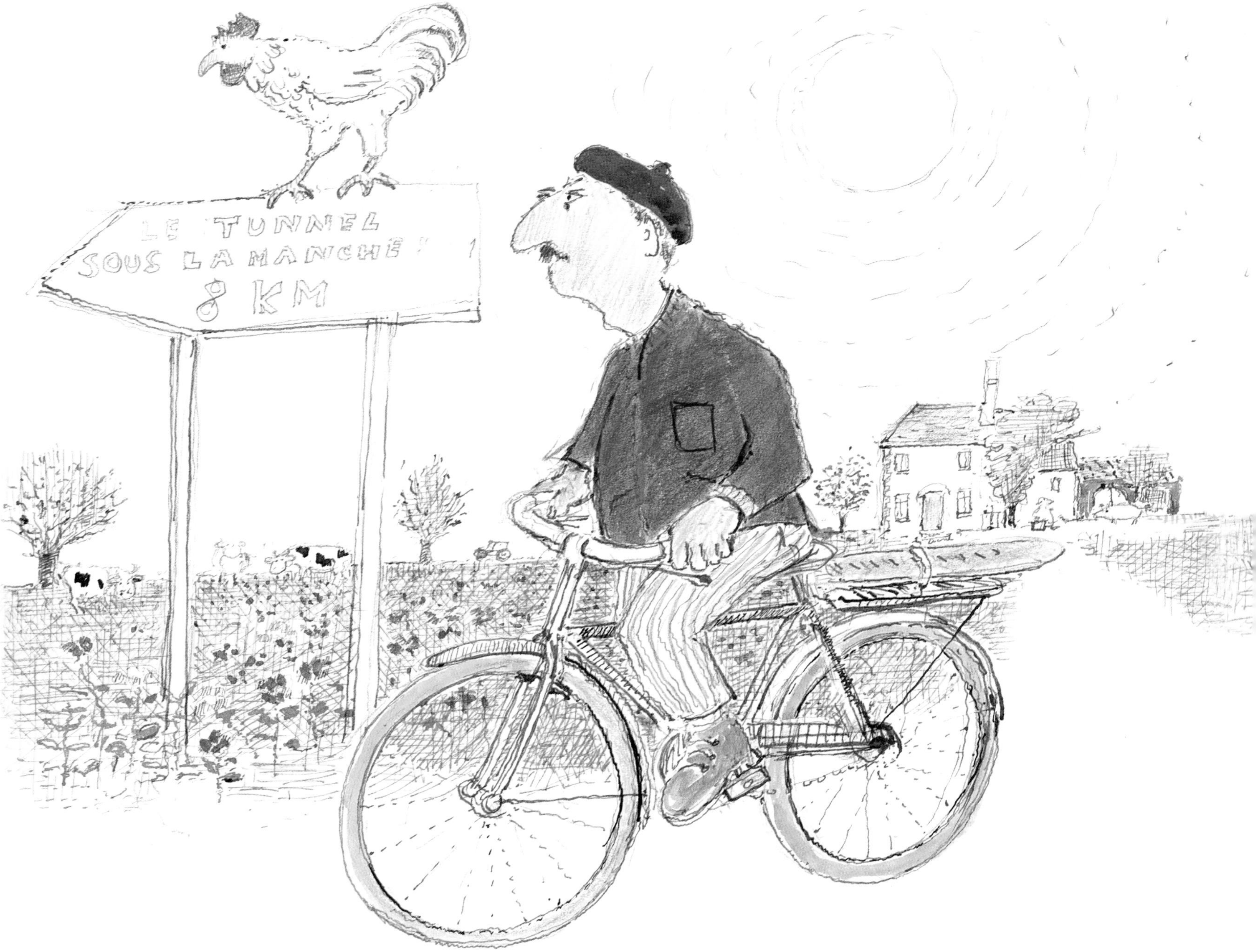
LE TUNNEL
SOUS LA MANCHE
8 KM

John Burningham's
FRANCE

A DK INK BOOK
DK PUBLISHING, INC.

DK Publishing, Inc.
95 Madison Avenue
New York, New York 10016

Visit us on the World Wide Web at http://www.dk.com

Library of Congress Cataloging-in-Publication Data
Burningham, John
        John Burningham's France
                    p.   cm.
        "A DK Ink book"
        ISBN 0-7894-2557-2
            1. France--Social life and customs--20th century--Humor.
2. French wit and humor, Pictorial. 3. National characteristics,
French--Humor. I. Title
DC33.7.B85   1998   98-3523
944.081--dc21   CIP

Printed and bound in Singapore.

First American Edition, 1998
10 9 8 7 6 5 4 3 2 1

Published simultaneously in the United Kingdom by Jonathan Cape, London.

'Well, how can you expect any kind of agreement from Frenchmen in a country where there are 270 different kinds of cheese?'

Charles de Gaulle

The King then asked the name of the castle he saw near him: he was told it was called Azincourt. 'Then,' said he, 'since all battles should bear the name of the fortress nearest to the spot where they were fought, this battle shall from henceforth, and for ever, bear the name of AZINCOURT.'

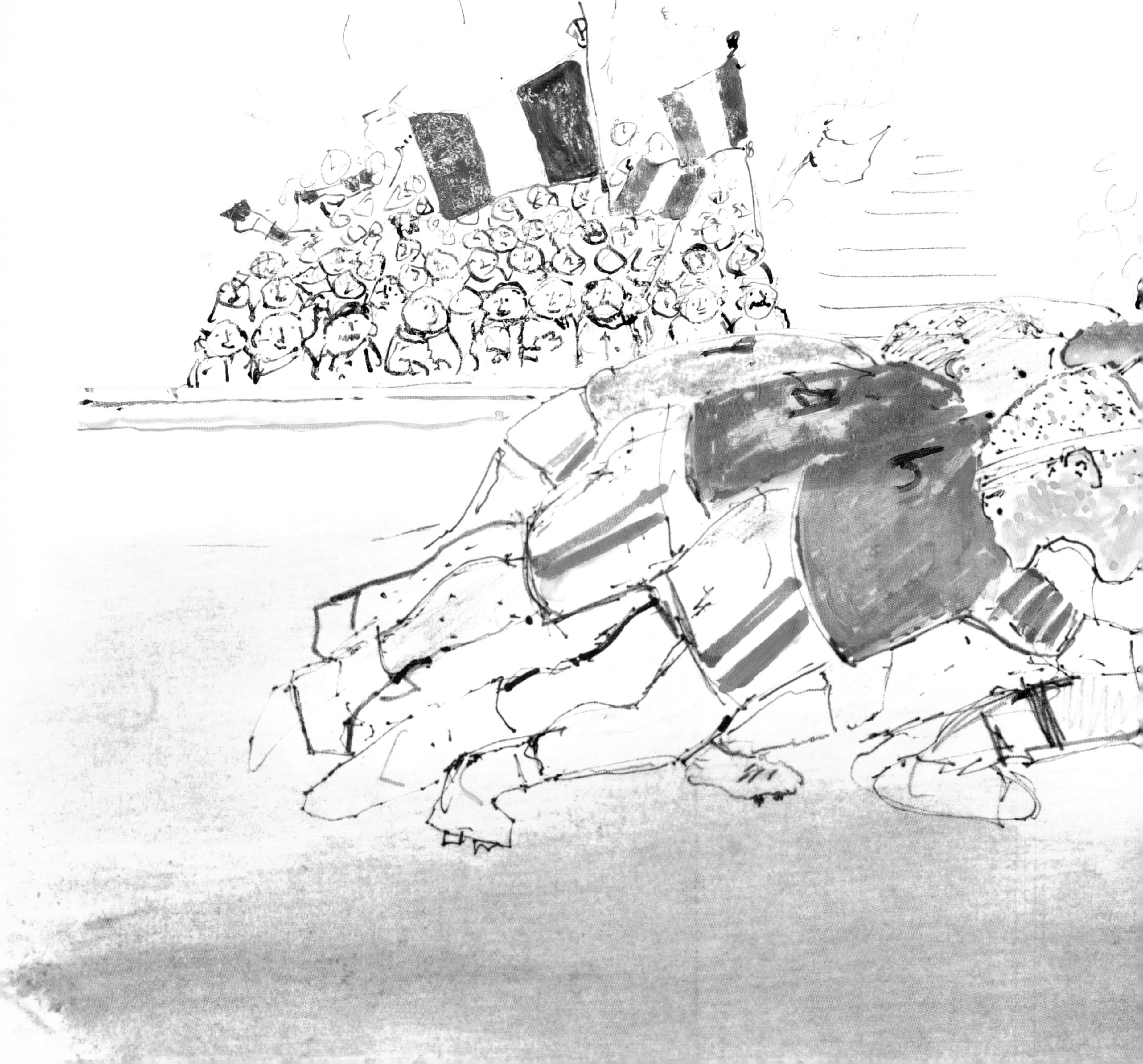

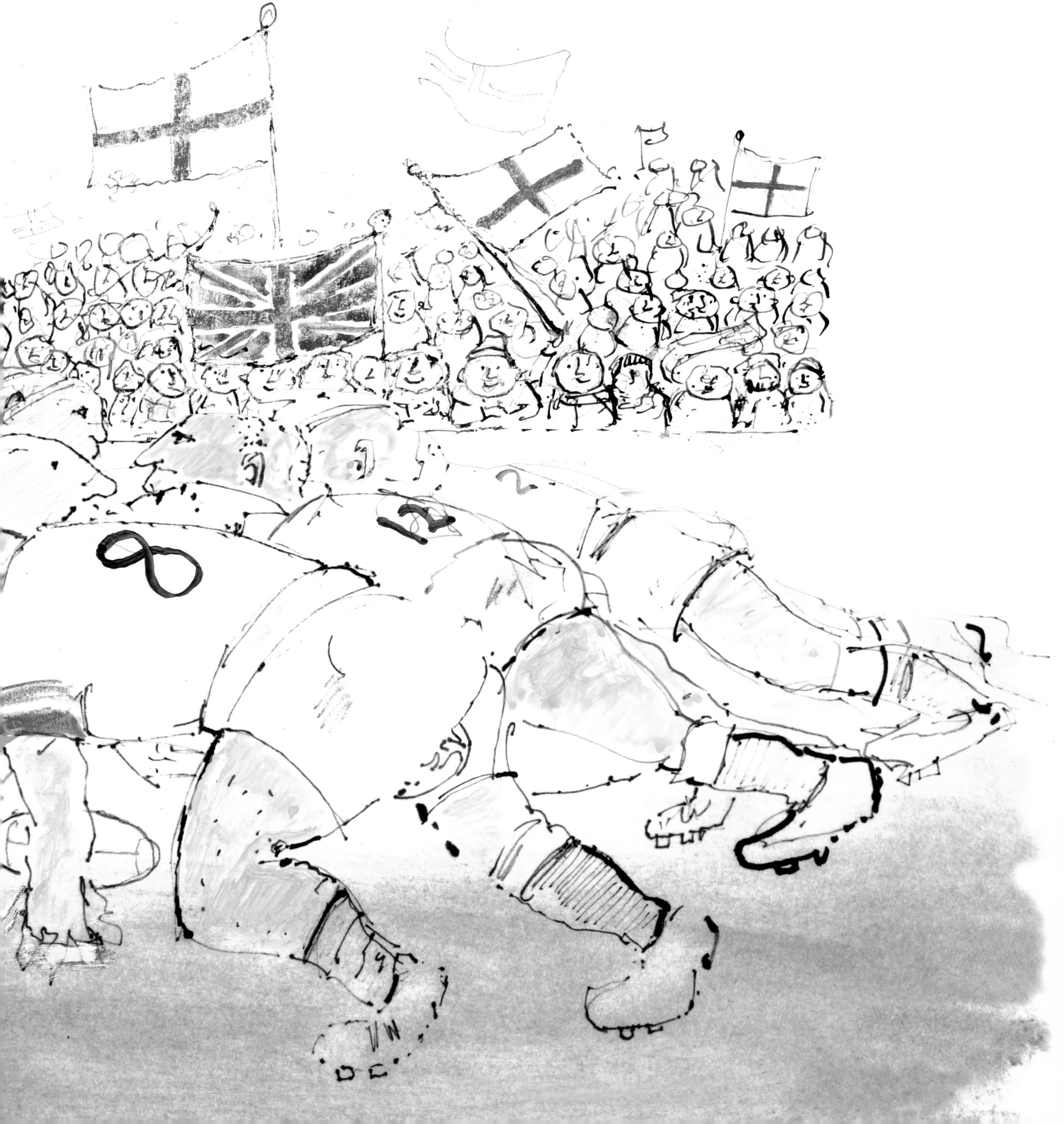

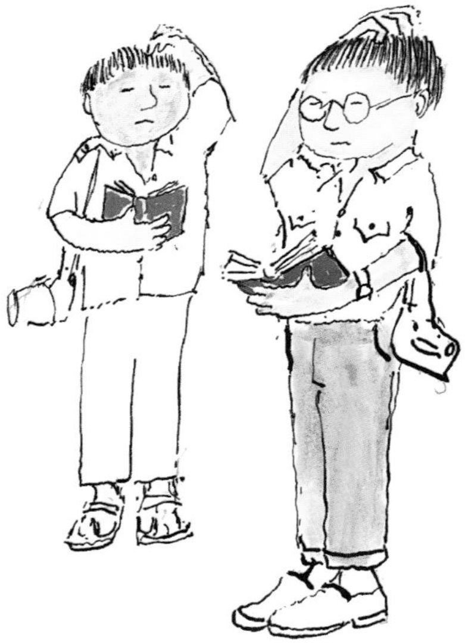

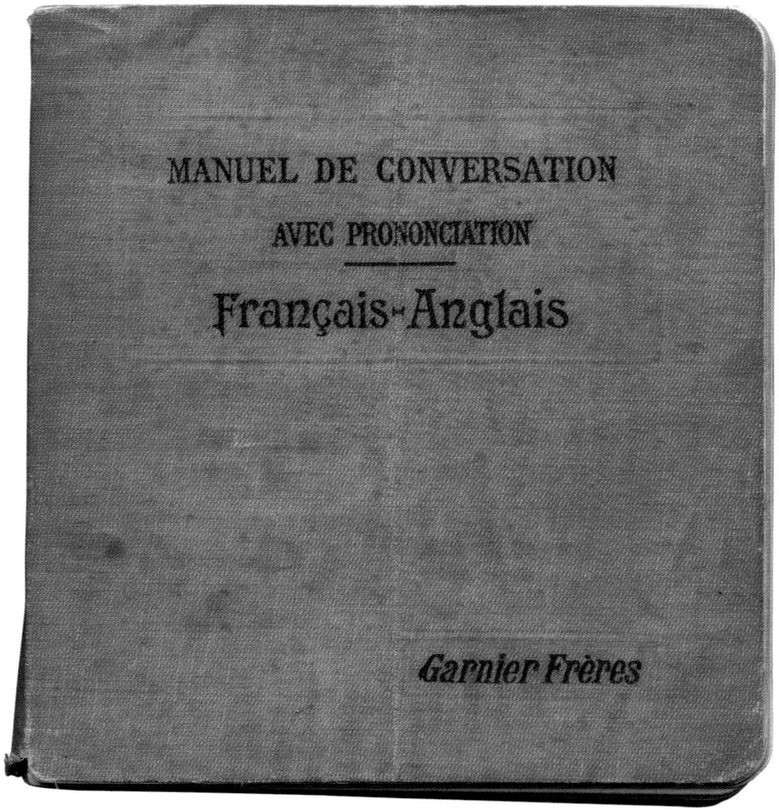
MANUEL DE CONVERSATION
AVEC PRONONCIATION
Français-Anglais
Garnier Frères

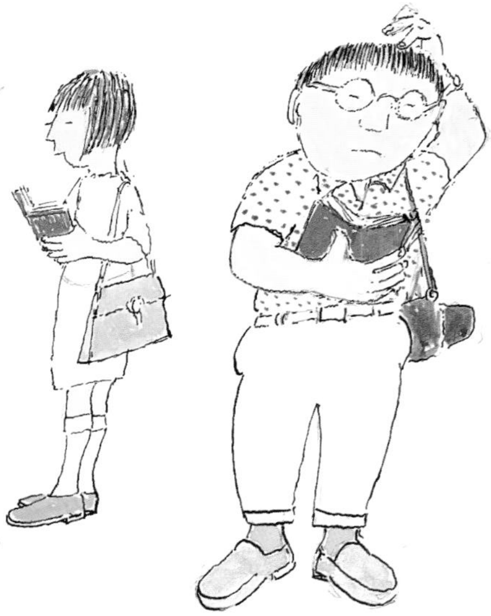

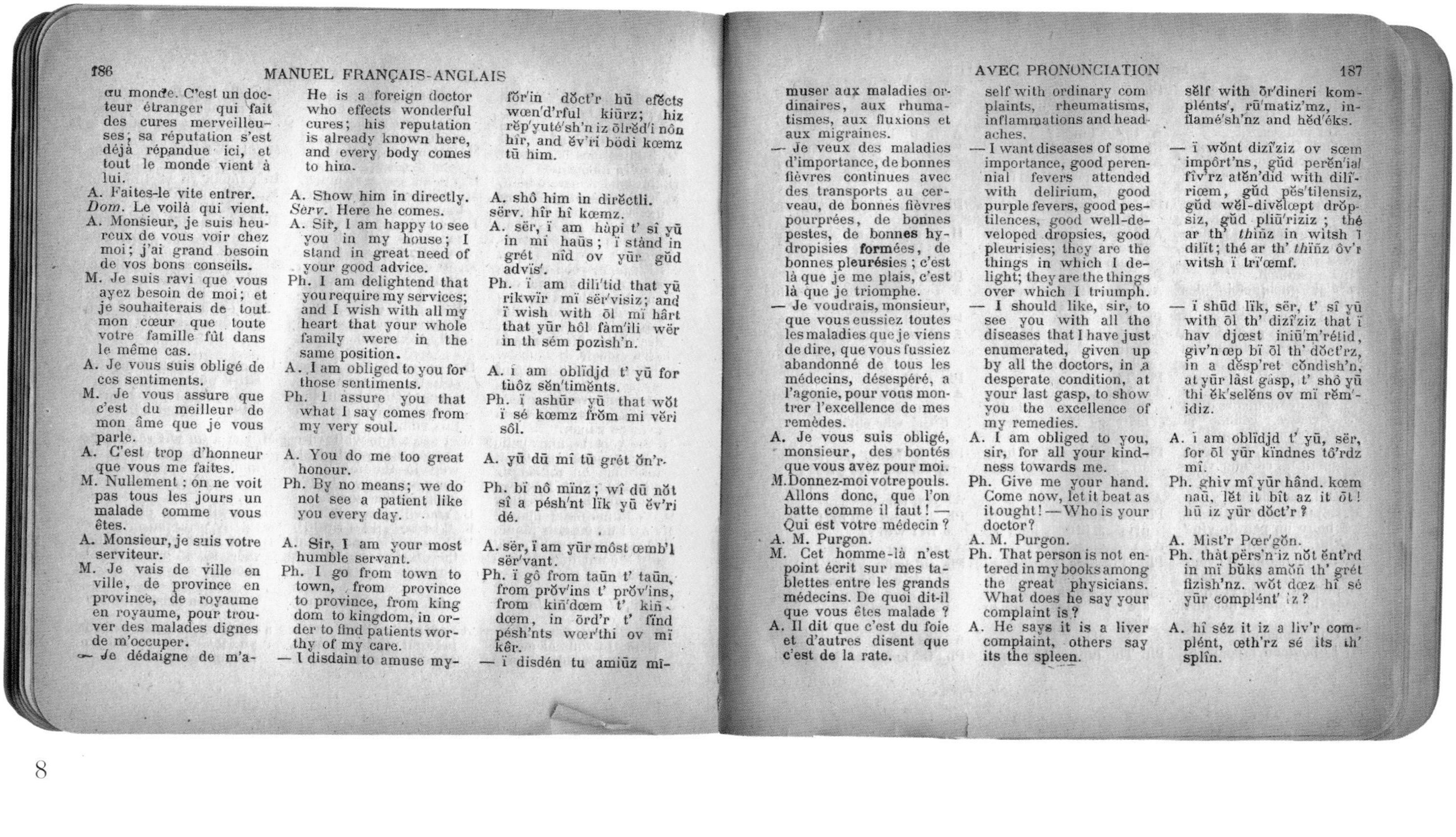

186 MANUEL FRANÇAIS-ANGLAIS

au monde. C'est un docteur étranger qui fait des cures merveilleuses; sa réputation s'est déjà répandue ici, et tout le monde vient à lui.	He is a foreign doctor who effects wonderful cures; his reputation is already known here, and every body comes to him.	fŏr'in dŏct'r hū efĕcts wœn'd'rful kiūrz; hiz rĕp'yuté'sh'n iz ōlrĕd'i nôn hîr, and ĕv'ri bödi kœmz tū him.
A. Faites-le vite entrer.	A. Show him in directly.	A. shô him in dirĕctli.
Dom. Le voilà qui vient.	*Serv.* Here he comes.	sërv. hîr hî kœmz.
A. Monsieur, je suis heureux de vous voir chez moi; j'ai grand besoin de vos bons conseils.	A. Sir, I am happy to see you in my house; I stand in great need of your good advice.	A. sër, ï am hàpi t' sî yū in mï haūs; ï stànd in grét nîd ov yūr gŭd advïs'.
M. Je suis ravi que vous ayez besoin de moi; et je souhaiterais de tout mon cœur que toute votre famille fût dans le même cas.	Ph. I am delightend that you require my services; and I wish with all my heart that your whole family were in the same position.	Ph. ï am dili'tid that yū rikwïr mï sër'visiz; and ï wish with ōl mï hârt that yūr hôl fàm'ili wër in th sém pozish'n.
A. Je vous suis obligé de ces sentiments.	A. I am obliged to you for those sentiments.	A. ï am oblïdjd t' yū for thôz sĕn'timĕnts.
M. Je vous assure que c'est du meilleur de mon âme que je vous parle.	Ph. I assure you that what I say comes from my very soul.	Ph. ï ashūr yū that wŏt ï sé kœmz frŏm mi vĕri sôl.
A. C'est trop d'honneur que vous me faites.	A. You do me too great honour.	A. yū dū mî tū grét ŏn'r.
M. Nullement : on ne voit pas tous les jours un malade comme vous êtes.	Ph. By no means; we do not see a patient like you every day.	Ph. bï nô mïnz ; wî dū nŏt sî a pésh'nt lïk yū ĕv'ri dé.
A. Monsieur, je suis votre serviteur.	A. Sir, I am your most humble servant.	A. sër, ï am yūr môst œmb'l sër'vant.
M. Je vais de ville en ville, de province en province, de royaume en royaume, pour trouver des malades dignes de m'occuper.	Ph. I go from town to town, from province to province, from king dom to kingdom, in order to find patients worthy of my care.	Ph. ï gô from taūn t' taūn, from prŏv'ins t' prŏv'ins, from kiñ'dœm t' kiñ-dœm, in ōrd'r t' fïnd pésh'nts wœr'thi ov mï kêr.
— Je dédaigne de m'a-	— I disdain to amuse my-	— ï disdén tu amiūz mï-

AVEC PRONONCIATION 187

muser aux maladies ordinaires, aux rhumatismes, aux fluxions et aux migraines.	self with ordinary complaints, rheumatisms, inflammations and headaches.	sĕlf with ōr'dineri komplénts', rū'matiz'mz, inflamé'sh'nz and hĕd'éks.
— Je veux des maladies d'importance, de bonnes fièvres continues avec des transports au cerveau, de bonnes fièvres pourprées, de bonnes pestes, de bonnes hydropisies formées, de bonnes pleurésies ; c'est là que je me plais, c'est là que je triomphe.	— I want diseases of some importance, good perennial fevers attended with delirium, good purple fevers, good pestilences, good well-developed dropsies, good pleurisies; they are the things in which I delight; they are the things over which I triumph.	— ï wŏnt dizï'ziz ov sœm impôrt'ns, gŭd perĕn'ial fïv'rz atĕn'did with dilï'riœm, gŭd pĕs'tilensiz, gŭd wĕl-divĕlœpt drŏpsiz, gŭd pliū'riziz ; thé ar th' *th*iñz in witsh ï dilït; thé ar th' *th*iñz ôv'r witsh ï trï'œmf.
— Je voudrais, monsieur, que vous eussiez toutes les maladies que je viens de dire, que vous fussiez abandonné de tous les médecins, désespéré, a l'agonie, pour vous montrer l'excellence de mes remèdes.	— I should like, sir, to see you with all the diseases that I have just enumerated, given up by all the doctors, in a desperate condition, at your last gasp, to show you the excellence of my remedies.	— ï shūd lïk, sër, t' sî yū with ōl th' dizï'ziz that ï hav djœst iniū'm'rétid, gìv'n œp bï ōl th' dŏct'rz, in a dĕsp'ret cŏndish'n, at yūr lâst gàsp, t' shô yū thi ĕk'selĕns ov mï rĕm'-idiz.
A. Je vous suis obligé, monsieur, des bontés que vous avez pour moi.	A. I am obliged to you, sir, for all your kindness towards me.	A. ï am oblïdjd t' yū, sër, for ōl yūr kïndnes tô'rdz mî.
M. Donnez-moi votre pouls. Allons donc, que l'on batte comme il faut ! — Qui est votre médecin ?	Ph. Give me your hand. Come now, let it beat as it ought! — Who is your doctor?	Ph. ghiv mî yūr hând. kœm naū, lĕt it bît az it ōt ! hū iz yūr dŏct'r ?
A. M. Purgon.	A. M. Purgon.	A. Mist'r Pœr'gŏn.
M. Cet homme-là n'est point écrit sur mes tablettes entre les grands médecins. De quoi dit-il que vous êtes malade ?	Ph. That person is not entered in my books among the great physicians. What does he say your complaint is?	Ph. thàt pĕrs'n iz nŏt ĕnt'rd in mï bŭks amŏñ th' grét fizish'nz. wŏt dœz hî sé yūr complént' iz ?
A. Il dit que c'est du foie et d'autres disent que c'est de la rate.	A. He says it is a liver complaint, others say its the spleen.	A. hî séz it iz a liv'r complént, œth'rz sé its th' splîn.

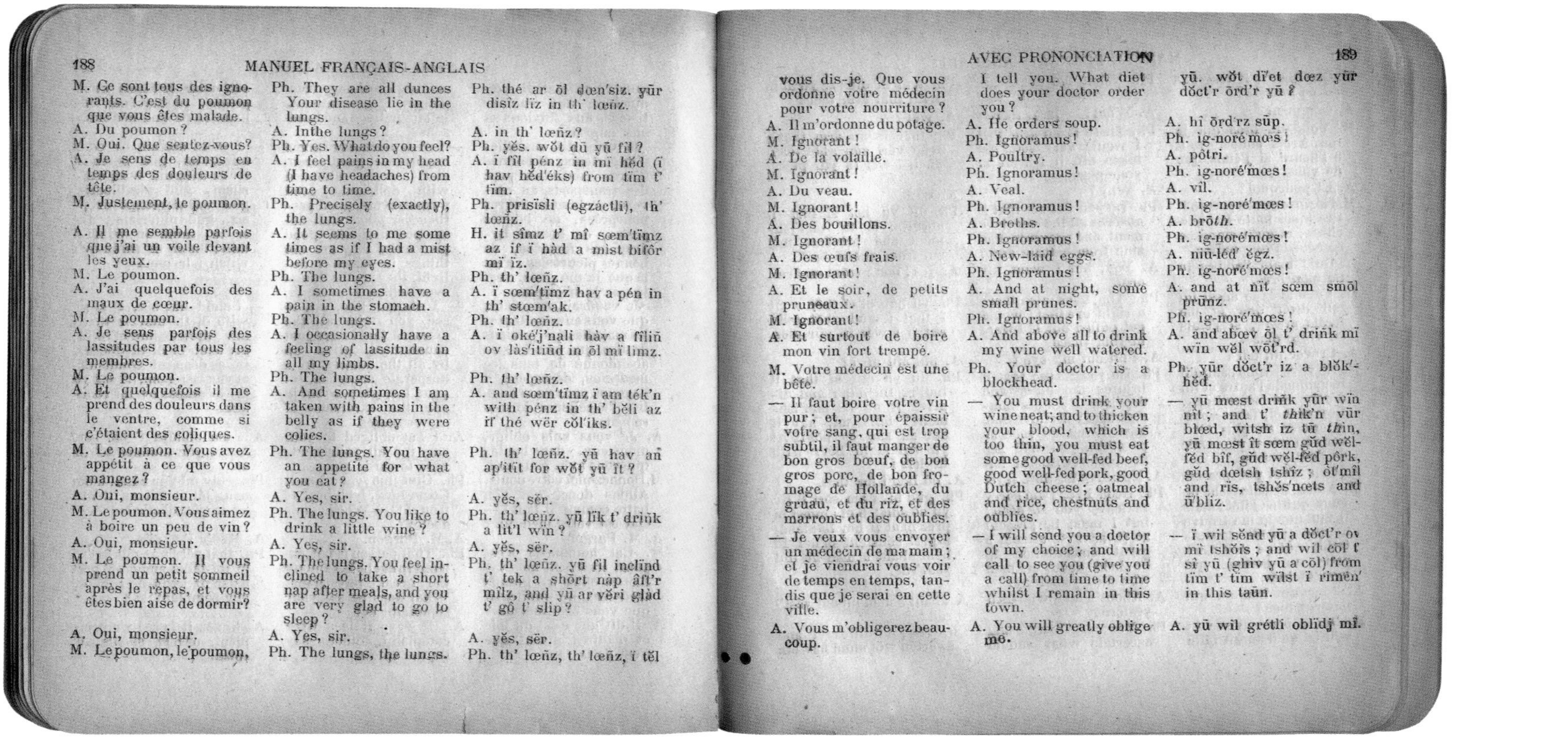

M. Ce sont tous des ignorants. C'est du poumon que vous êtes malade.	Ph. They are all dunces Your disease lie in the lungs.	Ph. thé ar ōl dœn'siz. yūr disîz lïz in th' lœñz.
A. Du poumon ?	A. Inthe lungs ?	A. in th' lœñz ?
M. Oui. Que sentez-vous?	Ph. Yes. What do you feel?	Ph. yĕs. wŏt dū yū fïl ?
A. Je sens de temps en temps des douleurs de tête.	A. I feel pains in my head (I have headaches) from time to time.	A. ï fïl pénz in mï hĕd (ï hav hĕd'éks) from tïm t' tïm.
M. Justement, le poumon.	Ph. Precisely (exactly), the lungs.	Ph. prisïsli (egzáctli), th' lœñz.
A. Il me semble parfois que j'ai un voile devant les yeux.	A. It seems to me some times as if I had a mist before my eyes.	H. it sîmz t' mî sœm'tïmz az if ï hàd a mist bifôr mï ïz.
M. Le poumon.	Ph. The lungs.	Ph. th' lœñz.
A. J'ai quelquefois des maux de cœur.	A. I sometimes have a pain in the stomach.	A. ï sœm'tïmz hav a pén in th' stœm'ak.
M. Le poumon.	Ph. The lungs.	Ph. th' lœñz.
A. Je sens parfois des lassitudes par tous les membres.	A. I occasionally have a feeling of lassitude in all my limbs.	A. ï oké'j'nali hàv a fîliñ ov làs'itiūd in ōl mï limz.
M. Le poumon.	Ph. The lungs.	Ph. th' lœñz.
A. Et quelquefois il me prend des douleurs dans le ventre, comme si c'étaient des coliques.	A. And sometimes I am taken with pains in the belly as if they were colics.	A. and sœm'tïmz ï am ték'n with pénz in th' bĕli az if thé wĕr cŏl'iks.
M. Le poumon. Vous avez appétit à ce que vous mangez ?	Ph. The lungs. You have an appetite for what you eat ?	Ph. th' lœñz. yū hav an ap'itït for wŏt yū ît ?
A. Oui, monsieur.	A. Yes, sir.	A. yĕs, sĕr.
M. Le poumon. Vous aimez à boire un peu de vin ?	Ph. The lungs. You like to drink a little wine ?	Ph. th' lœñz. yū lïk t' driñk a lit'l wïn ?
A. Oui, monsieur.	A. Yes, sir.	A. yĕs, sĕr.
M. Le poumon. Il vous prend un petit sommeil après le repas, et vous êtes bien aise de dormir?	Ph. The lungs. You feel inclined to take a short nap after meals, and you are very glad to go to sleep ?	Ph. th' lœñz. yū fil inclïnd t' tek a shŏrt nàp âft'r mîlz, and yū ar vĕri glàd t' gô t' slip ?
A. Oui, monsieur.	A. Yes, sir.	A. yĕs, sĕr.
M. Le poumon, le poumon,	Ph. The lungs, the lungs.	Ph. th' lœñz, th' lœñz, ï tĕl

vous dis-je. Que vous ordonne votre médecin pour votre nourriture ?	I tell you. What diet does your doctor order you ?	yū. wŏt dïet dœz yūr dŏct'r ōrd'r yū ?
A. Il m'ordonne du potage.	A. He orders soup.	A. hî ōrd'rz sūp.
M. Ignorant !	Ph. Ignoramus !	Ph. ig-noré'mœs !
A. De la volaille.	A. Poultry.	A. pôtri.
M. Ignorant !	Ph. Ignoramus !	Ph. ig-noré'mœs !
A. Du veau.	A. Veal.	A. vîl.
M. Ignorant !	Ph. Ignoramus !	Ph. ig-noré'mœs !
A. Des bouillons.	A. Broths.	A. brō*th*.
M. Ignorant !	Ph. Ignoramus !	Ph. ig-noré'mœs !
A. Des œufs frais.	A. New-laid eggs.	A. niū-léd' ĕgz.
M. Ignorant !	Ph. Ignoramus !	Ph. ig-noré'mœs !
A. Et le soir, de petits pruneaux.	A. And at night, some small prunes.	A. and at nït sœm smōl prūnz.
M. Ignorant !	Ph. Ignoramus !	Ph. ig-noré'mœs !
A. Et surtout de boire mon vin fort trempé.	A. And above all to drink my wine well watered.	A. and abœv ōl t' driñk mï wïn wĕl wōt'rd.
M. Votre médecin est une bête.	Ph. Your doctor is a blockhead.	Ph. yūr dŏct'r iz a blŏk'-hĕd.
— Il faut boire votre vin pur ; et, pour épaissir votre sang, qui est trop subtil, il faut manger de bon gros bœuf, de bon gros porc, de bon fromage de Hollande, du gruau, et du riz, et des marrons et des oublies.	— You must drink your wine neat; and to thicken your blood, which is too thin, you must eat some good well-fed beef, good well-fed pork, good Dutch cheese ; oatmeal and rice, chestnuts and oublies.	— yū mœst driñk yūr wïn nît ; and t' *th*ik'n yūr blœd, witsh iz tū *th*in, yū mœst ît sœm gŭd wĕl-fĕd bîf, gŭd wĕl-fĕd pôrk, gŭd dœtsh tshîz ; ōt'mîl and rïs, tshĕs'nœts and ū'bliz.
— Je veux vous envoyer un médecin de ma main ; et je viendrai vous voir de temps en temps, tandis que je serai en cette ville.	— I will send you a doctor of my choice ; and will call to see you (give you a call) from time to time whilst I remain in this town.	— ï wil sĕnd yū a dŏct'r ov mï tshŏïs ; and wil cōl t' sï yū (ghiv yū a cōl) from tïm t' tïm wïlst ï rimén' in this taūn.
A. Vous m'obligerez beaucoup.	A. You will greatly oblige me.	A. yū wil grétli oblïdj mî.

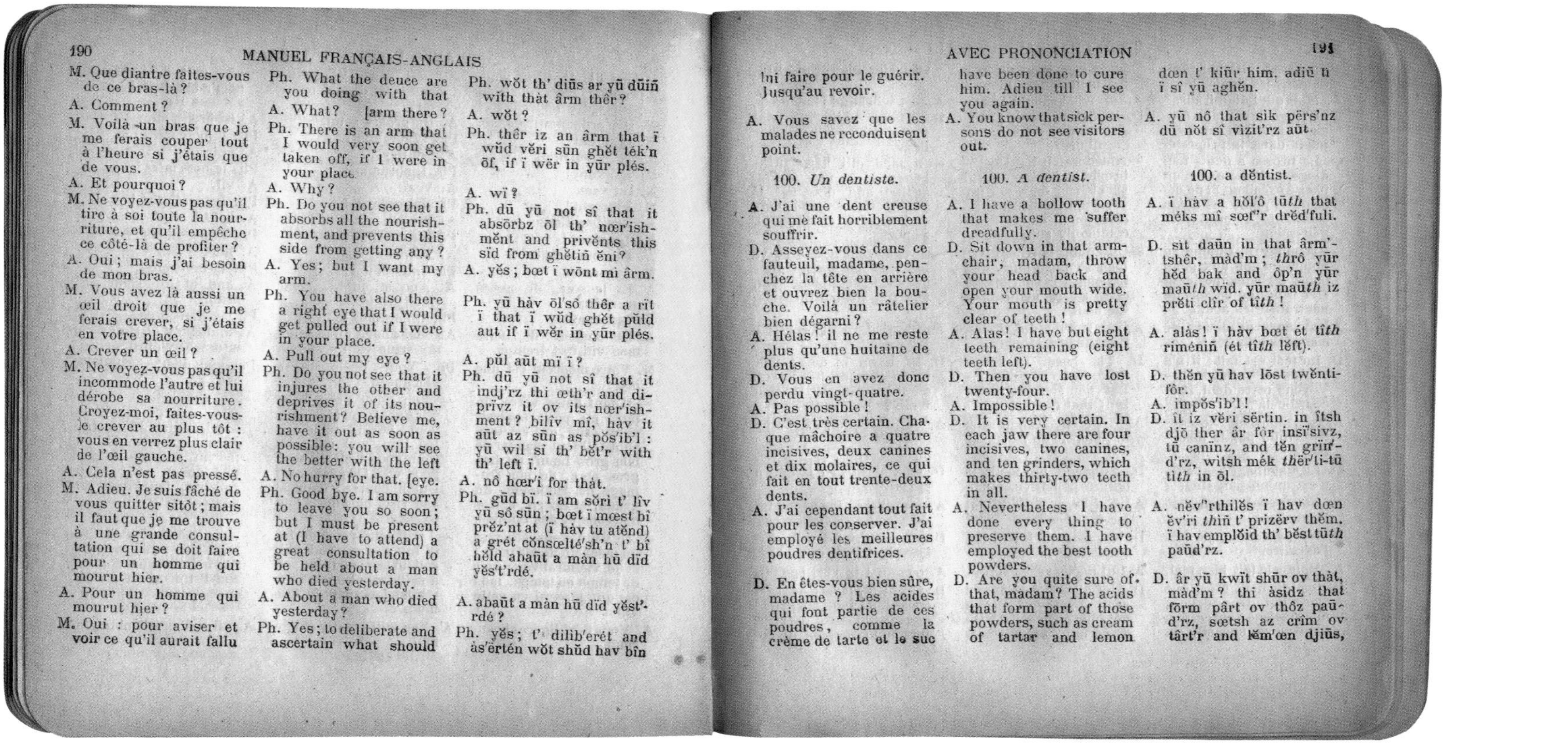

M. Que diantre faites-vous de ce bras-là ?	Ph. What the deuce are you doing with that arm there ?	Ph. wŏt th' diūs ar yū dūiñ with thàt ârm thêr ?
A. Comment ?	A. What?	A. wŏt ?
M. Voilà un bras que je me ferais couper tout à l'heure si j'étais que de vous.	Ph. There is an arm that I would very soon get taken off, if I were in your place.	Ph. thêr iz an ârm that ï wŭd vĕri sūn ghĕt ték'n ōf, if ï wĕr in yūr plés.
A. Et pourquoi ?	A. Why ?	A. wï ?
M. Ne voyez-vous pas qu'il tire à soi toute la nourriture, et qu'il empêche ce côté-là de profiter ?	Ph. Do you not see that it absorbs all the nourishment, and prevents this side from getting any ?	Ph. dū yū not sî that it absōrbz ōl th' nœr'ishmĕnt and privĕnts this sïd from ghĕtiñ ĕni ?
A. Oui ; mais j'ai besoin de mon bras.	A. Yes ; but I want my arm.	A. yĕs ; bœt ï wōnt mi ârm.
M. Vous avez là aussi un œil droit que je me ferais crever, si j'étais en votre place.	Ph. You have also there a right eye that I would get pulled out if I were in your place.	Ph. yū hàv ōl'sô thêr a rït ï that ï wŭd ghĕt pŭld aut if ï wĕr in yūr plés.
A. Crever un œil ?	A. Pull out my eye ?	A. pŭl aūt mï ï ?
M. Ne voyez-vous pas qu'il incommode l'autre et lui dérobe sa nourriture. Croyez-moi, faites-vous le crever au plus tôt : vous en verrez plus clair de l'œil gauche.	Ph. Do you not see that it injures the other and deprives it of its nourishment ? Believe me, have it out as soon as possible : you will see the better with the left eye.	Ph. dū yū not sî that it indj'rz thi œth'r and diprïvz it ov its nœr'ishment ? bilîv mî, hàv it aūt az sūn as pŏs'ib'l : yū wil sî th' bĕt'r with th' left ï.
A. Cela n'est pas pressé.	A. No hurry for that.	A. nô hœr'i for thàt.
M. Adieu. Je suis fâché de vous quitter sitôt ; mais il faut que je me trouve à une grande consultation qui se doit faire pour un homme qui mourut hier.	Ph. Good bye. I am sorry to leave you so soon ; but I must be present at (I have to attend) a great consultation to be held about a man who died yesterday.	Ph. gŭd bï. ï am sŏri t' lïv yū sô sūn ; bœt ï mœst bî prĕz'nt at (ï hàv tu atĕnd) a grét cŏnsœlté'sh'n t' bî hĕld abaūt a màn hū dïd yĕs't'rdé.
A. Pour un homme qui mourut hier ?	A. About a man who died yesterday ?	A. abaūt a màn hū dïd yĕst'rdé ?
M. Oui : pour aviser et voir ce qu'il aurait fallu	Ph. Yes ; to deliberate and ascertain what should	Ph. yĕs ; t' dilib'erét and às'ĕrtén wŏt shŭd hav bîn

lui faire pour le guérir. Jusqu'au revoir.	have been done to cure him. Adieu till I see you again.	dœn t' kiūr him. adiū ti ï sî yū aghĕn.
A. Vous savez que les malades ne reconduisent point.	A. You know that sick persons do not see visitors out.	A. yū nô that sik pĕrs'nz dū nŏt sî vìzit'rz aūt.
100. *Un dentiste.*	100. *A dentist.*	100. a dĕntist.
A. J'ai une dent creuse qui me fait horriblement souffrir.	A. I have a hollow tooth that makes me suffer dreadfully.	A. ï hàv a hŏl'ô tū*th* that méks mî sœf''r drĕd'fuli.
D. Asseyez-vous dans ce fauteuil, madame, penchez la tête en arrière et ouvrez bien la bouche. Voilà un râtelier bien dégarni ?	D. Sit down in that armchair, madam, throw your head back and open your mouth wide. Your mouth is pretty clear of teeth !	D. sit daūn in that ârm'-tshêr, màd'm ; *th*rô yūr hĕd bak and ôp'n yūr maū*th* wïd. yūr maū*th* iz prĕti clîr of tî*th* !
A. Hélas ! il ne me reste plus qu'une huitaine de dents.	A. Alas ! I have but eight teeth remaining (eight teeth left).	A. alás ! ï hàv bœt ét tî*th* riméniñ (ét tî*th* lĕft).
D. Vous en avez donc perdu vingt-quatre.	D. Then you have lost twenty-four.	D. thĕn yū hav lōst twĕnti-fôr.
A. Pas possible !	A. Impossible !	A. impŏs'ib'l !
D. C'est très certain. Chaque mâchoire a quatre incisives, deux canines et dix molaires, ce qui fait en tout trente-deux dents.	D. It is very certain. In each jaw there are four incisives, two canines, and ten grinders, which makes thirty-two teeth in all.	D. ït iz vĕri sĕrtin. in îtsh djō ther âr fòr insï'sivz, tū canïnz, and tĕn grïn'-d'rz, witsh mék *th*ĕr'ti-tū tî*th* in ōl.
A. J'ai cependant tout fait pour les conserver. J'ai employé les meilleures poudres dentifrices.	A. Nevertheless I have done every thing to preserve them. I have employed the best tooth powders.	A. nĕv''rthilĕs ï hav dœn ĕv'ri *th*iñ t' prizërv thĕm. ï hav emplŏïd th' bĕst tū*th* paūd'rz.
D. En êtes-vous bien sûre, madame ? Les acides qui font partie de ces poudres, comme la crème de tarte et le suc	D. Are you quite sure of that, madam ? The acids that form part of those powders, such as cream of tartar and lemon	D. âr yū kwït shūr ov thàt, màd'm ? thi àsidz that fōrm pârt ov thôz paū-d'rz, sœtsh az crîm ov târt'r and lĕm'œn djiūs,

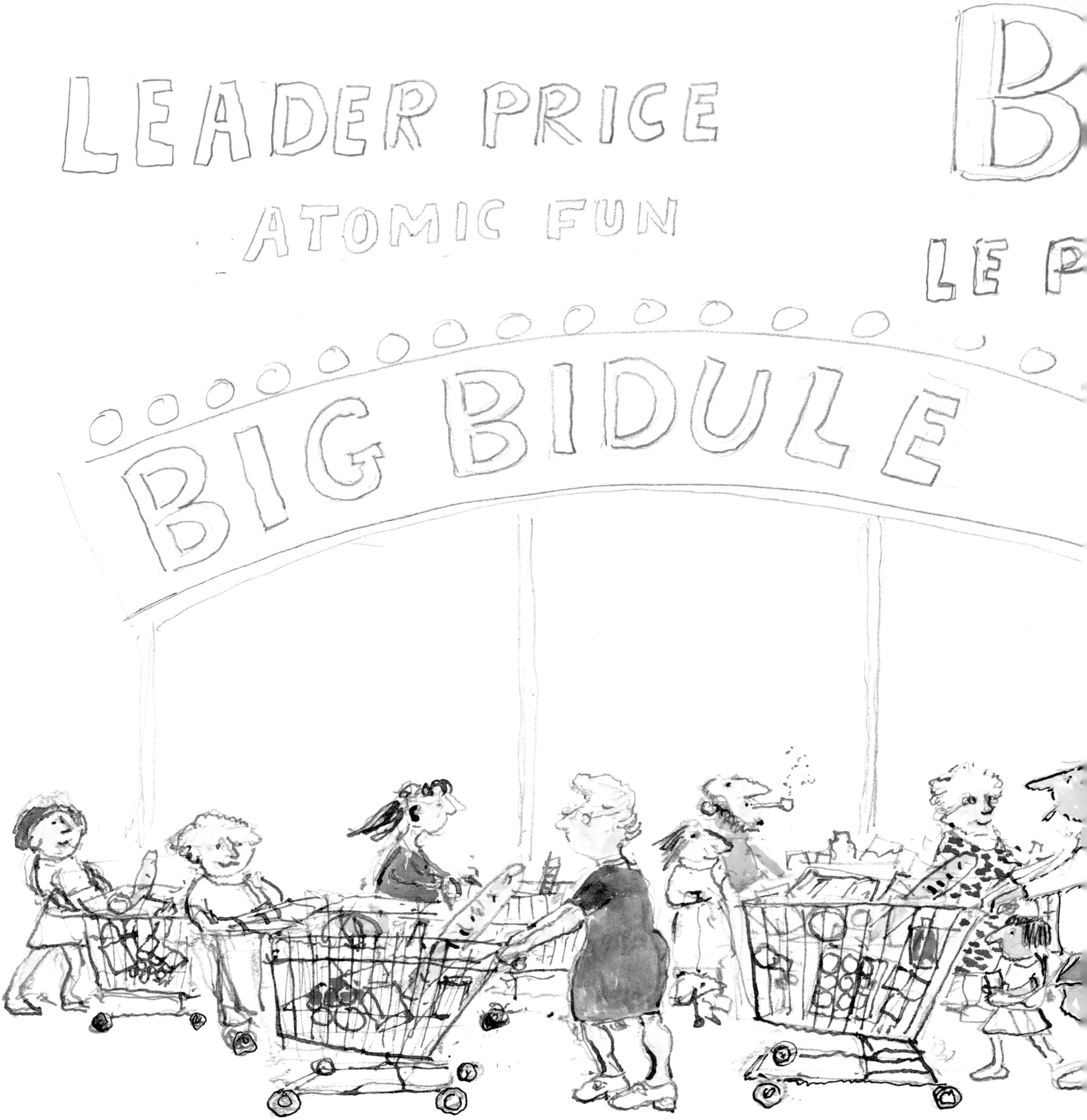
LEADER PRICE
ATOMIC FUN
B
LE P
BIG BIDULE

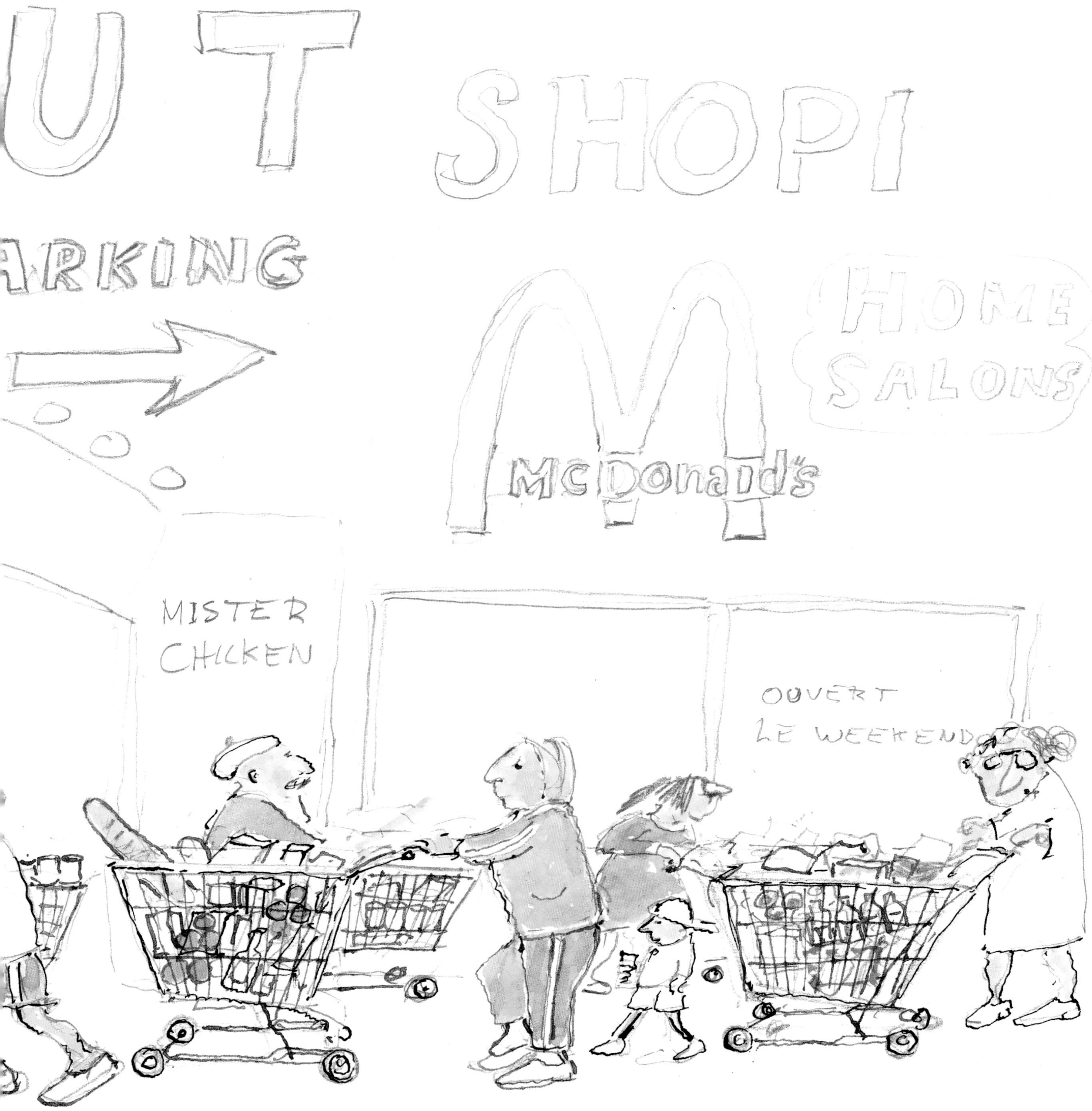
UT
SHOPI
ARKING
HOME SALONS
McDonald's
MISTER CHICKEN
OUVERT LE WEEKEND

French defends its *raison d'être*

The Times 24/2/94
FROM CHARLES BREMNER IN PARIS

France has unveiled a long-awaited law designed to turn back the tide of 'franglais' at home and combat the supremacy of English as the dominant world language.

When the law takes effect, the language police will crack down with fines, the removal of subsidies and other punishments on anyone using English in advertising, official communications or broadcasting. Radio stations, for example, will no longer be able to refer to their 'hit parade' or theatres to their 'one-man shows'.

Broadcasters will be liable to prosecution for using foreign words if there is a French equivalent. At present such terms are used in abundance. They range from the common 'le job' instead of *emploi* to 'le challenge' instead of *le défi*.

The state-run post office bank will have to stop boasting of its 'Authentic Revenue' account. Indeed, no state-run body will be allowed to use any name containing English as a trademark.

All congresses and debates held in France, as well as academic and scientific communications, will have to be in French, not English as is now common.

The Bill, introduced yesterday, has the support of all political parties and the intellectual classes. It seeks to extend a neglected 1975 decree on the use of French, taking its momentum from the furore last year over the 'cultural invasion' of Europe by the American entertainment industry.

Introducing the Bill, Jacques Toubon, the Culture Minister, said his government had decided to 'turn the policy of French language into a national cause' and was seeking to protect the right of the French to be addressed in their own language.

'A foreign language often becomes a tool of domination, uniformity, a factor of social exclusion and, when used snobbishly, a language of contempt,' he said.

French Words (Prohibition)

Hansard 5/7/94
3.35 pm

Mr. Anthony Steen (South Hams): I beg to move, That leave be given to bring in a Bill to prohibit the use of French words in written and spoken English; and for connected purposes.

I seek the leave of the House to introduce a Bill to outlaw the use of everyday French words in the English language, whether spoken or written, which, if infringed, would be punishable by a fine. I am doing this principally to make a point, not to be taken too seriously, to highlight the bizarre situation which has resulted in the French language prohibition Bill or le roi relatif à l'emploi de la langue Française tabled by Jacques Toubon, the Gaullist Culture Minister, which passed all its stages in the French National Assembly and the Senate last Friday.

That Bill banned the use of English words or expressions such as software, hamburger, football and tee-shirt on advertising boards, in the media, on television or radio, in work contracts and instruction leaflets; and, even where English is the chosen language at international congresses held in France, all French contributions must be delivered in French. If someone were to flout the law and sneak in an English word or two, that person could be sent to the Bastille for six months or fined £5,000. Mr. Toubon's Bill tears up completely the entente cordiale which was signed by Edward VII on 8 April 1904 at the end of 100 years of hostilities between the French and the English…

I stress that my bill is solely retaliatory - a cause célèbre. My aim is to introduce an equivalent measure as a tit-for-tat response…

…We should forget words like baguette or croissant - they are out. We would not be able to visit a café or brasserie. There would be no apéritifs or hors d'oeuvres - in fact, there would be no restaurants. We should forget the table d'hôte; there is no question of the à la carte instead. There would be no left or right-hand side of the menu and no nouvelle cuisine. Bon viveurs would be banned. One would not be able to shower one's fiancée with bouquets, meet at a secret rendezvous, or buy her haute couture clothes. There would be great difficulties in having a ménage-à-trois. Crime passionnel would be out of the question and négligée would make a liaison dangereuse a little risquée.

If one is a gambling man, one would no longer hear the familiar words faites vos jeux or rien ne va plus when playing the tables. There would be no question of feeling déjà vu and there is no way that one could live in a pied-à-terre. If by chance one drives in a cul-de-sac, that would be a bit of a faux pas. In short, everyone in the country would have to mind their language and pardon their French because Mr. Toubon's Bill is a fait accompli. However, he does not realise that, if he ever came to Britain, he would be refused entry unless he changed his name to Mr. Allgood.

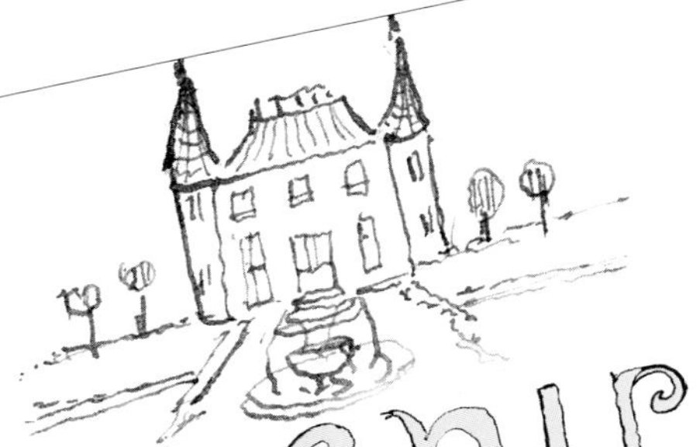

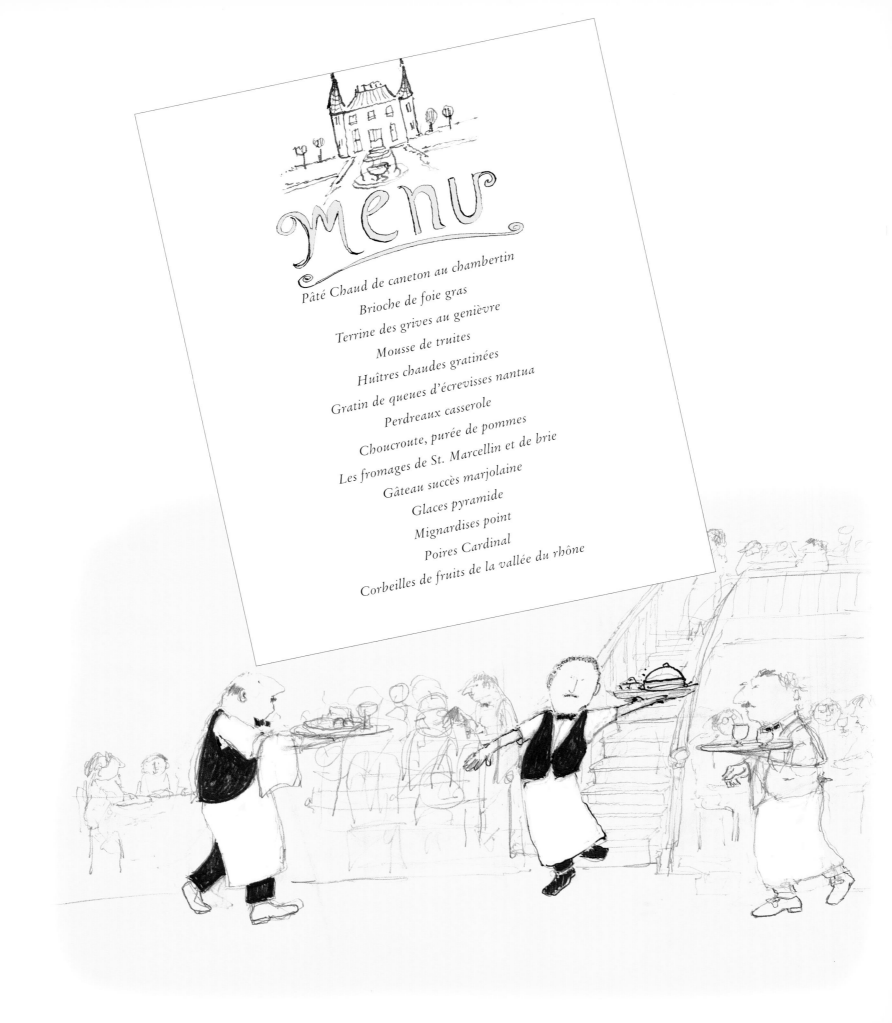

Menu

Pâté Chaud de caneton au chambertin

Brioche de foie gras

Terrine des grives au genièvre

Mousse de truites

Huîtres chaudes gratinées

Gratin de queues d'écrevisses nantua

Perdreaux casserole

Choucroute, purée de pommes

Les fromages de St. Marcellin et de brie

Gâteau succès marjolaine

Glaces pyramide

Mignardises point

Poires Cardinal

Corbeilles de fruits de la vallée du rhône

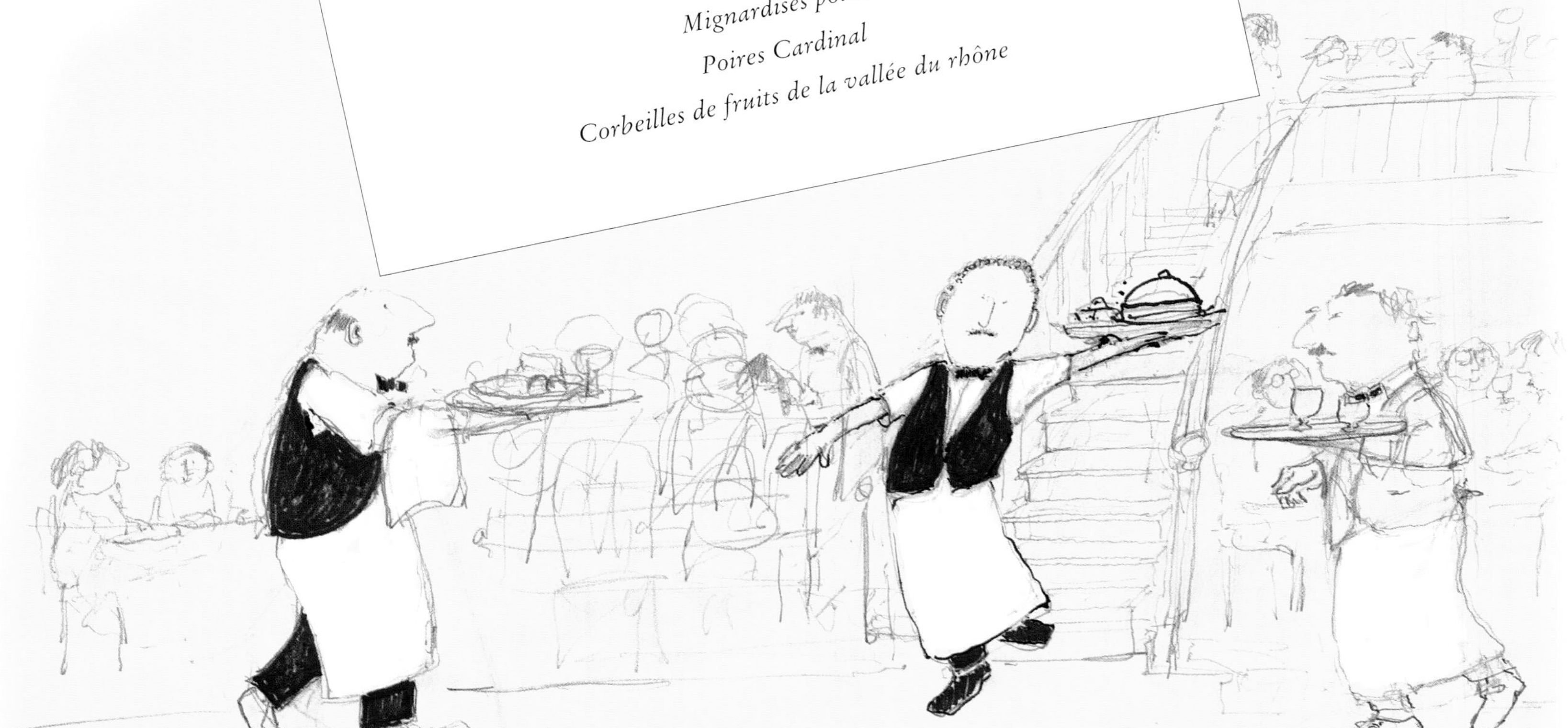

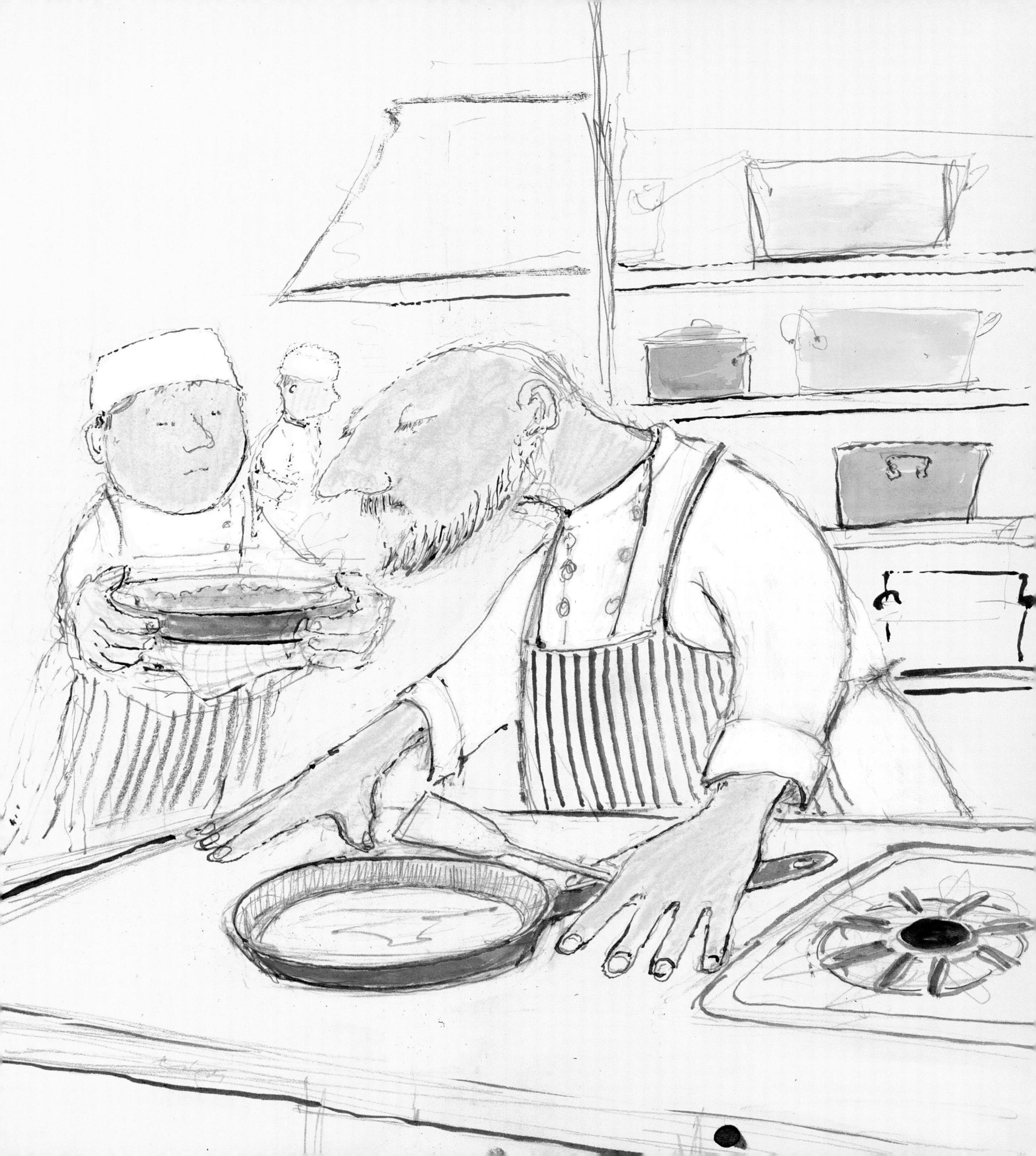

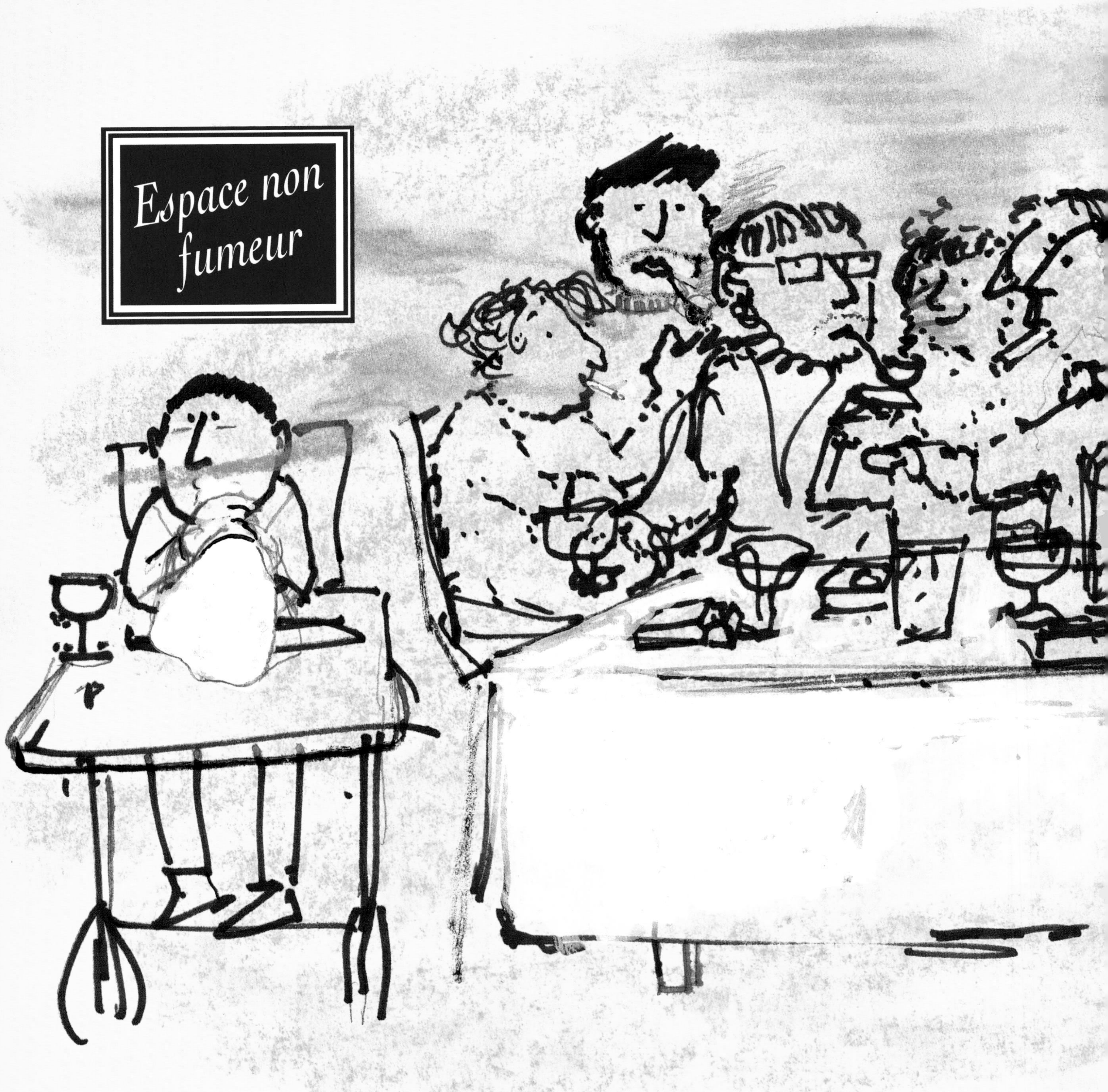
Espace non fumeur

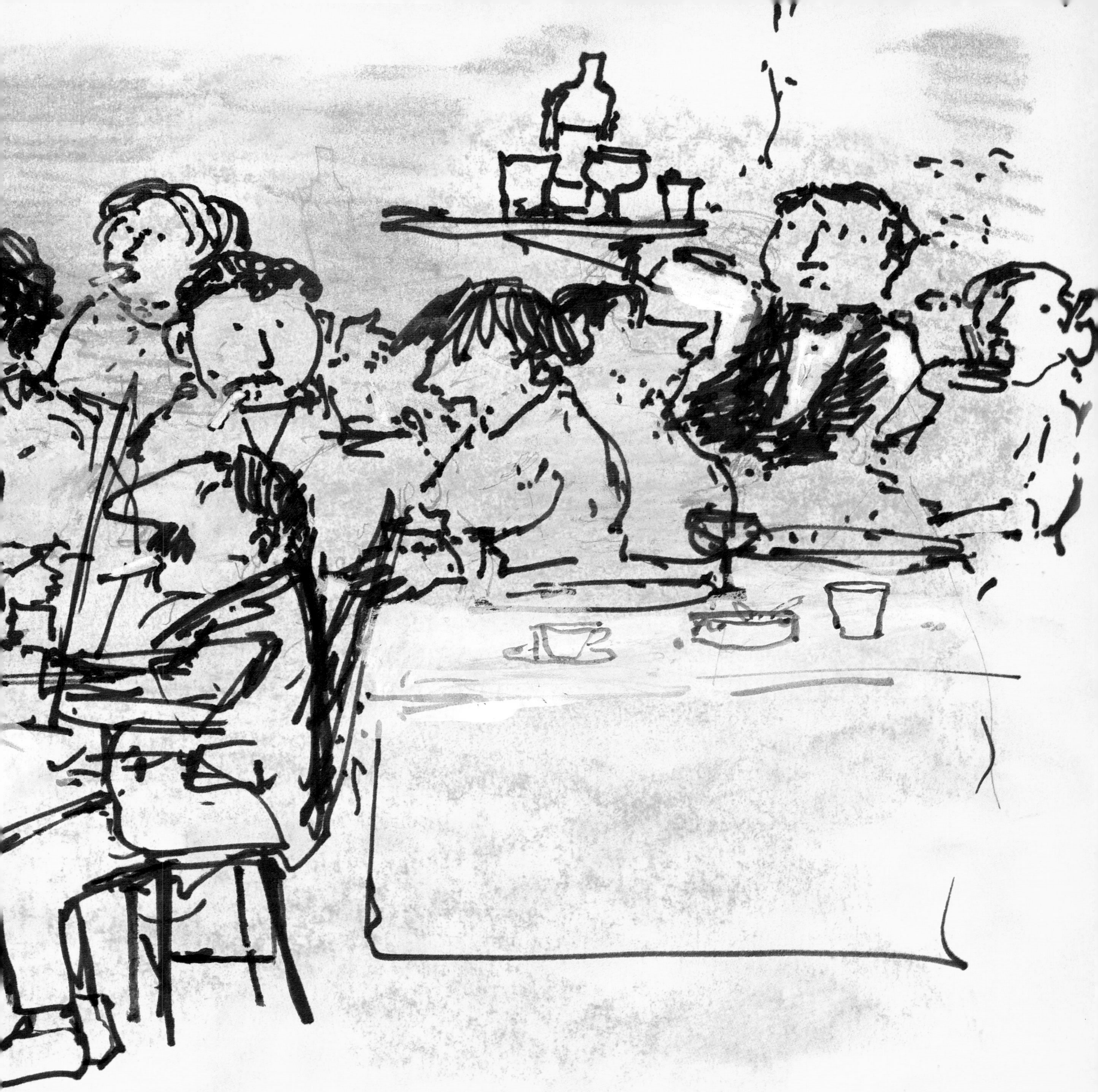

The Influence of Gourmandism upon Conjugal Happiness

Gourmandism, when it is shared, has the most marked influence upon the happiness attainable in the married state.

Let the twain be gourmands, and at least once a day they have occasion to enjoy each other's company; for even those who sleep apart (and there are many such) eat at the same table; they have a theme of conversation which never grows stale, for they talk not only of what they are eating, but of what they are about to eat, what they have met with on the tables of their acquaintances, fashionable dishes, new inventions, etc., etc.; and such table-talk is full of charm.

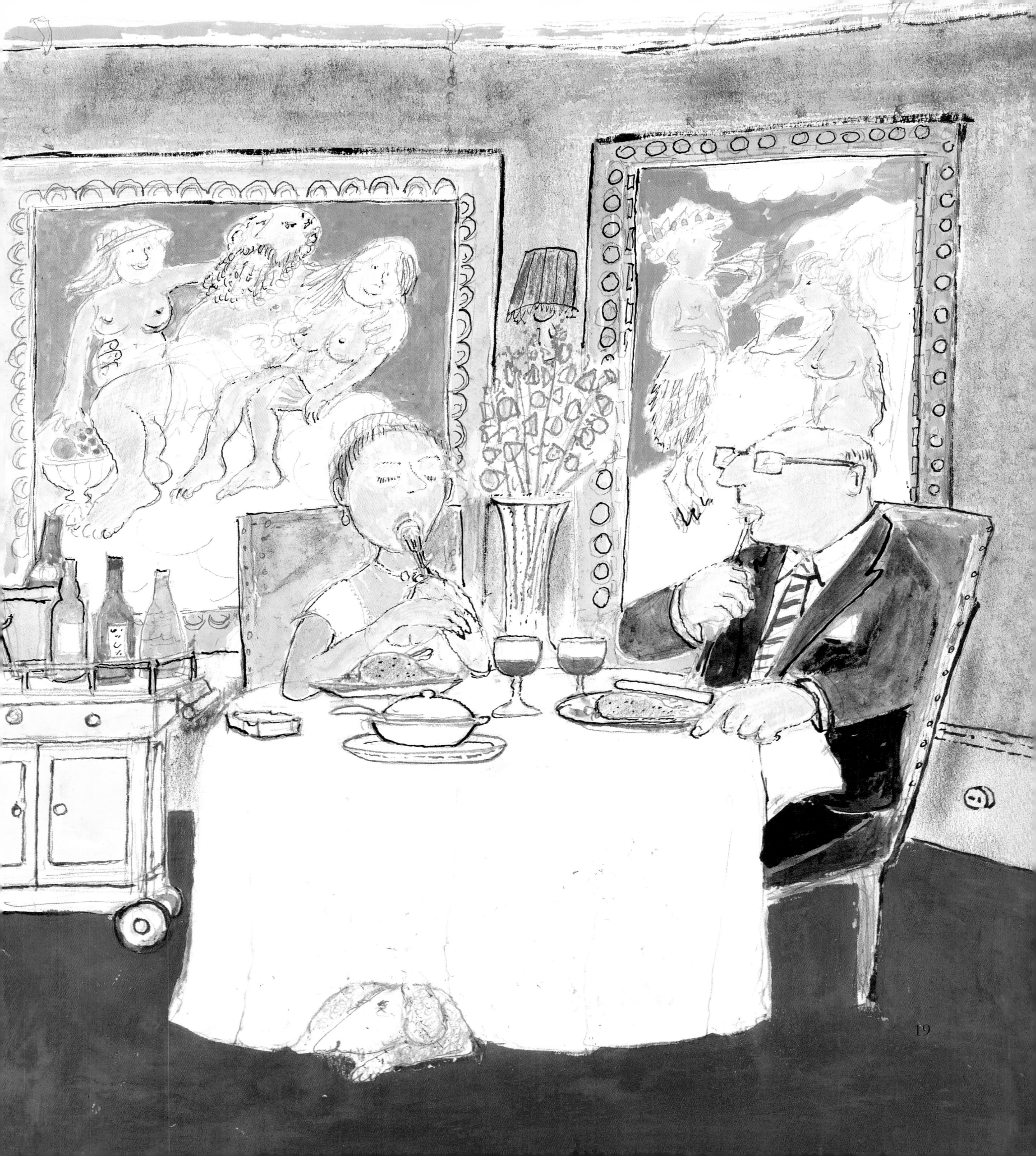

Lalbenque

Sunday 3 March 1996

Sixth Truffle-Hunting Trials
Arranged by the Truffle Syndicate of the
Lalbenque Region.

'Today is a day of relaxation and enjoyment.
Now, to the greatest possible satisfaction of all,
everyone present will have the chance to watch
the animals (pigs or dogs) at work. All
through the season, directed by their masters,
their talents have enabled them to detect the
precious Tuber Melanosporum in the truffle
grounds.

'In a little while, at the Town Hall, the cups
will be presented, the best will be rewarded.
To the pleasure felt by their masters, may I
add, after my congratulations to them, a pat to
all the animals who have done their duty so
well . . .

'Madame, Mademoiselle, Monsieur, thank you
again for visiting our canton.

'Come back often to Lalbenque, we shall be
very happy to welcome you.'

Raymond Lacan. County Councillor.

Rules of the Trial of Truffle Hunting - Dogs and Pigs

1. Points will be awarded out of a total of 100, apportioned as follows:

Truffles found: 60 One truffle = 10 points
Time taken: 30 One tenth point to be deducted per second.
General impression: 10

Dogs must work off the leash, with one or two handlers.
Pigs must work on the leash, with one or two handlers.
If a truffle is damaged by dog or hunter, it is worth 5 points only.
Three blind markings attract 5 penalty points. Marking on the side of a truffle already lifted: 2 penalty points.

2. Contestants must present themselves to the judge with their dog (or pig) when their number is called, without entering the truffle-ground, to avoid premature removal of truffles.

3. When the judge gives the word, the handler will take his dog (pig) and issue his command to the animal on arrival at the trial ground. The clock will start as soon as the animal reaches the search area and stop when the sixth truffle is found or after five minutes.

4. (Dogs) The dog's business in the truffle-ground is to search and trampling must be avoided as compressing the soil is unacceptable.

(Pigs) Trampling the truffle-ground must be avoided as compressing the soil is unacceptable.

5. (Dogs) The dog must mark the truffle. The handler will extract it without damage. The truffle must then be shown to the judge or the points will not be awarded. The handler must provide himself with an extracting tool and a receptacle for the truffles.

(Pigs) The pig must mark or lift the truffle with his snout. The handler will pick it up and then show it to the judge or the points will not be awarded. The handler must provide himself with an extracting tool and a receptacle for the truffles.

6. Each site shall be covered over and levelled immediately after the truffle has been lifted, either by the handler or his assistant, or points will be deducted.

7. Any dog (pig) eating a truffle or part of a truffle will be instantly disqualified.

8. Each contestant will work on an artificial truffle-ground, 5m x 5m, within which 6 truffles will have been hidden. Truffles will be ten metres [10 m] apart.

9. Any contestant leading his dog (pig) alongside the truffle-ground or among the onlookers, before or during the trials, will not be eligible to compete. Anyone doing so after competing will be disqualified.

10. Bitches on heat (sows or gilts in season) will be entered last in order not to disrupt the other entrants.

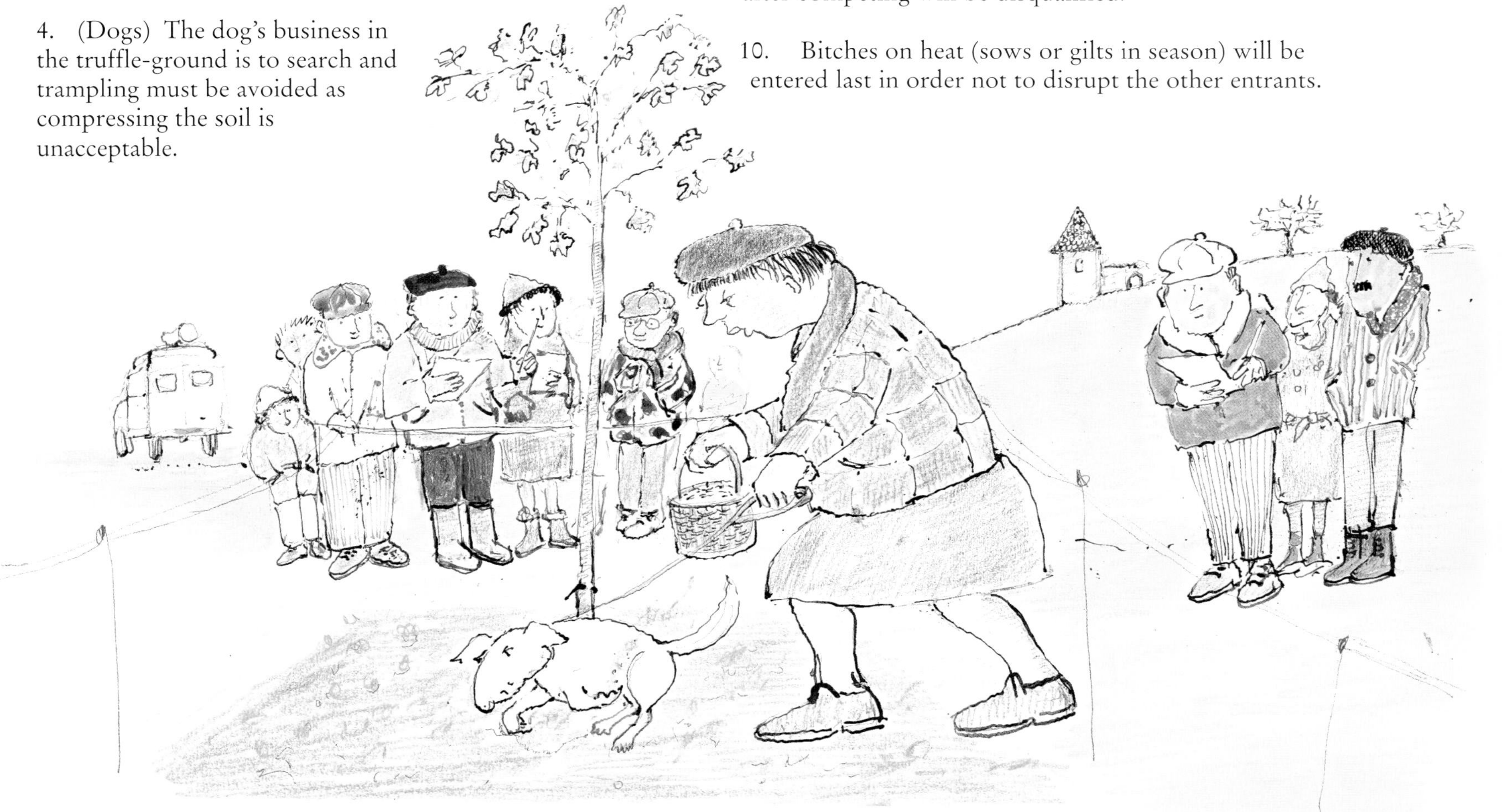

Foie Gras

The goose is nothing, but man has made of it an instrument for the output of a marvellous product, a kind of living hothouse in which there grows the supreme fruit of gastronomy.

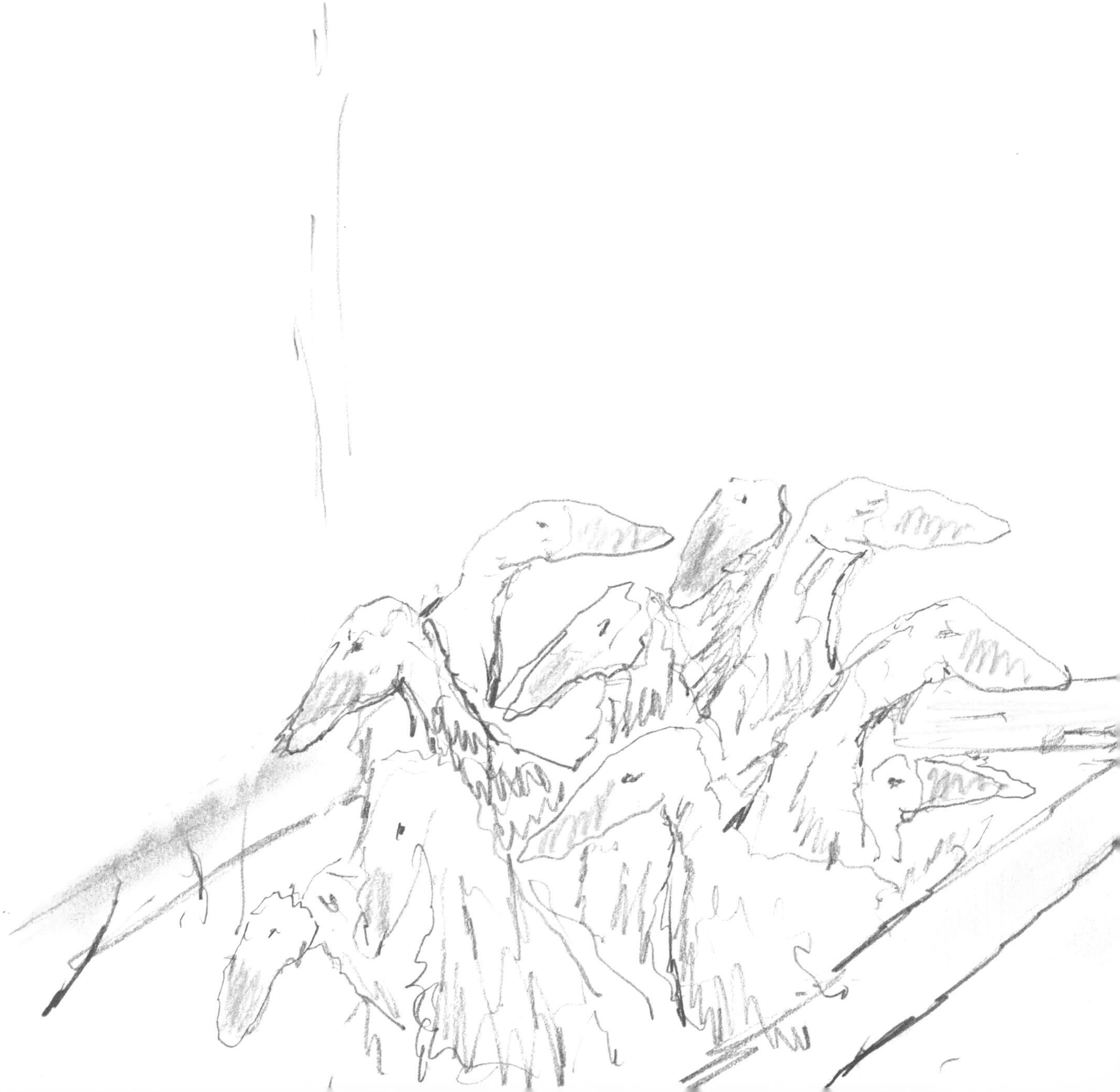

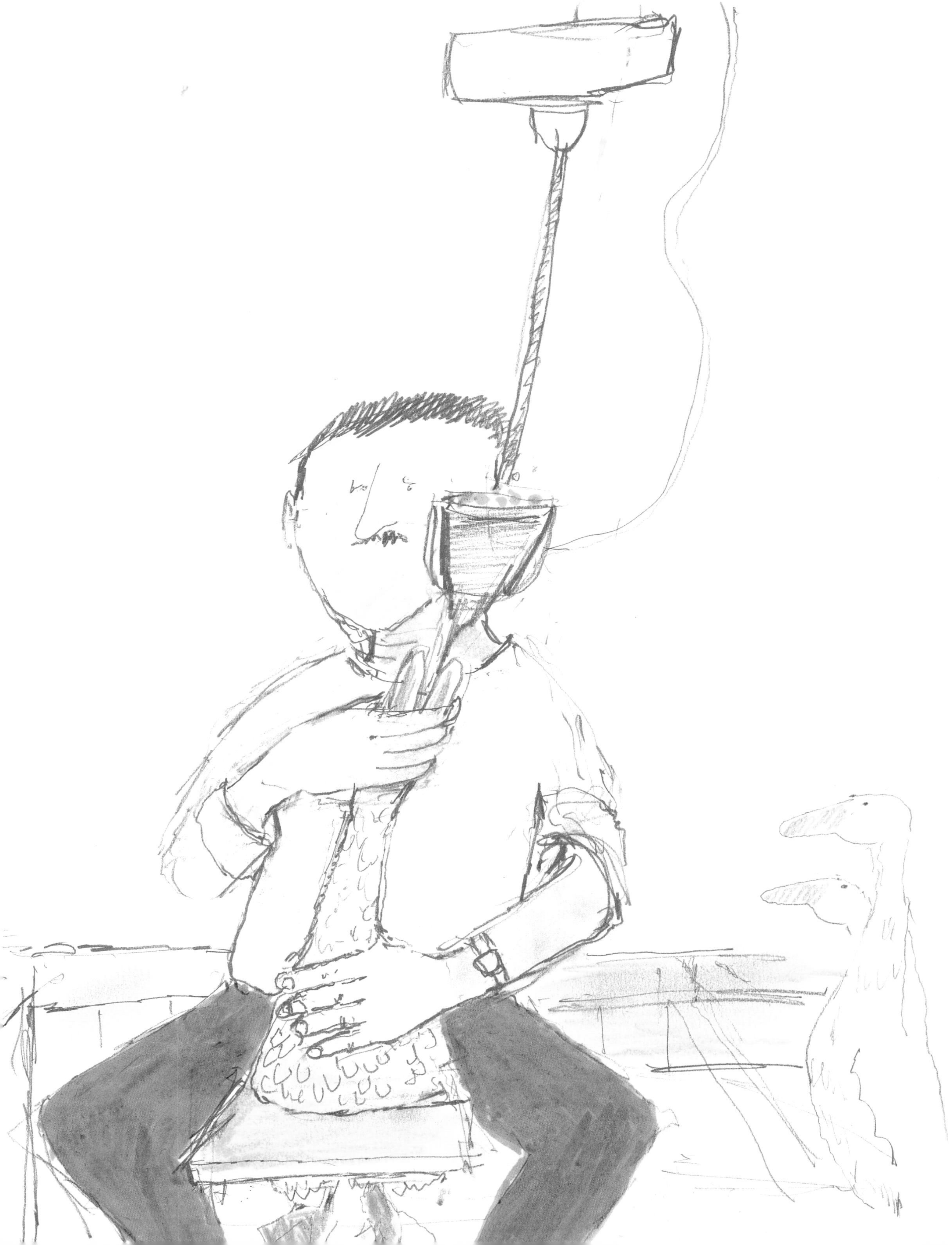

Le Marché

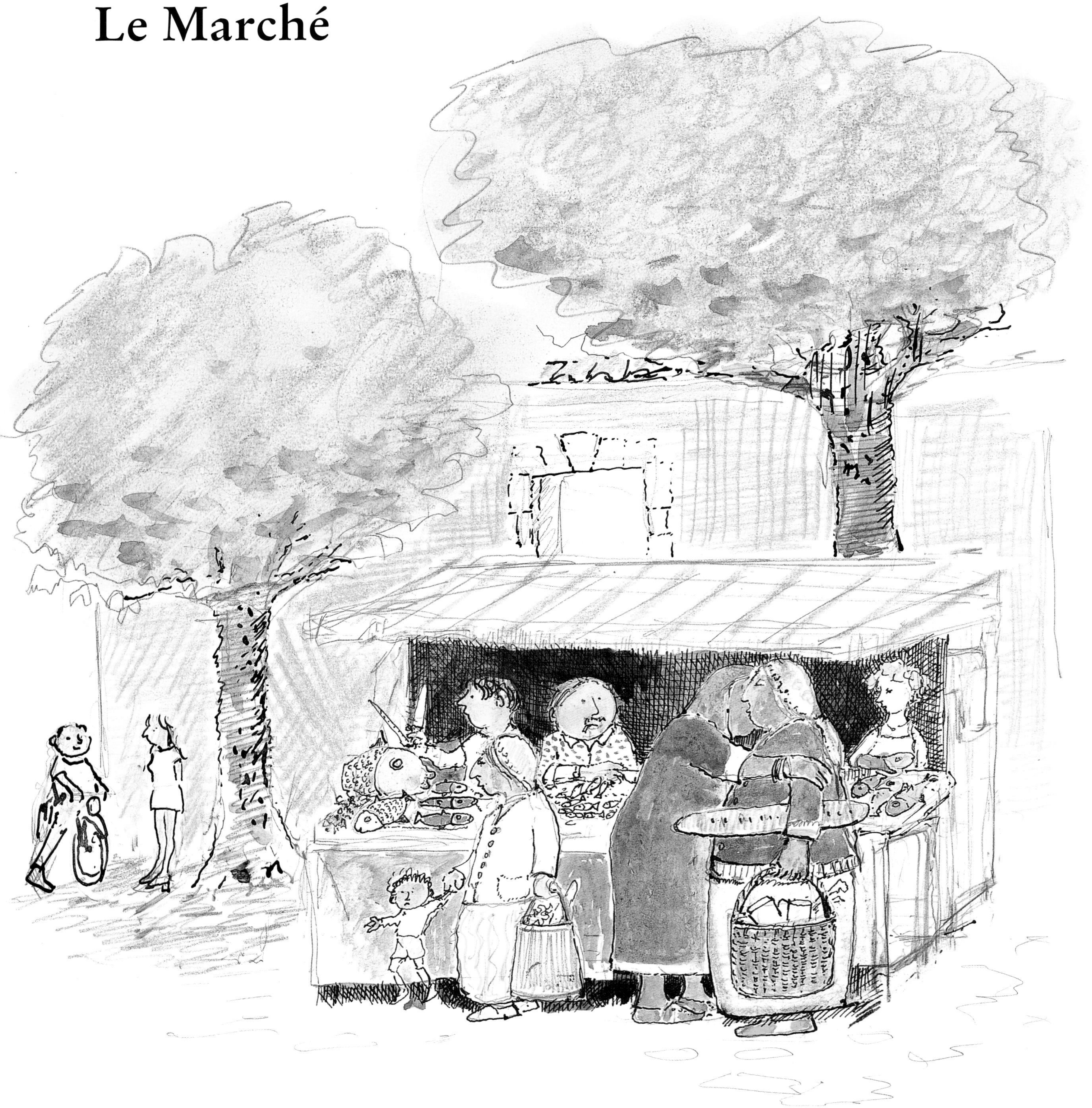

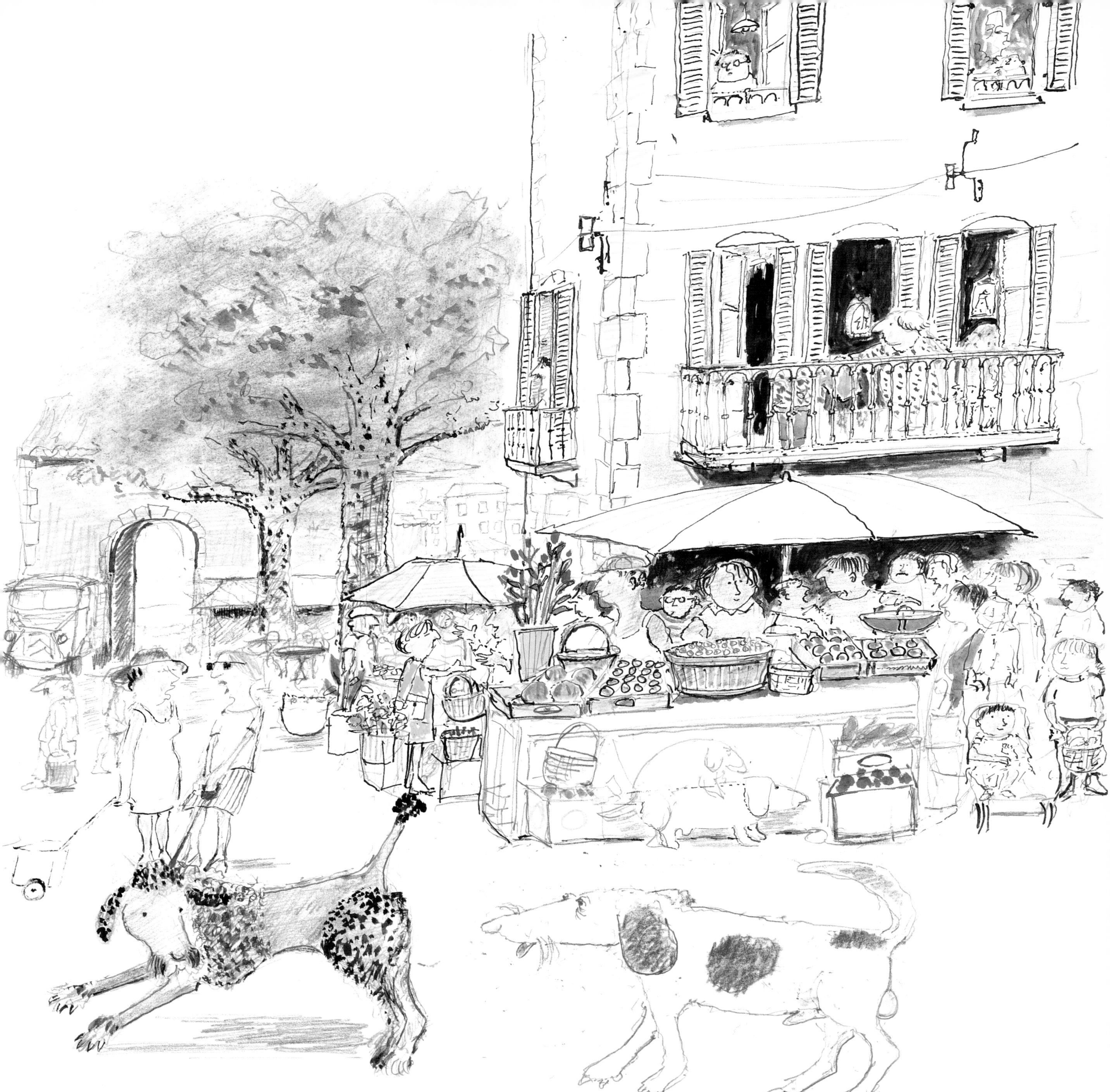

'Nuclear testing on Mururoa has not killed a single mosquito.'

Jean-Claude Martinez, French Member of the European Parliament

'When the bomb was detonated . . . all the water in the lagoon basin was sucked up
into the air, and then rained down. The islets on the encircling reef were all covered
with heaps of irradiated fish and clams, whose slowly rotting flesh continued to
stink for weeks.'

La Depêche de Tahiti (newspaper)

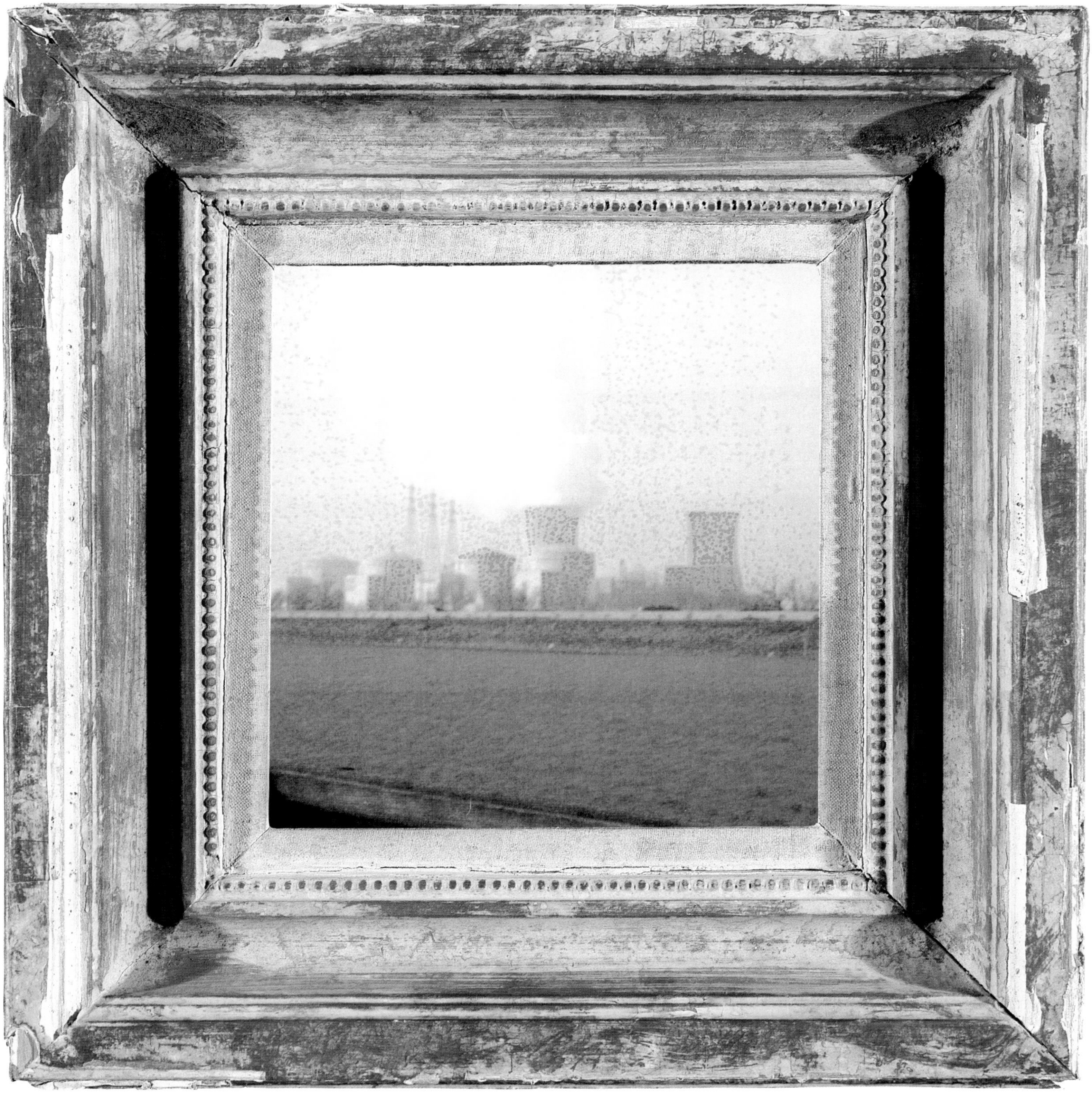

Nuclear Power Station, Donzère

BERCK-SUR-MER

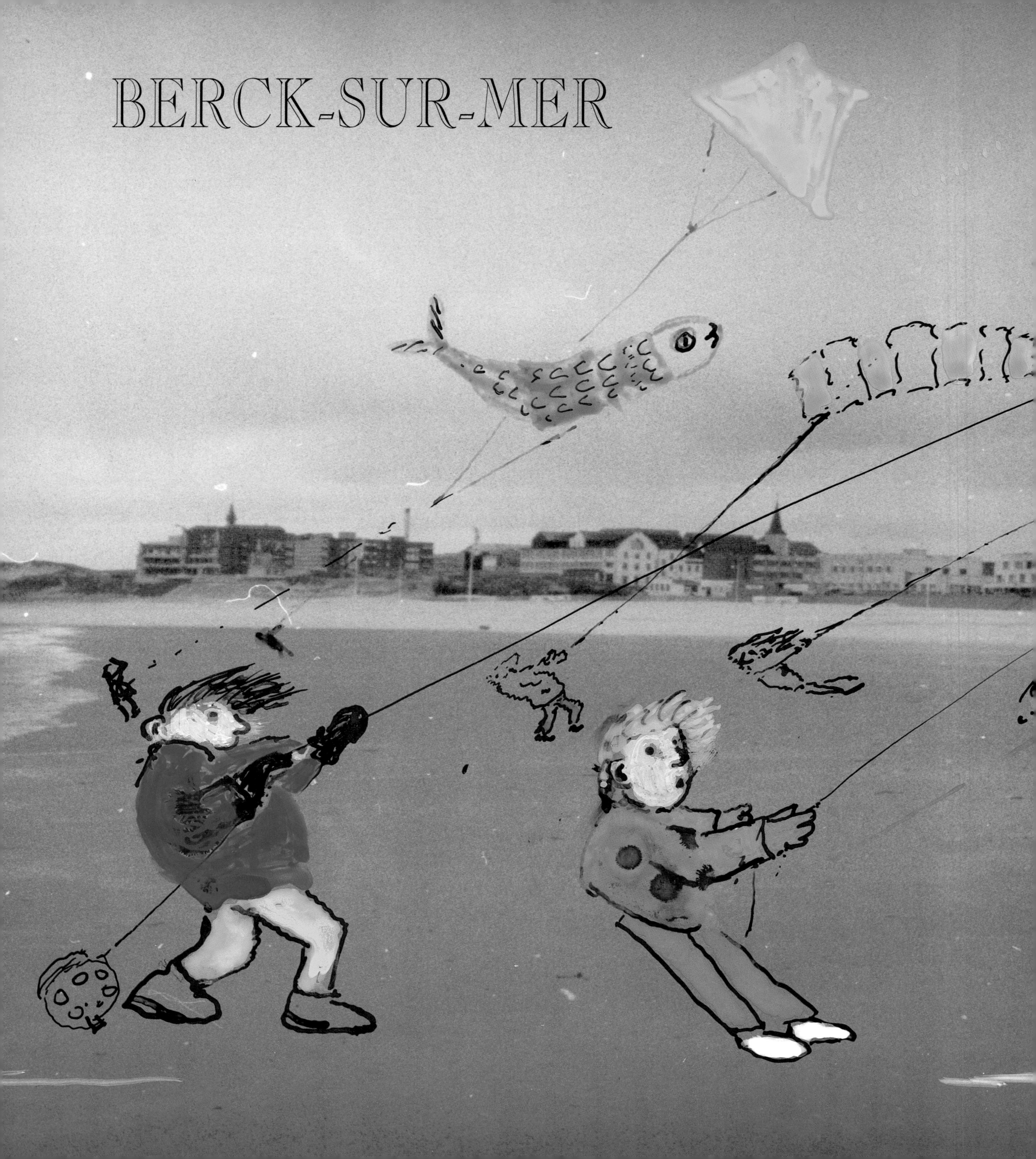

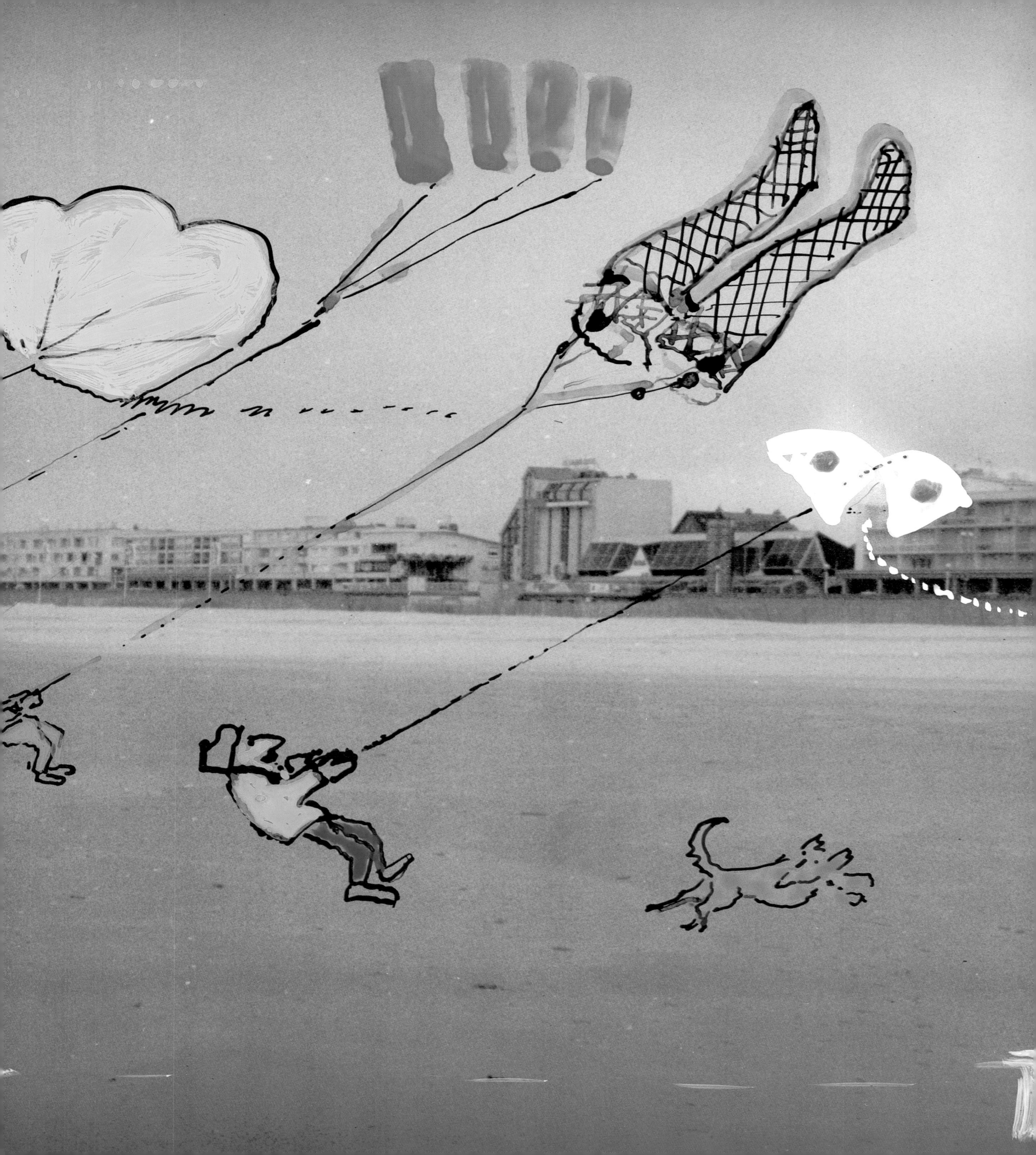

Lou Pouèmo dóu Rose

by Frédéric Mistral in Provençal

...La mistralado
Rounflo toujour Lis aubre, que saludon
En brounzissent, se giblon, s'estrigousson
Amand de s'estrounca...

'Boufo, bregand de coucho-mousco! Boufo,
Desbadarna de dieu, que te crebesses!
Liaura dounc jamais res, O Manjo-Fango
Que tapara lou trau de de Mounte Sortes?'

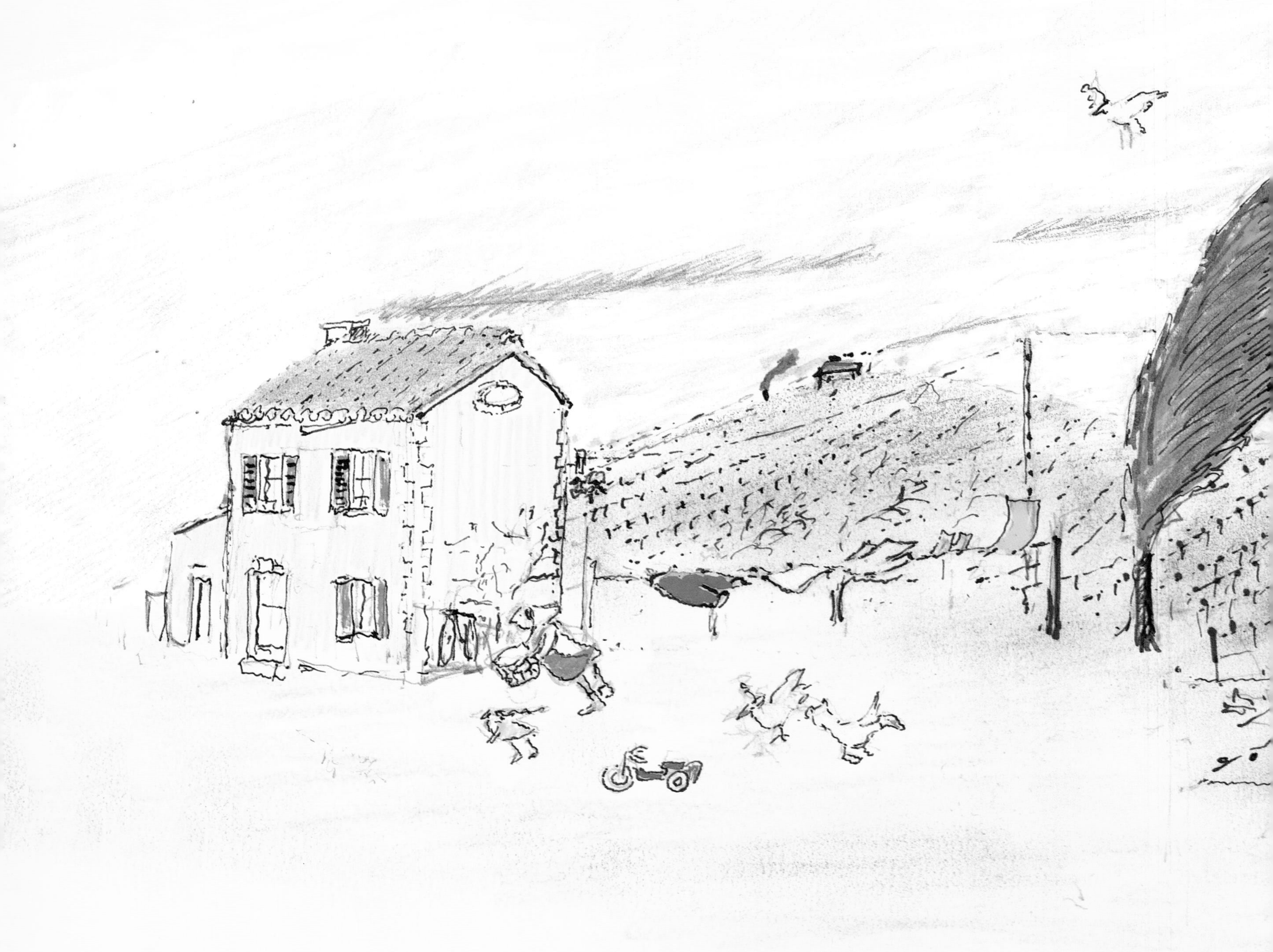

Le Poème du Rhône

by Frédéric Mistral in French

...le mistral en tempête
ronfle toujours. Les arbres, qui saluent
en mugissant, se courbent, se secouent
à arracher leurs troncs...

'Souffle, brigand de Chasse-mouches! Souffle,
ô débraillé de Dieu, à te crever!
Il n' y a donc personne, ô Mange-fange,
qui viendra boucher le trou d'où-tu sors?'

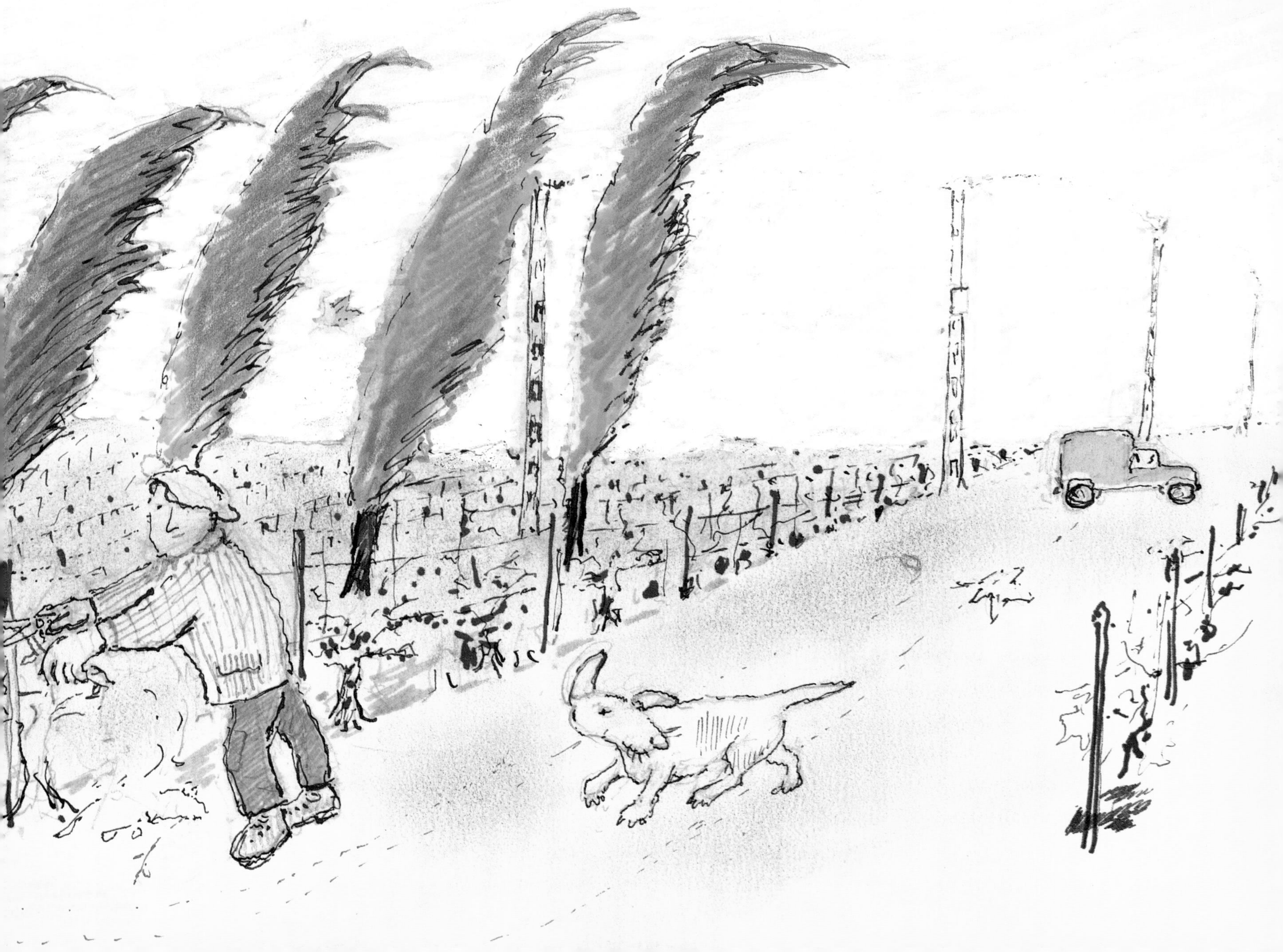

J'aimais la 2 CV, parce qu'elle était sommaire, comme un coucou de Blériot. Coucou couleur de zinc. Je l'aimais pour son habitacle, son odeur d'huile et de caoutchouc, son capot en tôlé ondulée, le bruit de son moteur, et la sensation qu'elle donnait, au-dessus de quarante kilomètres à l'heure, d'avoir le vent dans les voiles. Je l'aimais parce qu'elle était proche de l'invention.

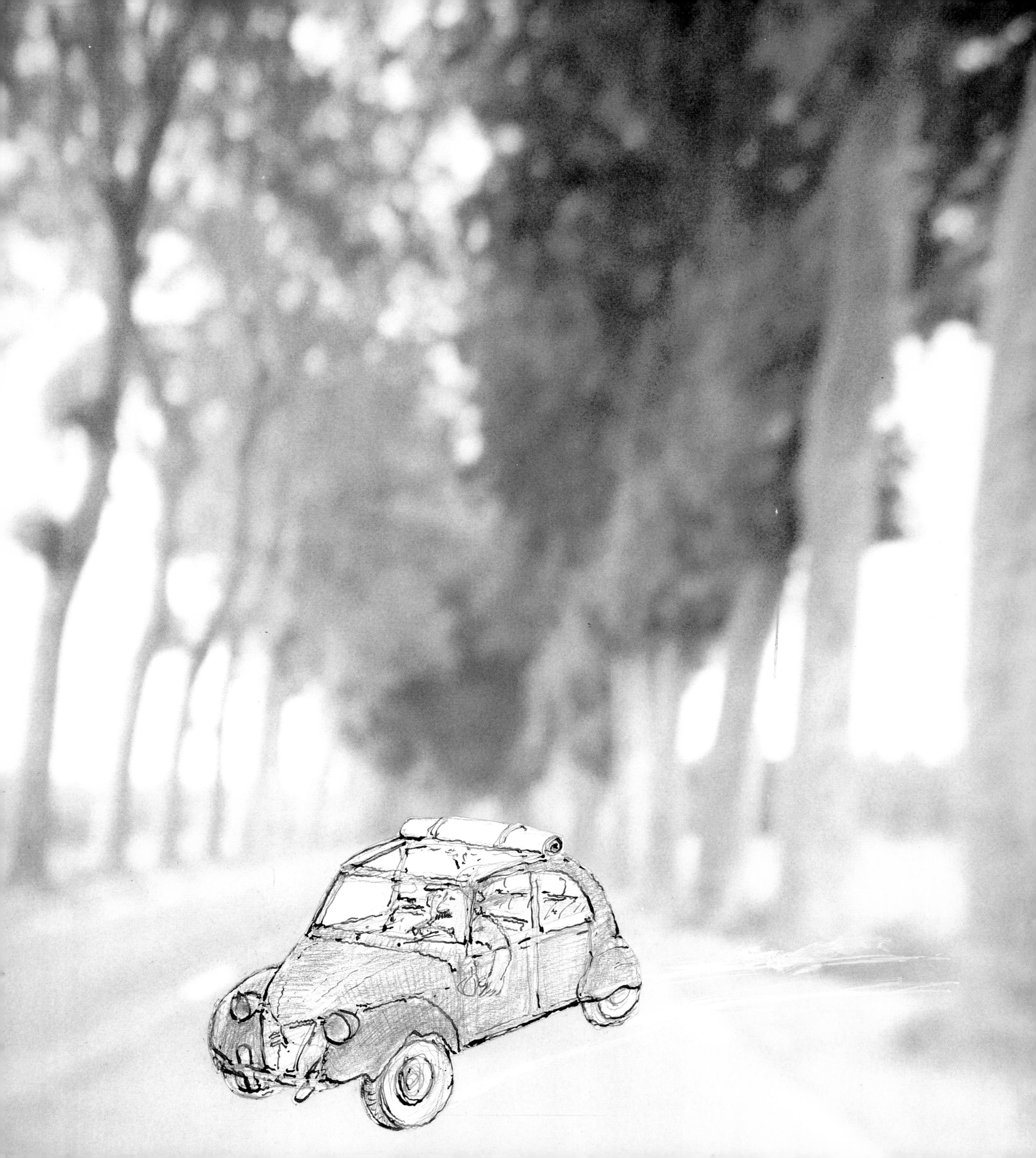

'I drink it when I'm sad. Sometimes I drink it when I'm alone. When I have company I consider it obligatory. I trifle with it when I'm not hungry and drink it when I am. Otherwise I never touch it - unless I'm thirsty.'

Madame Lily Bollinger, 1961

Enjoy the Moment

'Gentlemen, in the little moment that remains to us between the crisis and the catastrophe, we may as well drink a glass of champagne.'

Paul Claudel (1868-1955)

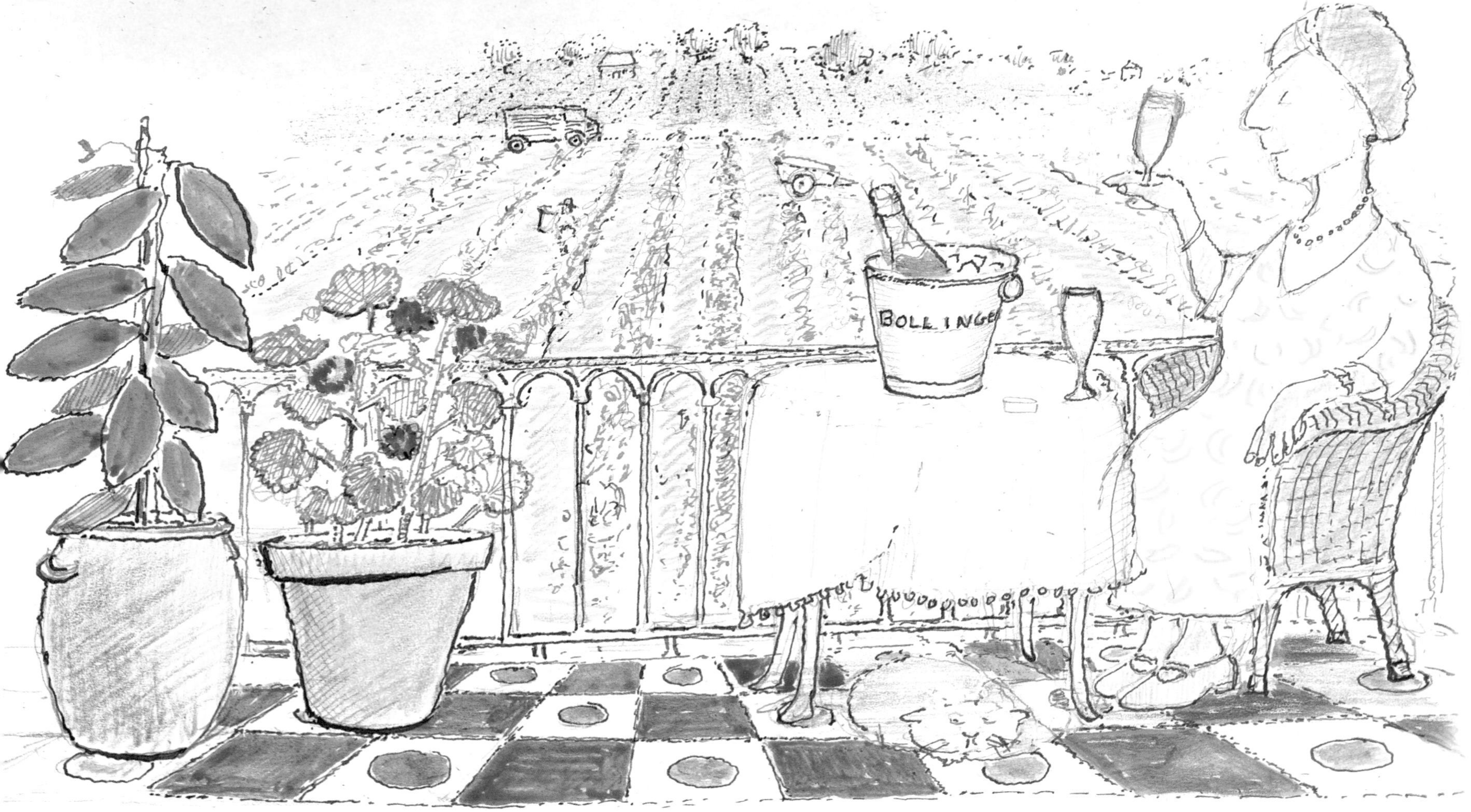
BOLLINGE

Code Rousseau de la Route, 1997

Pedestrian Crossings

A place where it is proper for pedestrians to cross the road is indicated by broad white stripes. One should slow down and stop if necessary to give way to pedestrians crossing.

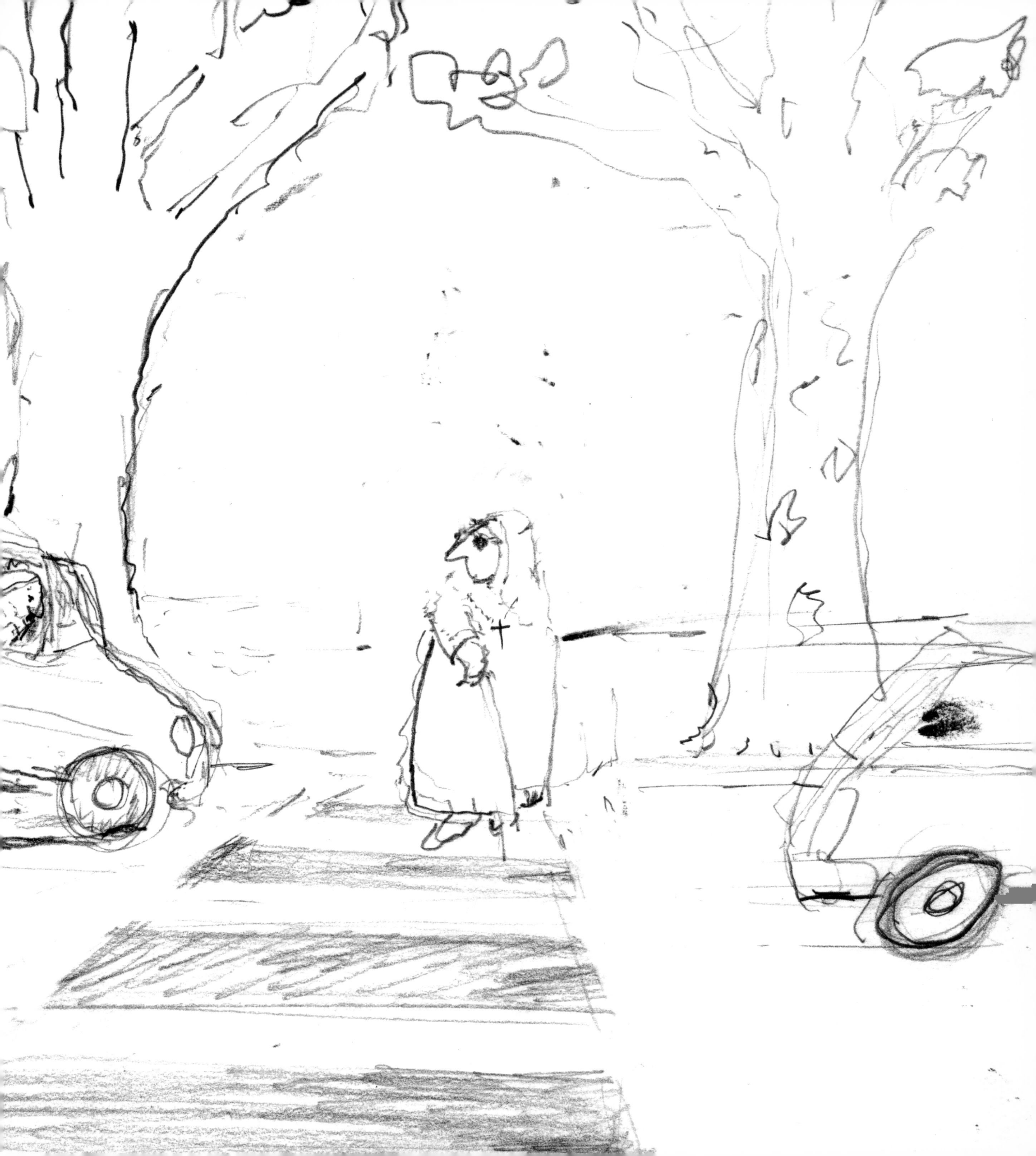

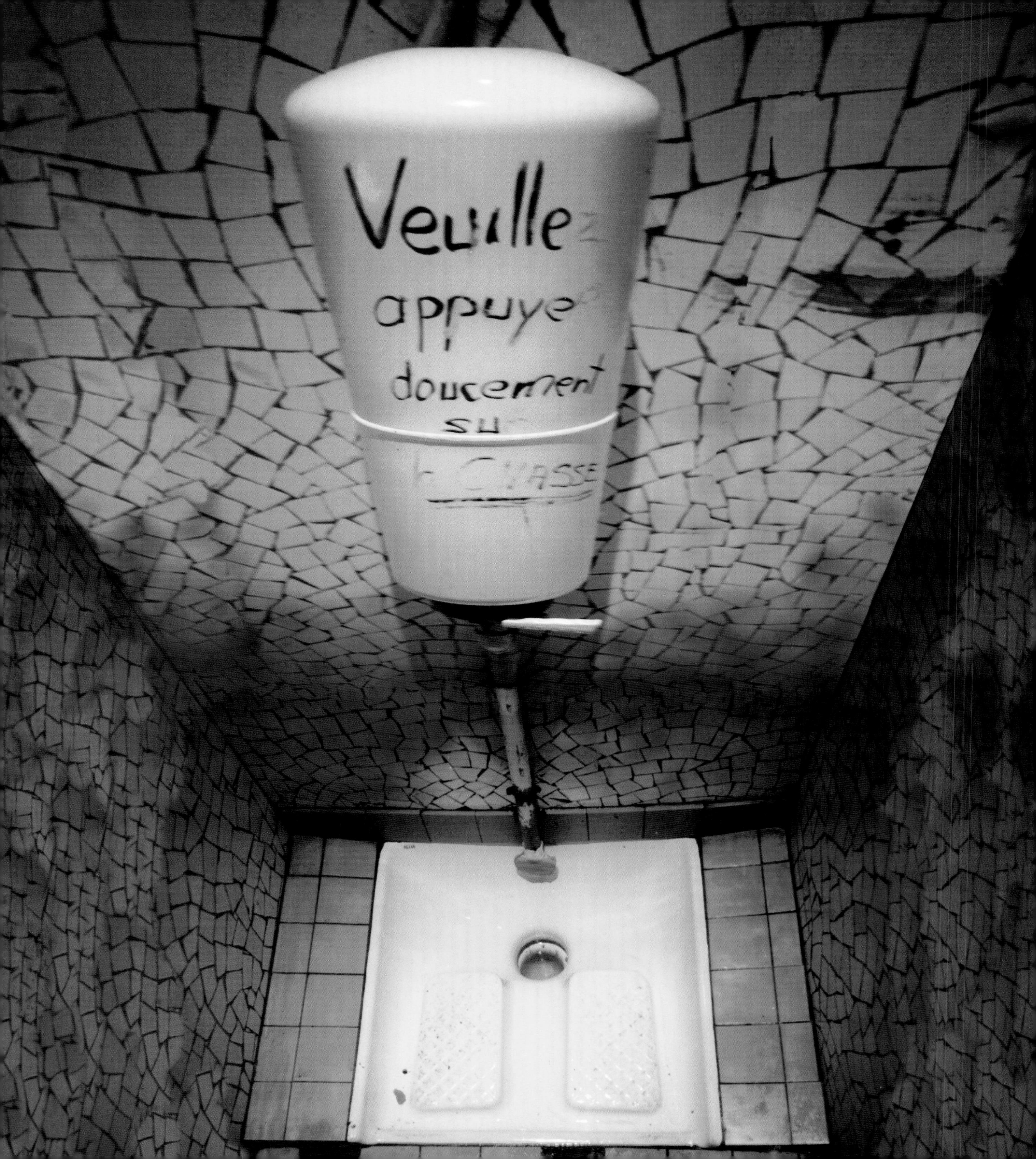
Veuille
appuye
doucement
su

Supporters of the Turkish system base their argument on anatomy: the crouching position has the advantage of facilitating evacuation of the bowels by contracting the abdominal muscles and raising the anus. Furthermore, the new seat carries the risk of infection, as Dr. Mangenot (*Revue d'hygiène et de police sanitaire*, 1897) explains: 'The English system is dangerous because, if not scrupulously cleaned after each visit, its front edge, 0.10 cm deep, can be the repository of a virus which, if picked up by tissue which is often damaged and invariably delicate, may result in a serious illness, the consequences of which, physical, moral and even social, are all the more damaging to the rash user in that others may be led to attribute it to sins he never committed.' Syphilis contracted from a lavatory seat was to become a persistent legend in the best bourgeois families.

In schools, where staff numbers are insufficient to provide adequate supervision, there is nothing to equal the old maxim: 'It is easy to maintain cleanliness when there is only a hole set in a sloping floor and the closet is walled with shiny tiles.' (Dr. A. Collineau, *L'hygiène à l'école, 1889).* Furthermore, there is a still more vital reason for perpetuating the inset foot-marks in the flooring. The crouching position is not a comfortable one, the balance is precarious, however brief the act of defecation, and consequently provides small incentive to linger in surroundings where solitude might give rise to unsavoury ideas…

But the last circle of hell is reached, all too often, by a descent into the conveniences of a café, three-quarters of the time 'à la turque'. 'Every time you pull the chain you get wet feet, they are blocked up, they are lacking in any amenities, they are dirty and they smell dreadful.' (Claude Sarraute, *Le Monde*, 16 February 1984.)

Roger-Henri Guerrand
Les Lieux, Histoire des Commodités

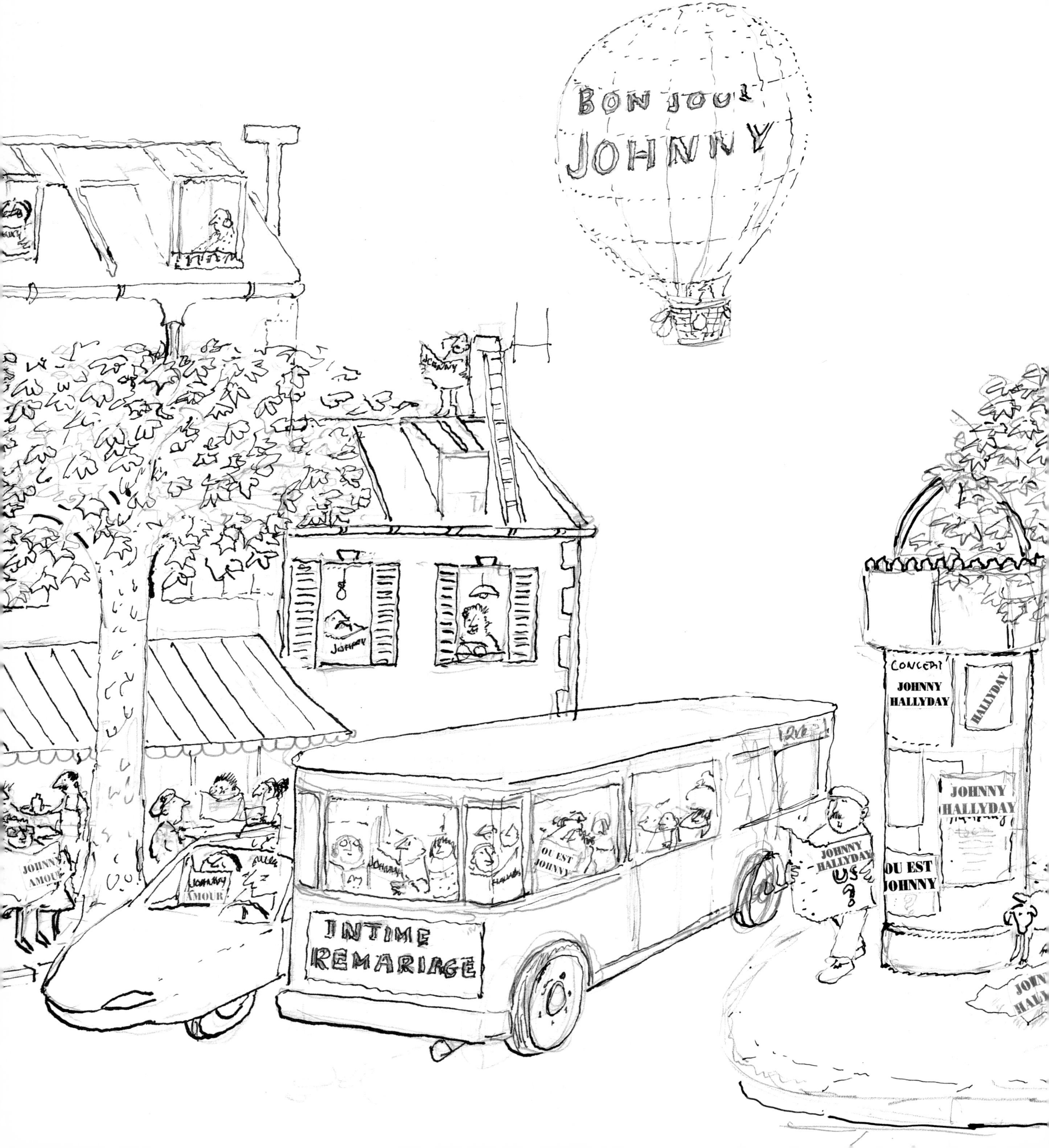
BON JOU
JOHNNY
CONCERT
JOHNNY HALLYDAY
HALLYDAY
JOHNNY HALLYDAY
OU EST JOHNNY
JOHNNY HALLYDAY
OU EST JOHNNY
JOHNNY AMOUR
AMOUR
INTIME REMARIAGE

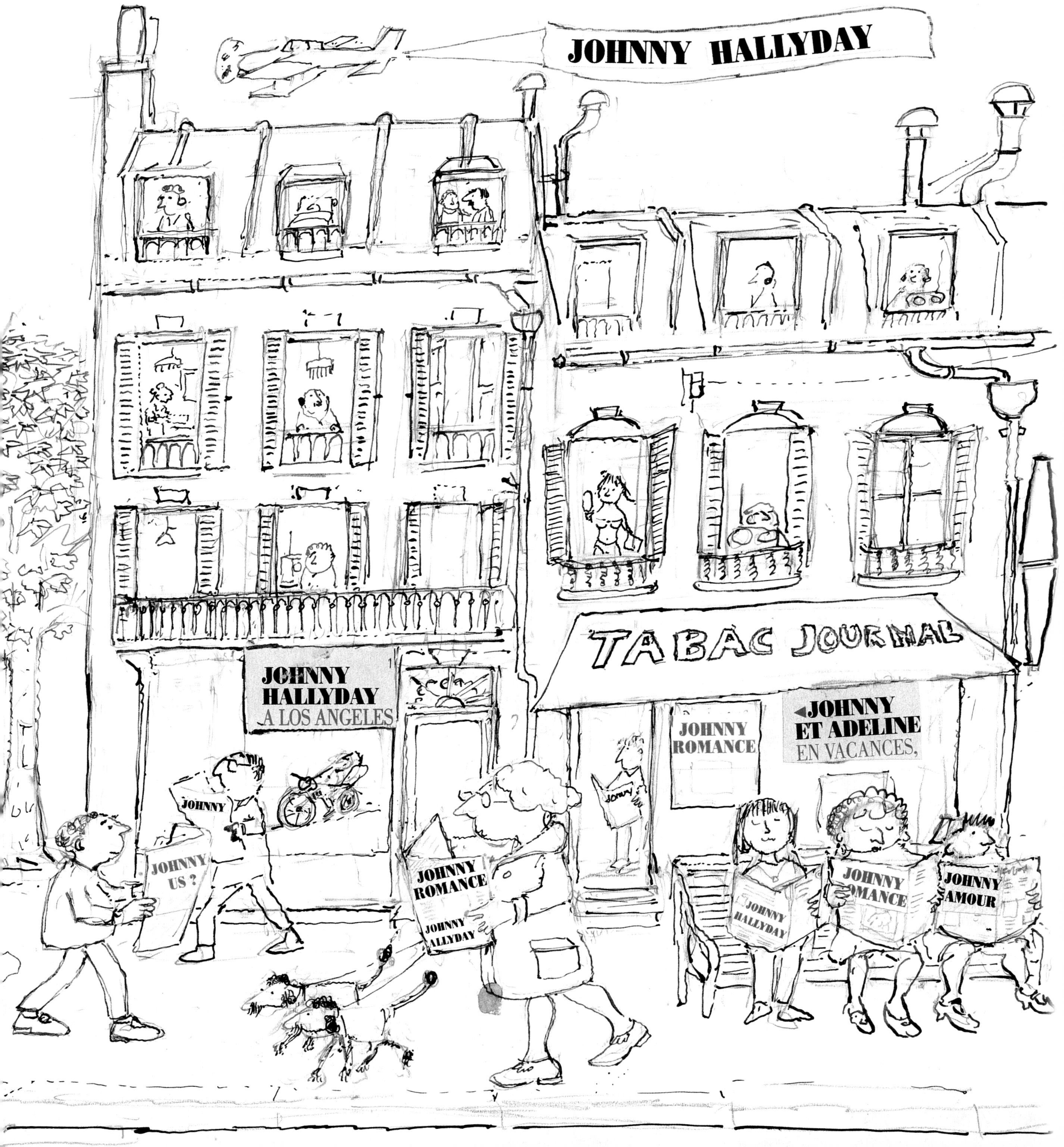
JOHNNY HALLYDAY
TABAC JOURNAL
JOHNNY HALLYDAY A LOS ANGELES
JOHNNY ROMANCE
◀ JOHNNY ET ADELINE EN VACANCES,
JOHNNY
JOHNNY US ?
JOHNNY ROMANCE JOHNNY HALLYDAY
JOHNNY HALLYDAY
JOHNNY ROMANCE
JOHNNY AMOUR

In certain provincial towns there are houses whose aspect inspires a melancholy equal to that provoked by the most sombre cloisters, the dreariest moorlands or the saddest ruins. Perhaps these houses contain at the same time the silence of a cloister, the aridity of a moor and the skeletal quality of ruins: life and movement in them are so still that a stranger would think them uninhabited, were he not suddenly to encounter the pale and cold gaze of a motionless figure whose half-monastic shape hovers behind the window, with the sound of an unknown tread.

Honoré de Balzac, *Eugénie Grandet*, 1833

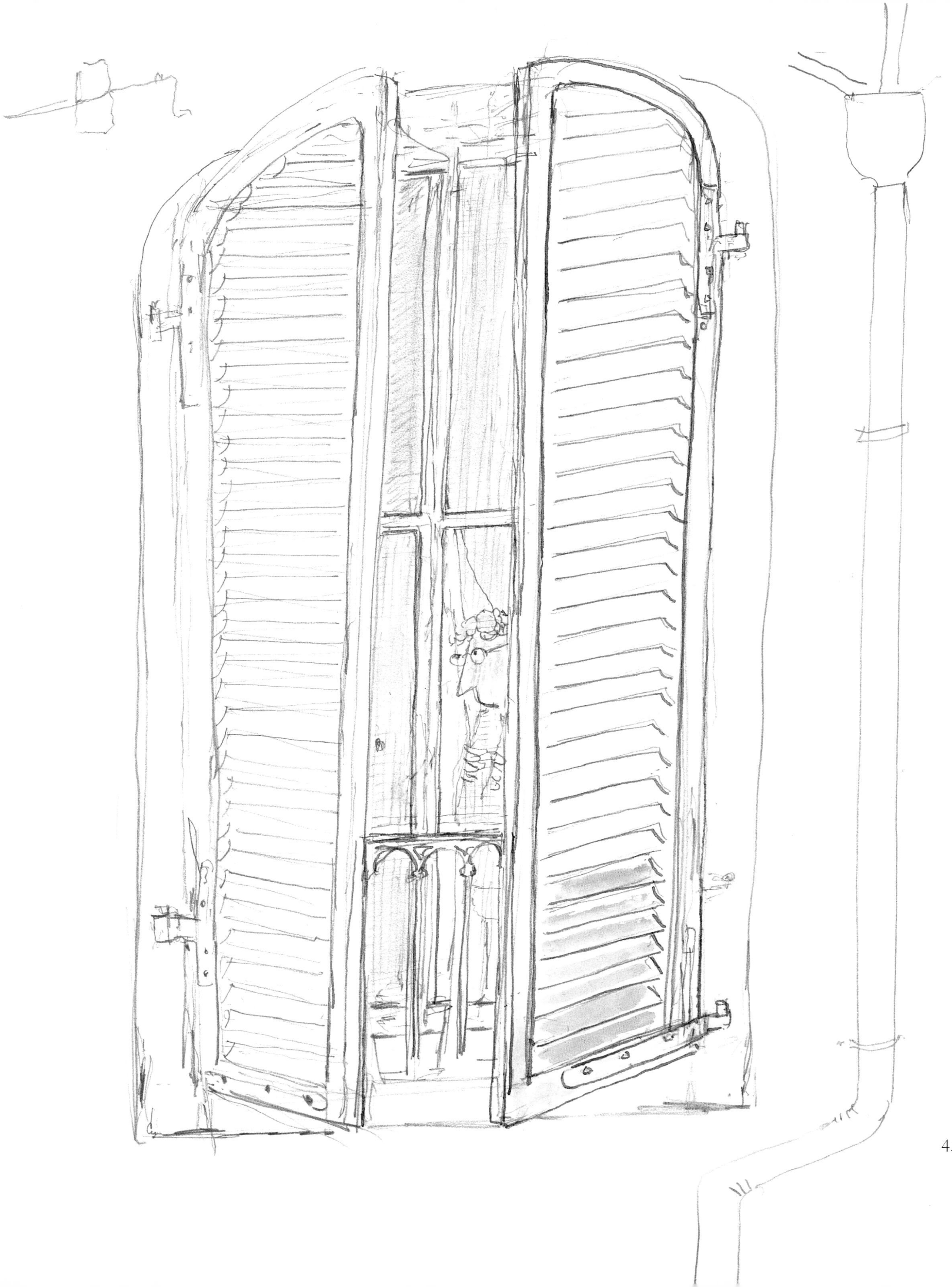

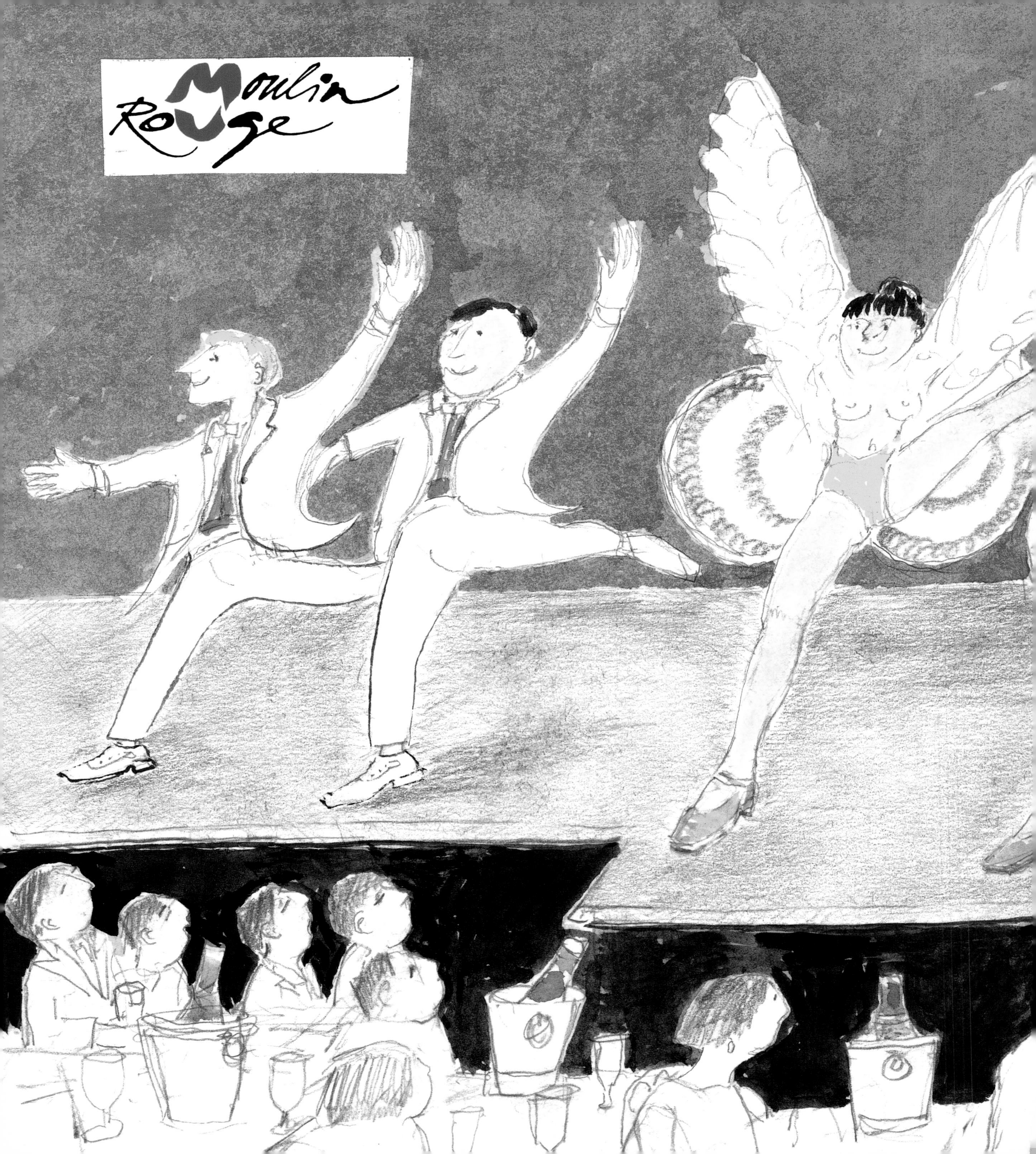
Moulin Rouge

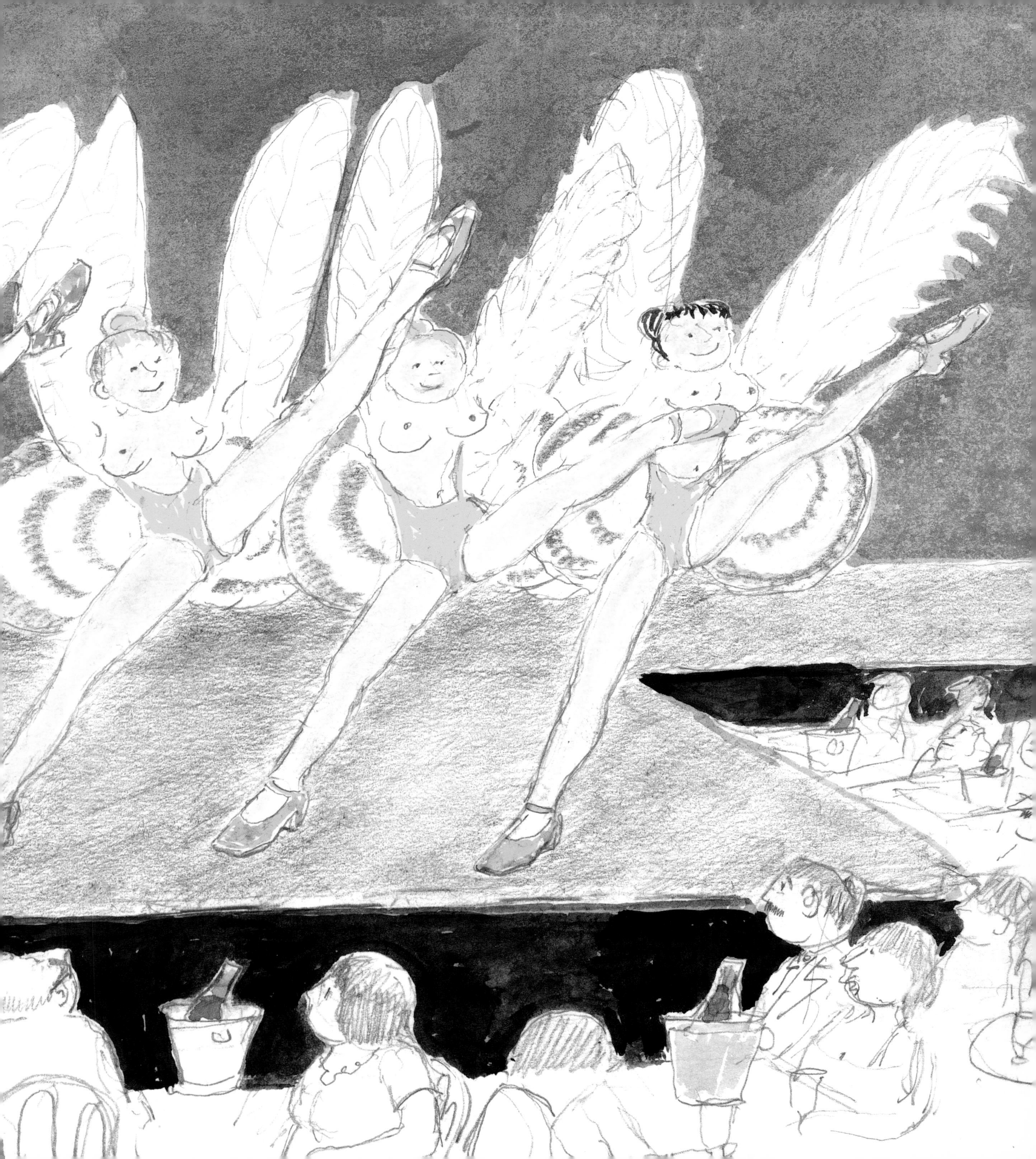

Under The Bridges Of Paris

(SOUS LES PONTS DE PARIS)

English lyric by DORCAS COCHRAN
French lyric by J. RODOR
Music by
VINCENT SCOTTO

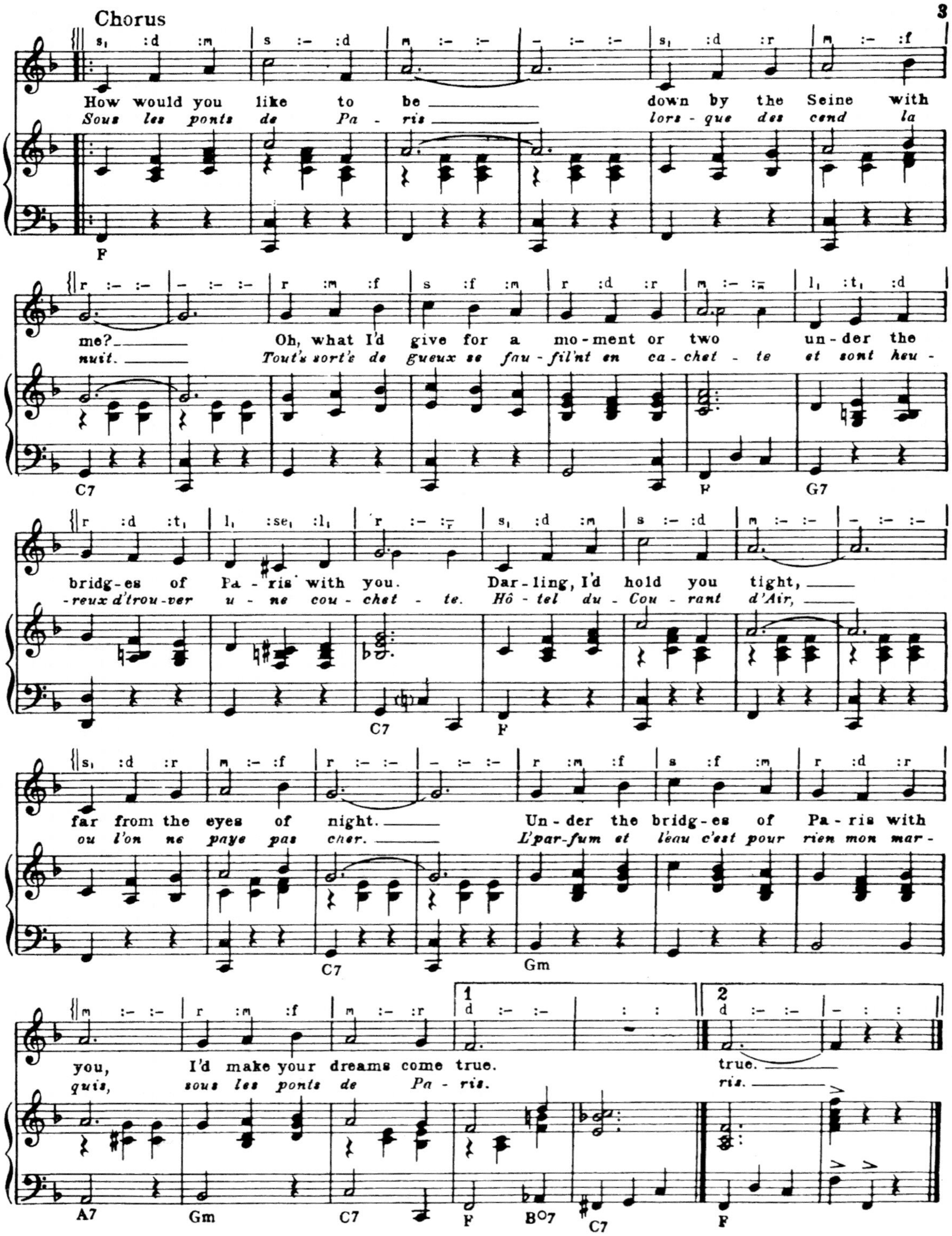
Chorus
How would you like to be ___ down by the Seine with me? ___ Oh, what I'd give for a mo-ment or two un-der the bridg-es of Pa-ris with you. Dar-ling, I'd hold you tight, ___ far from the eyes of night. ___ Un-der the bridg-es of Pa-ris with you, I'd make your dreams come true. true. ___
Sous les ponts de Pa-ris ___ lors-que des-cend la nuit. ___ Tout's sort's de gueux se fau-fil'nt en ca-chet-te et sont heu-reux d'trou-ver u-ne cou-chet-te. Hô-tel du Cou-rant d'Air, ___ ou l'on ne paye pas cher. ___ L'par-fum et l'eau c'est pour rien mon mar-quis, sous les ponts de Pa-ris. ris. ___
F
C7
G7
Gm
A7
B°7

SO. 71

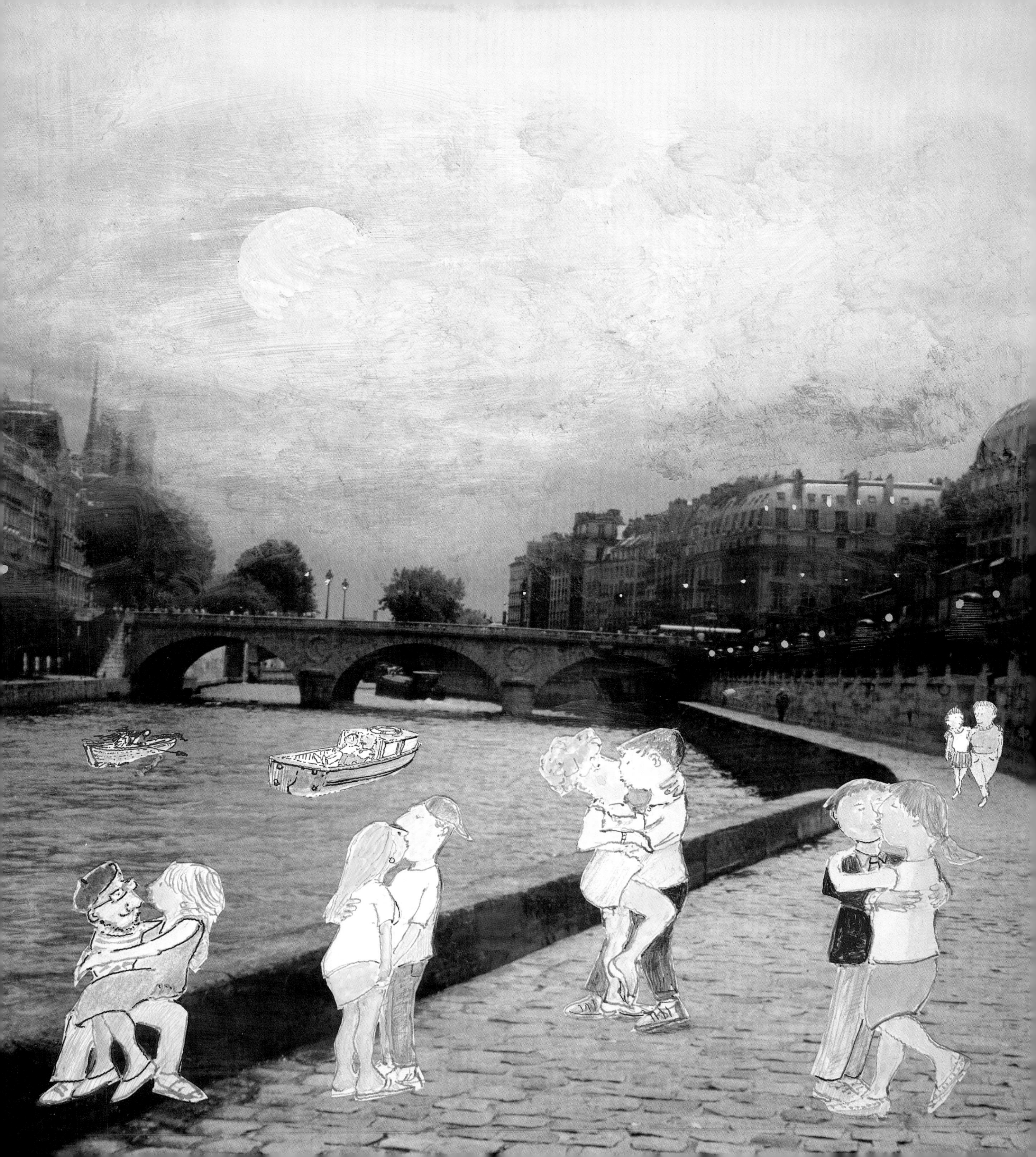

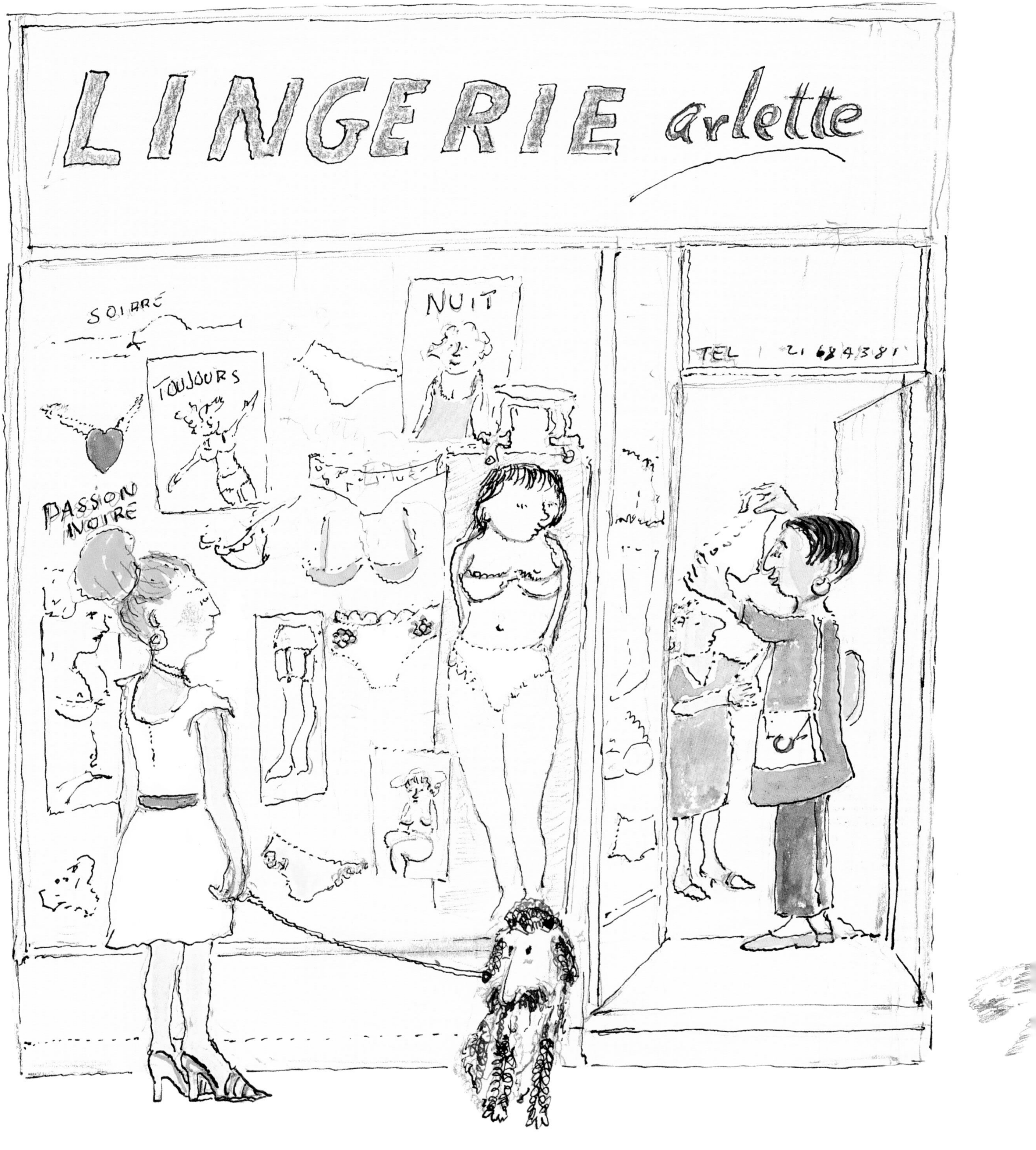

LINGERIE arlette
SOIRÉE
NUIT
TEL 21 68 43 81
TOUJOURS
PASSION NOIRE

Les Français sont jaloux de leurs maîtresses,
et jamais de leurs femmes.

Casanova de Seingalt *(1725-98),*
Mémoires, published 1826-38

'Cannes is where you lie on the beach and look at
the stars - or vice versa.'

Rex Reed, US film critic

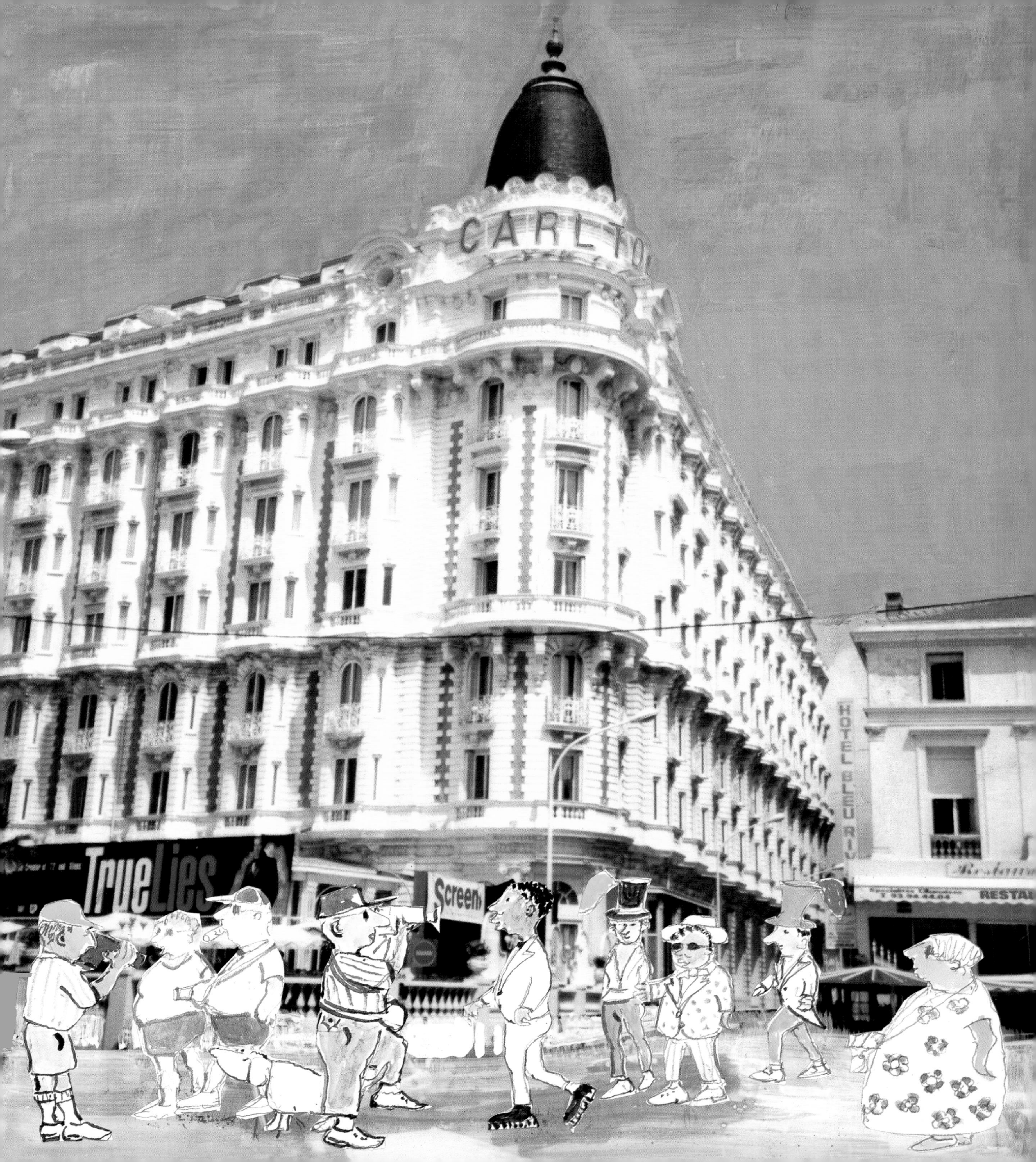
CARLTO
True Lies
Screen
HOTEL BLEU RIV
RESTAU

Corrigendum to 2221/92

As amended by EC Commission Reg No 3540/91, 2221/92, 3300/93, 1259/94,3239/94,786/95,2401/95,1511/96

COMMISSION REGULATION (EEC) NO. 1274/91

of 15 May 1991

introducing detailed rules for implementing Regulations (EEC) No. 1907/90 on certain marketing standards for eggs

THE COMMISSION OF THE EUROPEAN COMMUNITIES.

Having regard to the Treaty establishing the European Economic Community.

Having regard to Council Regulation (EEC) No. 1907/90 of 26 June 1990 on certain marketing standards for eggs[1] and in particular Articles 5(3), 10 (3), 11 (2), 20 (1) and 22 (2) thereof;

Whereas Regulation (EEC) No. 1907/90 contains a thorough revision of such marketing standards as were implemented in pursuance of previous Regulations; whereas provisions is made therein for detailed rules necessary for the implementation of such standards to be adopted in accordance with Article 17 of Council Regulation (EEC) No. 2771/75 [2] ; as last amended by Regulation (EEC) No. 1235/89[3] ; whereas such rules are in particular to be laid down as regards the conditions for registration of collectors and packing centres, the identification, frequency of collection and the delivery and handling of eggs, quality criteria and weight gradings, the particulars of indications on eggs and their packs, terms to be used for indications of the type of farming, and criteria concerning the origin of eggs, and exemption in the case of small quantities from the obligation for eggs to be packed in large packs;

Whereas both technological developments and consumer demand now make it appropriate to provide for prompter delivery, collection, grading and packing of eggs; whereas however certain producers are in a position to provide guarantees of maintaining the temperature at which the eggs are kept at a level such as would make possible a permanent exemption from the general requirement of daily collection or delivery in the case of eggs intended for labelling as 'extra' eggs as provided for in Article 12 of Regulation (EEC) No. 1907/90; whereas, however, for a transitional period, it is appropriate to provide for a general exemption for the benefit of all operators;

Whereas markets, access to which is restricted to authorised packing and processing undertakings, provide guarantees of correct handling such that they may be allowed to deliver eggs on the second working day following that of reception;

Whereas the deliberate cumulation of the various time limits, to the detriment of egg freshness, must be prevented in the case where a packing centre delivers ungraded eggs to another packing centre;

Whereas only undertakings whose premises and technical equipment are suited to the scale of their operations, which therefore permit the proper handling of the eggs, should be authorised to collect, or to grade eggs by quality and weight;

Whereas, for the avoidance of confusion and in order to facilitate identification of consignments of eggs for the purposes of the enforcement of this Regulation, each packing centre should be allotted a distinguishing registration number based on a uniform coding system;

Whereas, in order to ensure that the consumer is supplied with good quality produce, criteria of a high standard should be fixed for each quality grade;

---

(1) OJ No. L.173 .6. 7. 1990, p.5

(2) OJ No. L.232. 1.11.1975, p.49

(3) OJ No. L.123, 11. 5. 1989, p.19.

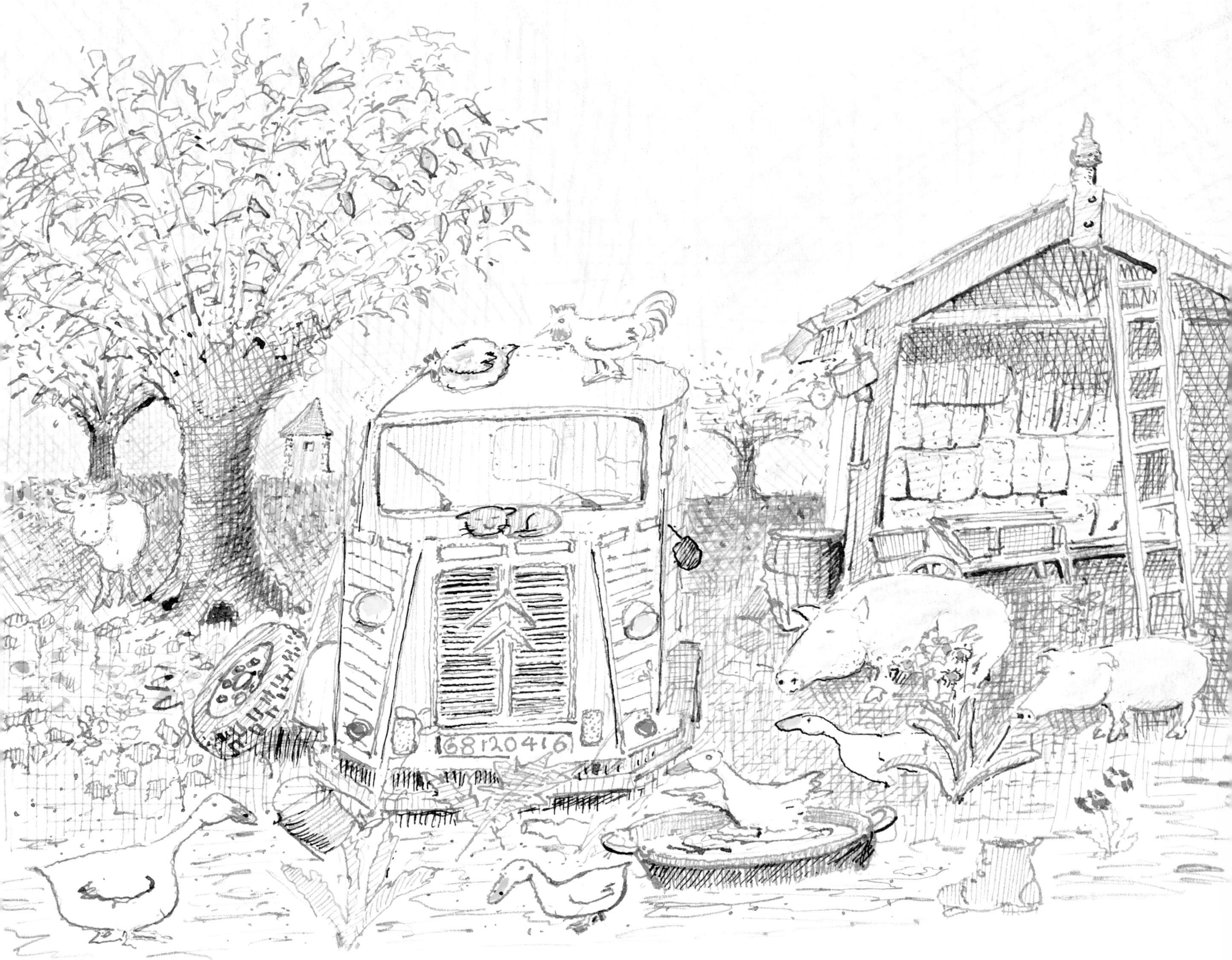
68r20416

Canal de Bourgogne

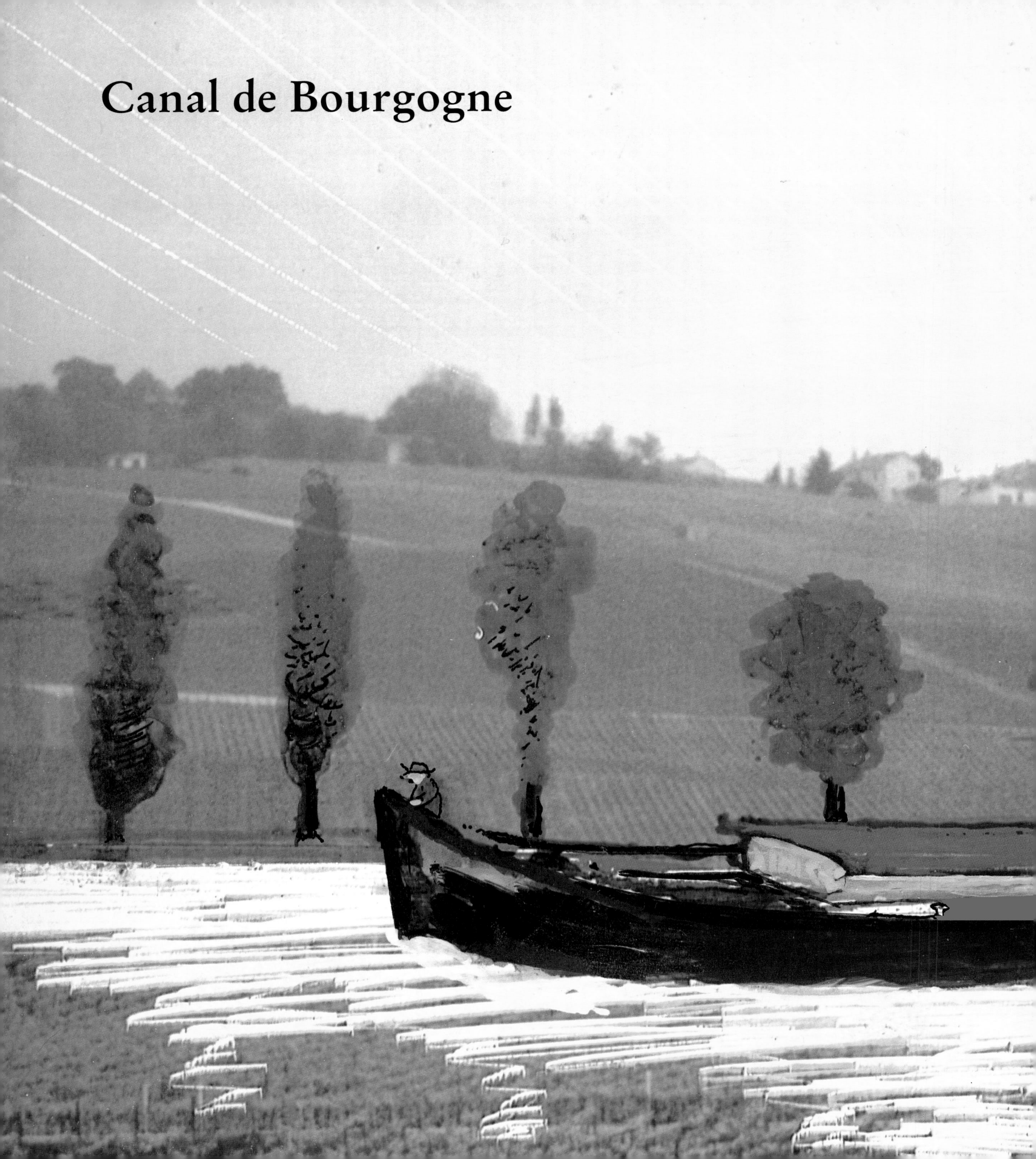

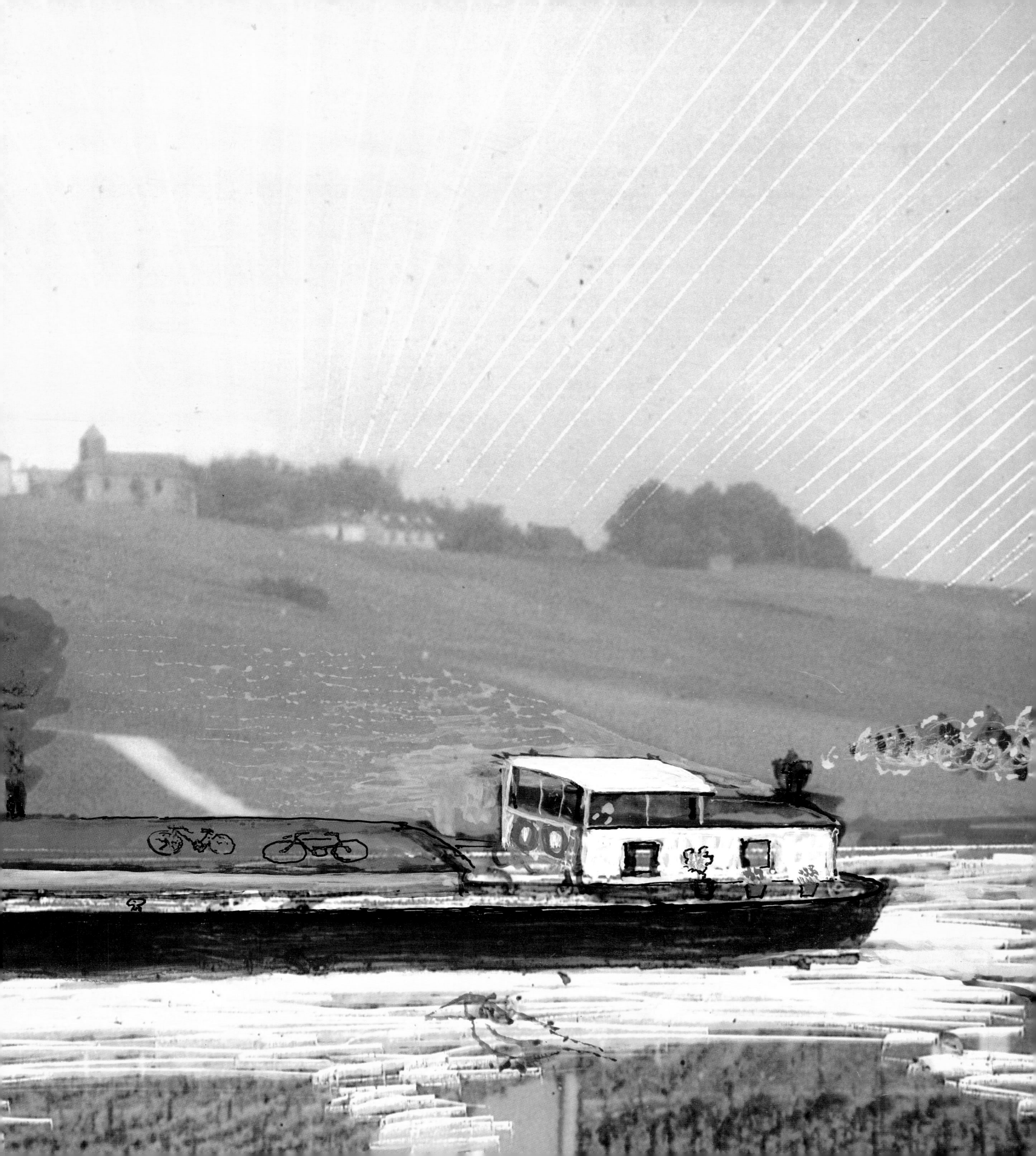

FNSEA
(Féderation nationale des syndicats d'exploitants agricoles)

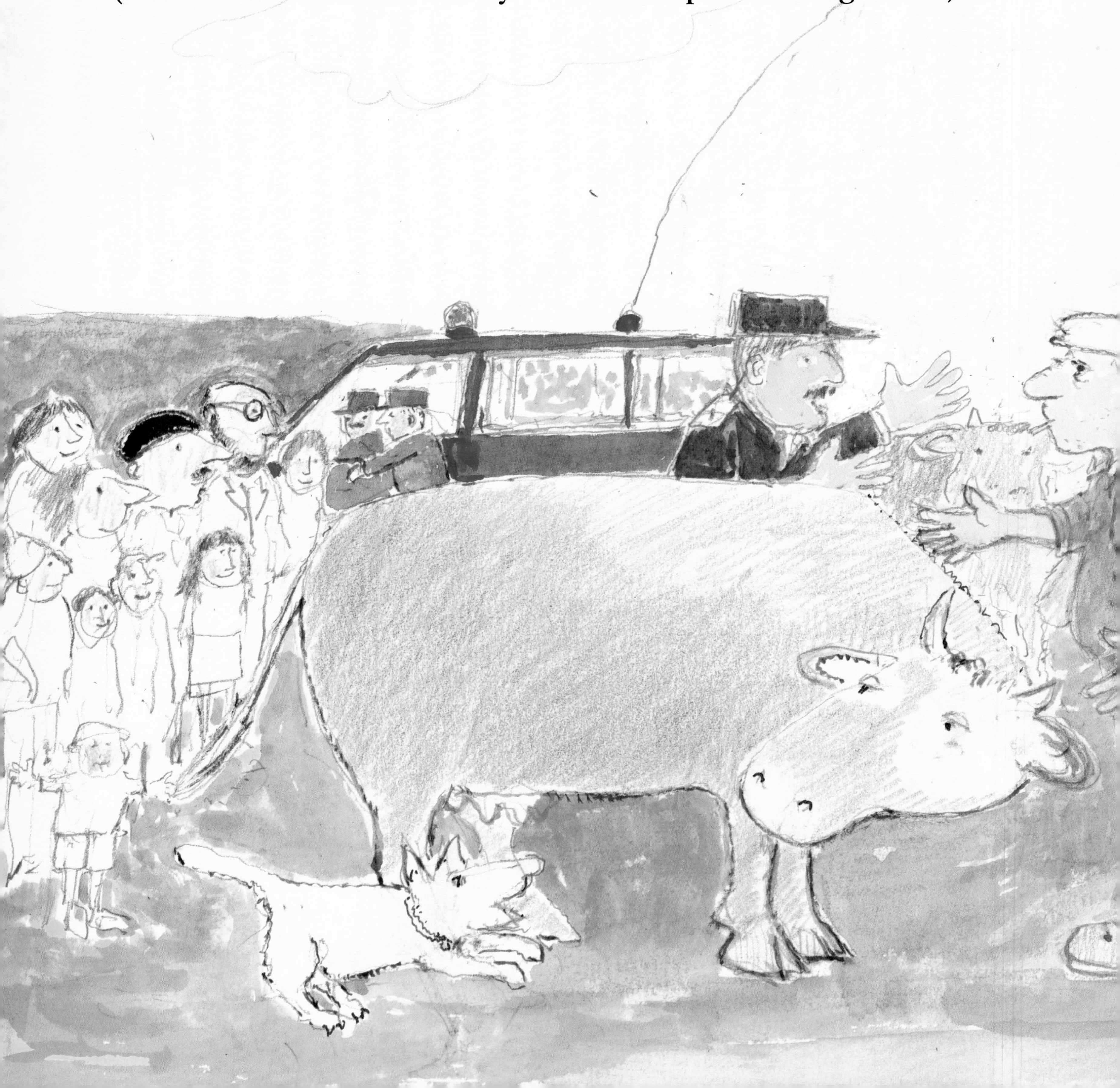

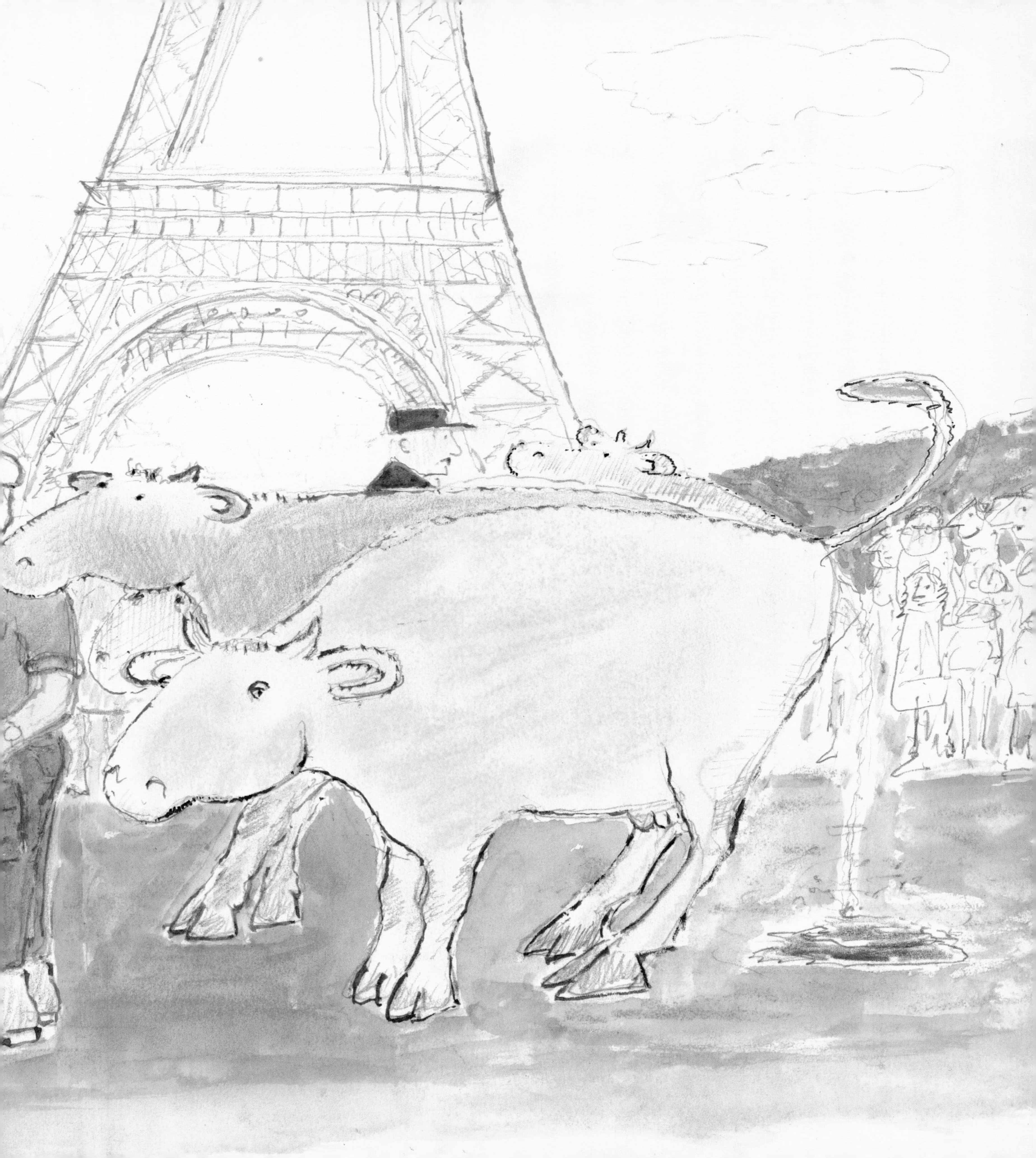

B ut let us return to the façade of
Notre-Dame as we find it today.
We gaze in reverent admiration upon this
solemn and mighty cathedral, awesome,
as its chroniclers express it: *Quae mole
sua terrorem incutit spectantibus.* *

*Which by its mass inspires terror in the spectators.

Victor Hugo, *The Hunchback of Notre-Dame*, 1831.

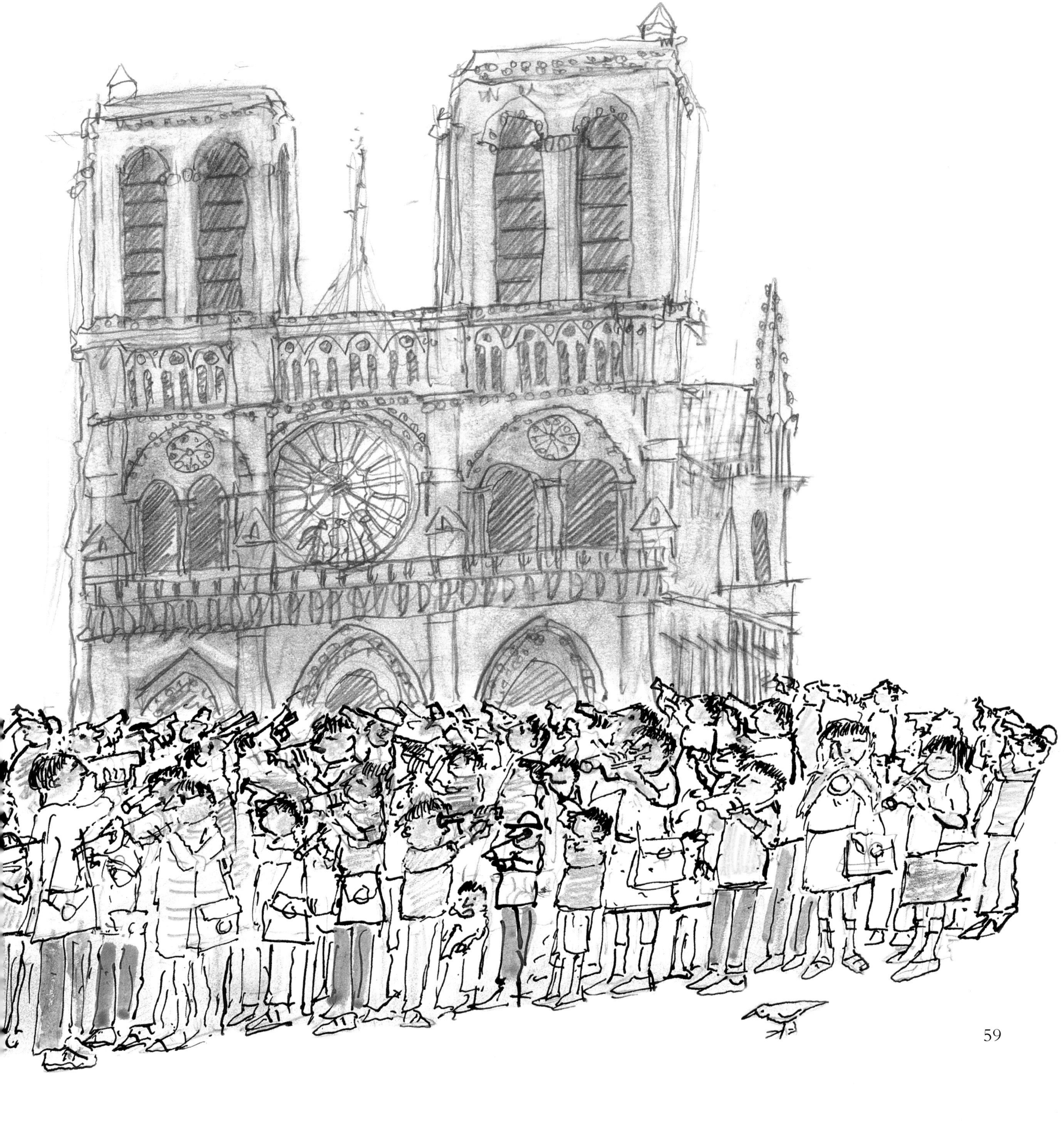

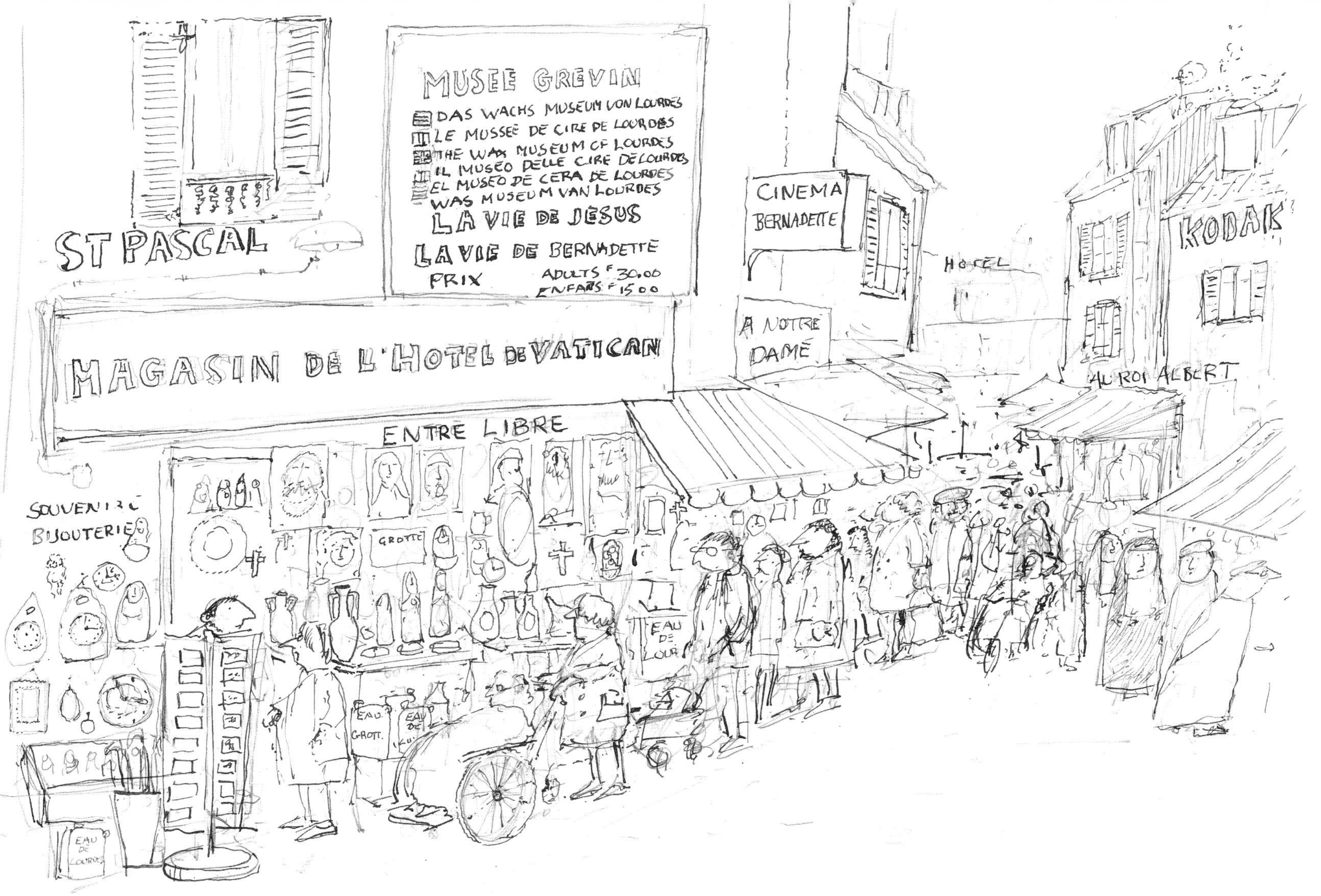
MUSEE GREVIN
DAS WACHS MUSEUM VON LOURDES
THE WAX MUSEUM OF LOURDES
EL MUSEO DE CERA DE LOURDES
WAS MUSEUM VAN LOURDES
LA VIE DE JESUS
LA VIE DE BERNADETTE
PRIX
ST PASCAL
CINEMA
BERNADETTE
A NOTRE DAME
KODAK
AU ROI ALBERT
MAGASIN DE L'HOTEL DE VATICAN
ENTRE LIBRE
BIJOUTERIE
GROTTE
EAU DE LOURDES

Lourdes

And there was also jewellery: rings, brooches and bracelets, loaded with stars and crosses, and ornamented with saintly figures. Finally there was the Paris article, which rose above and submerged all the rest: pencil-holders, purses, cigar-holders, paper-weights, paper-knives, even snuff-boxes; and innumerable other objects on which the Basilica, Grotto, and Blessed Virgin ever appeared, reproduced in every way, by every process that is known. Heaped together pell mell in one of the cases reserved to articles at fifty centimes apiece were napkin-rings, egg-cups, and wooden pipes, on which was carved the beaming apparition of Our Lady of Lourdes.

Little by little, M. de Guersaint, with the annoyance of a man who prides himself on being an artist, became disgusted and quite sad. ‘But all this is frightful, frightful!’ he repeated at every new article he took up to look at.

Émile Zola, *Lourdes,* 1894

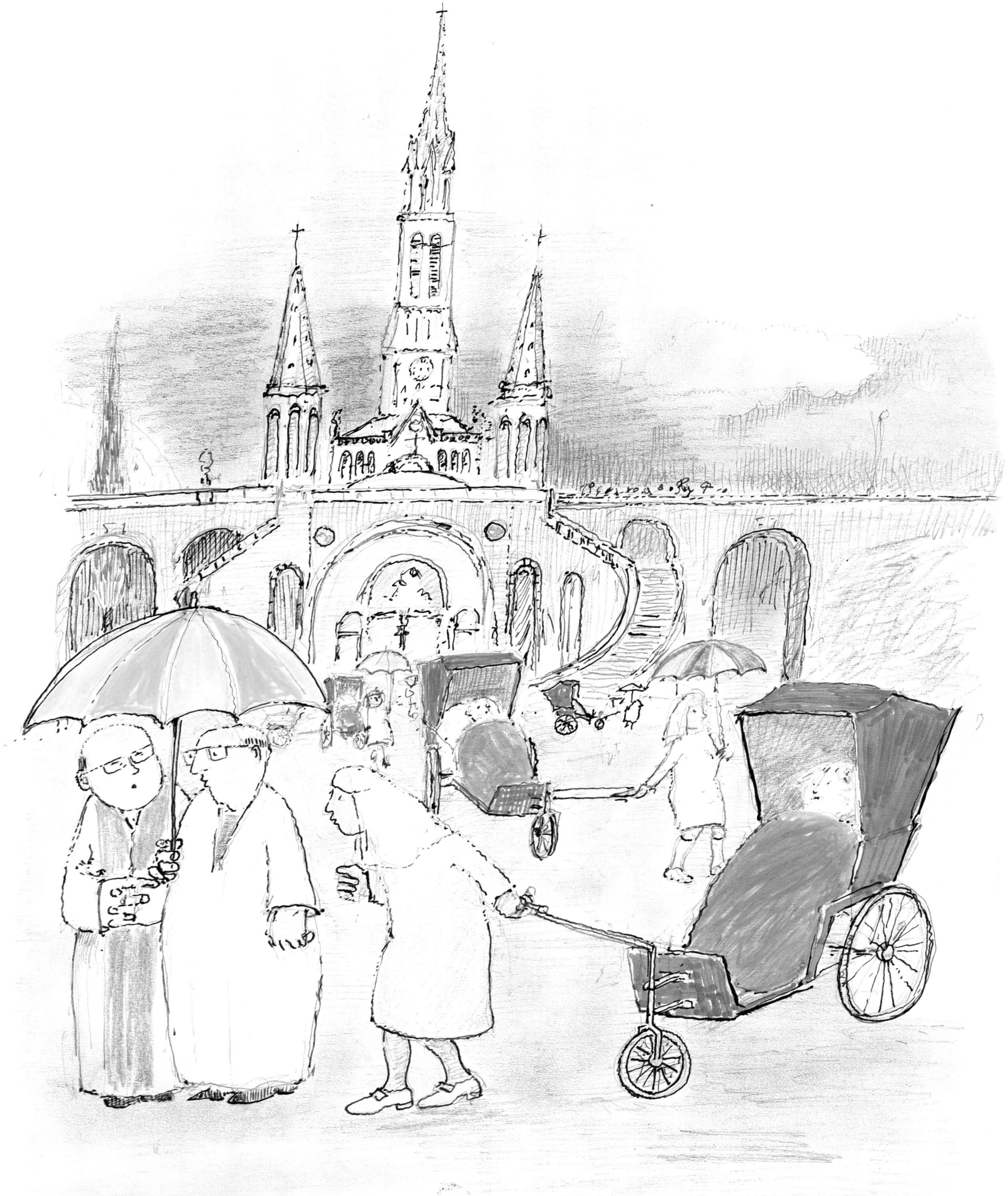

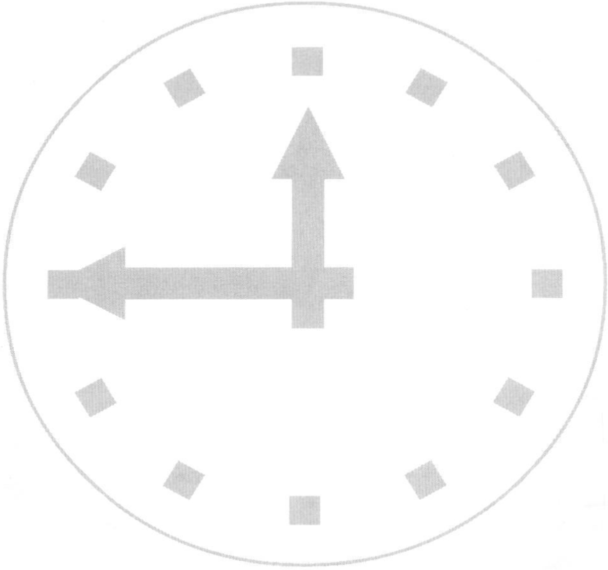

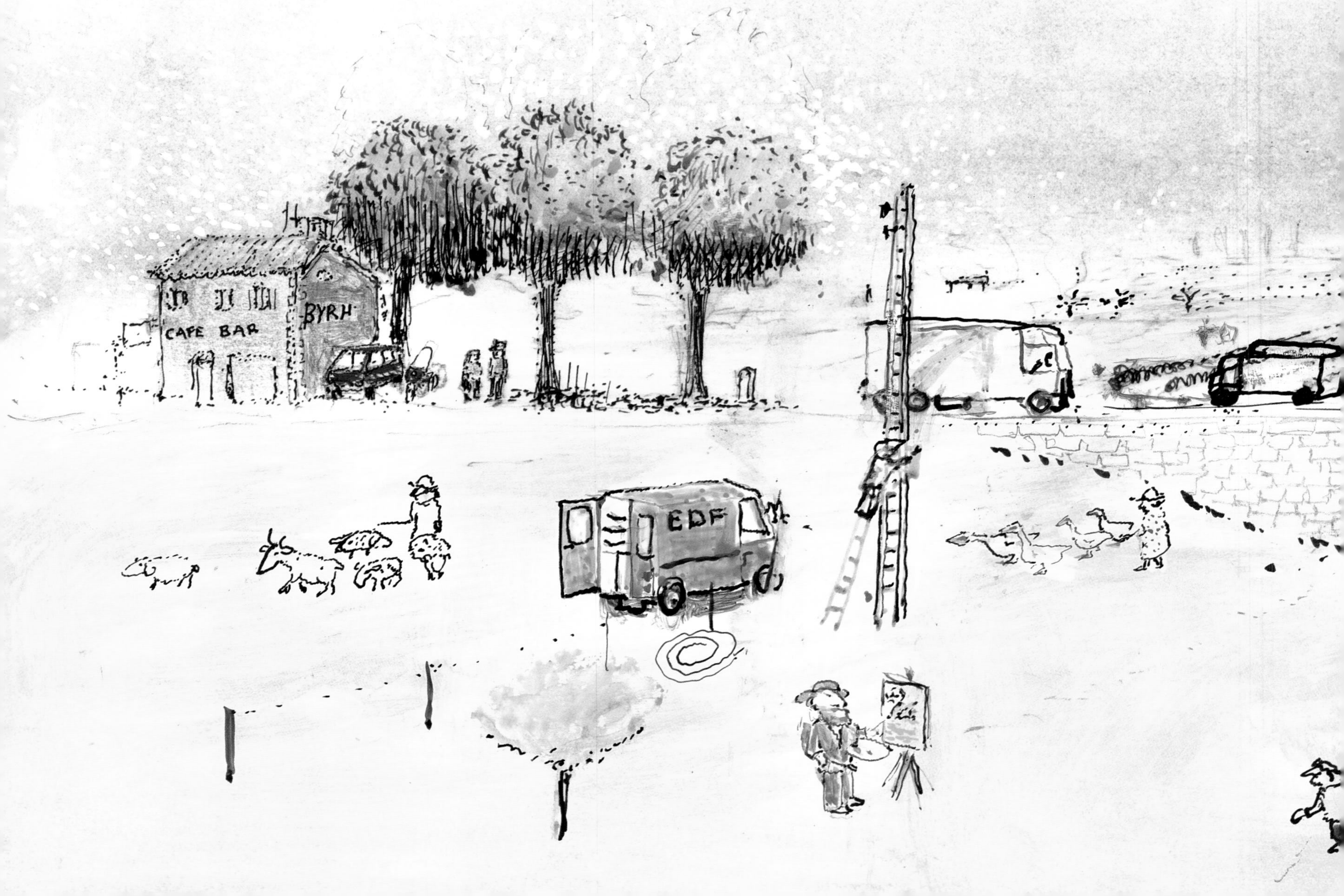
CAFE BAR
BYRH
EDF

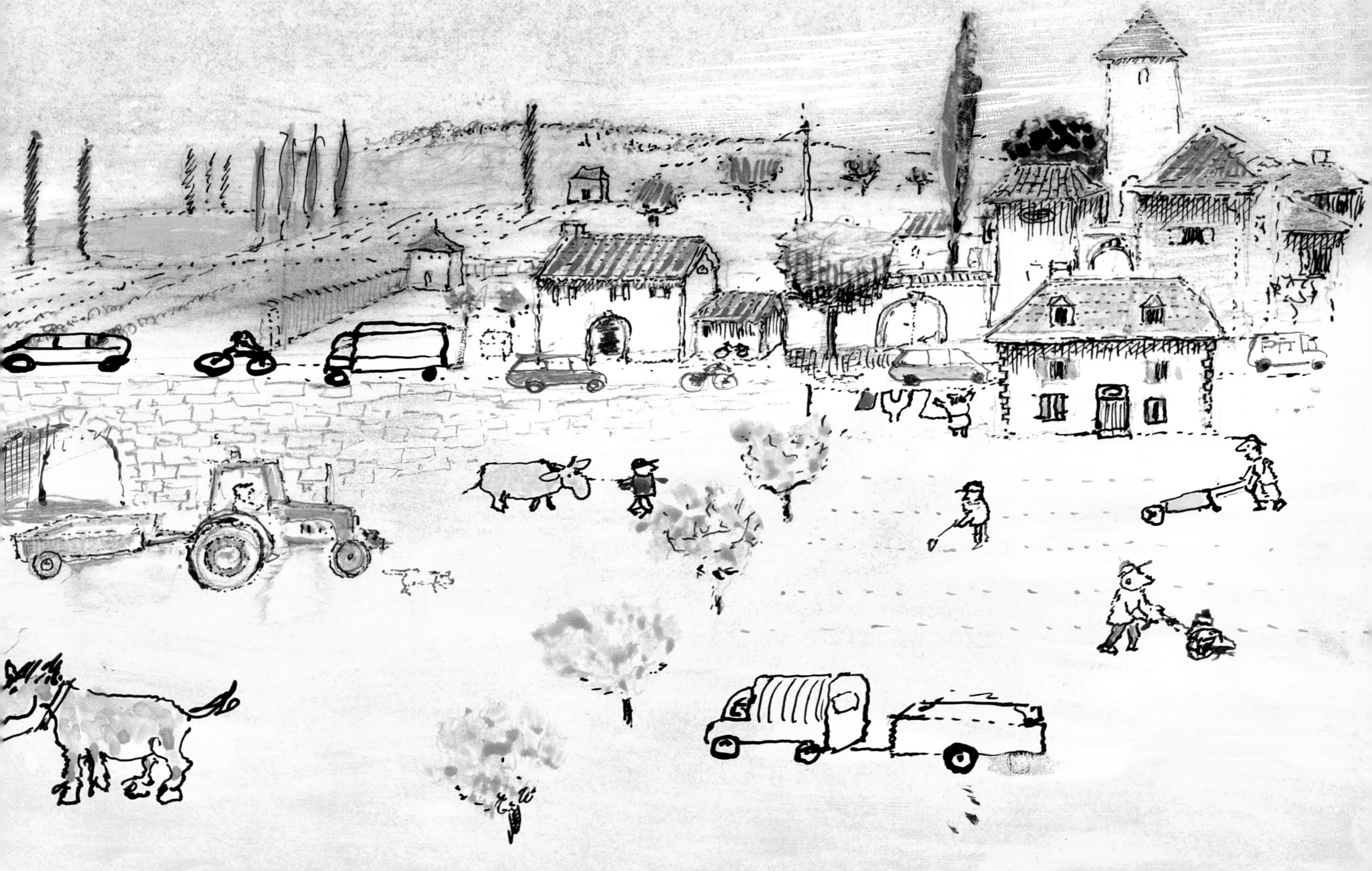
PTT

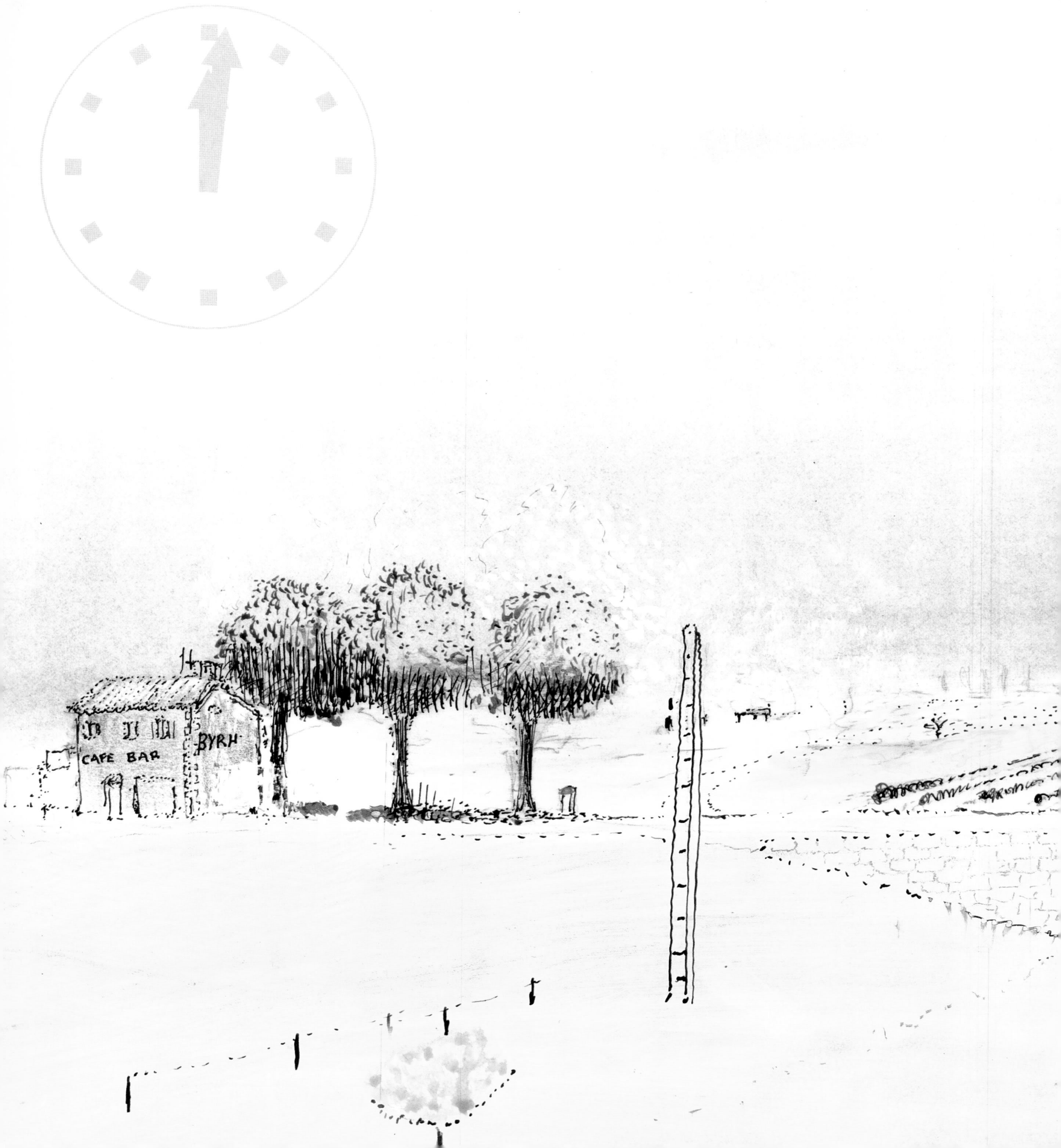
CAFE BAR
BYRH

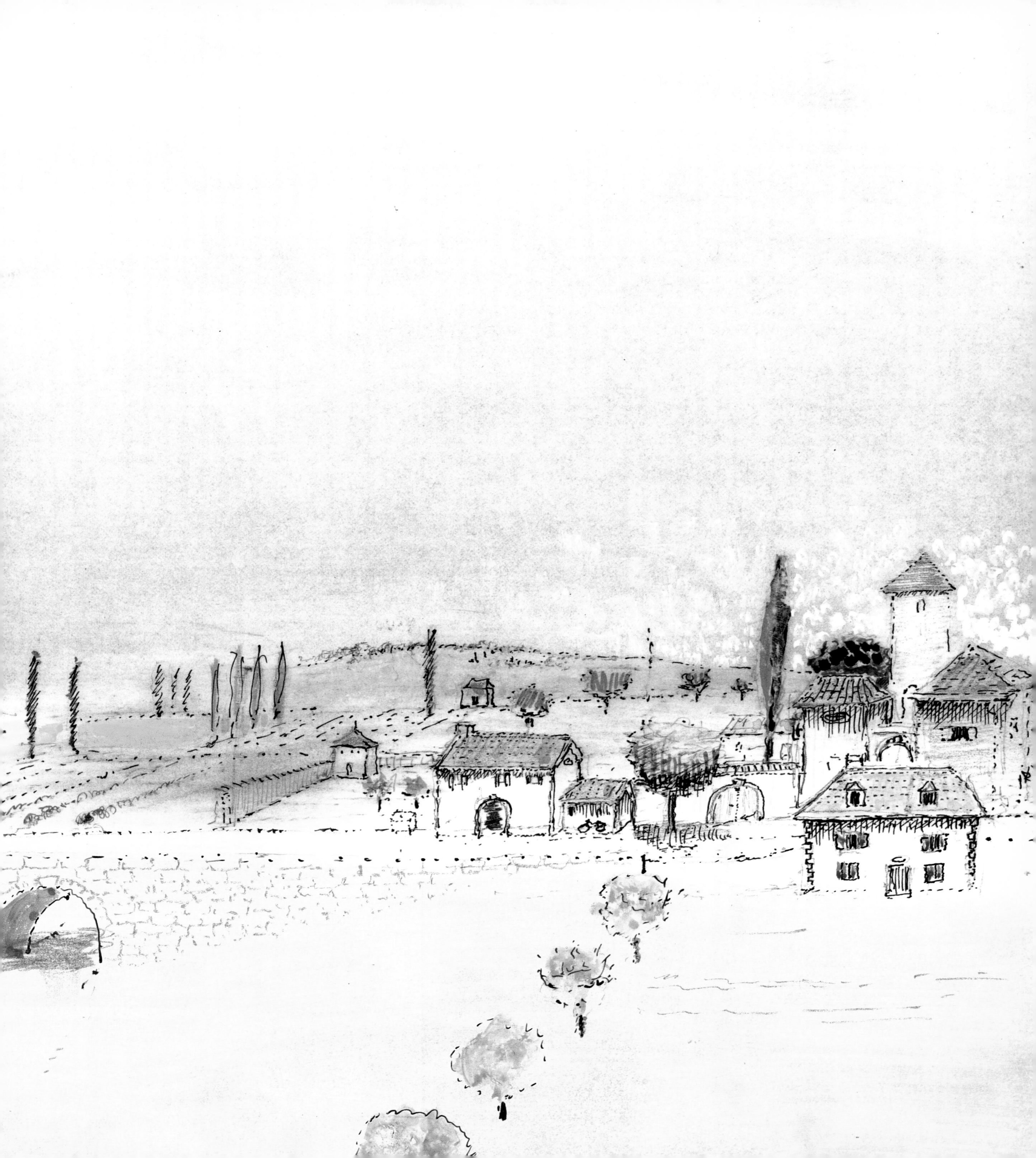

À Paris, à Paris, à Paris.

À Paris, à Paris, à Paris,
Sur un petit cheval gris;
À Rouen, à Rouen, à Rouen,
Sur un petit cheval blanc;
Au pas, pas, pas - au trot, trot, trot -
Au galop, au galop, au galop.

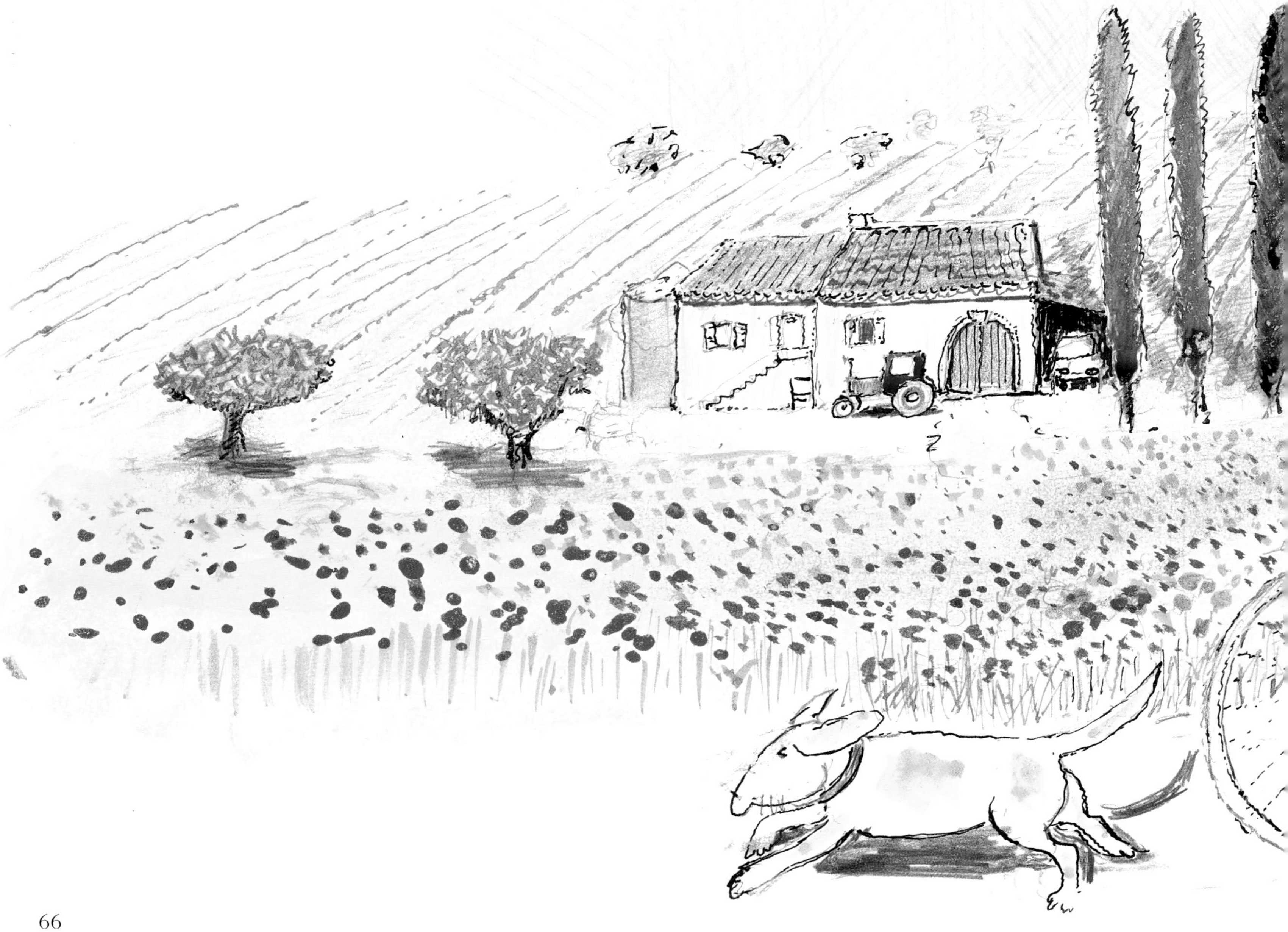

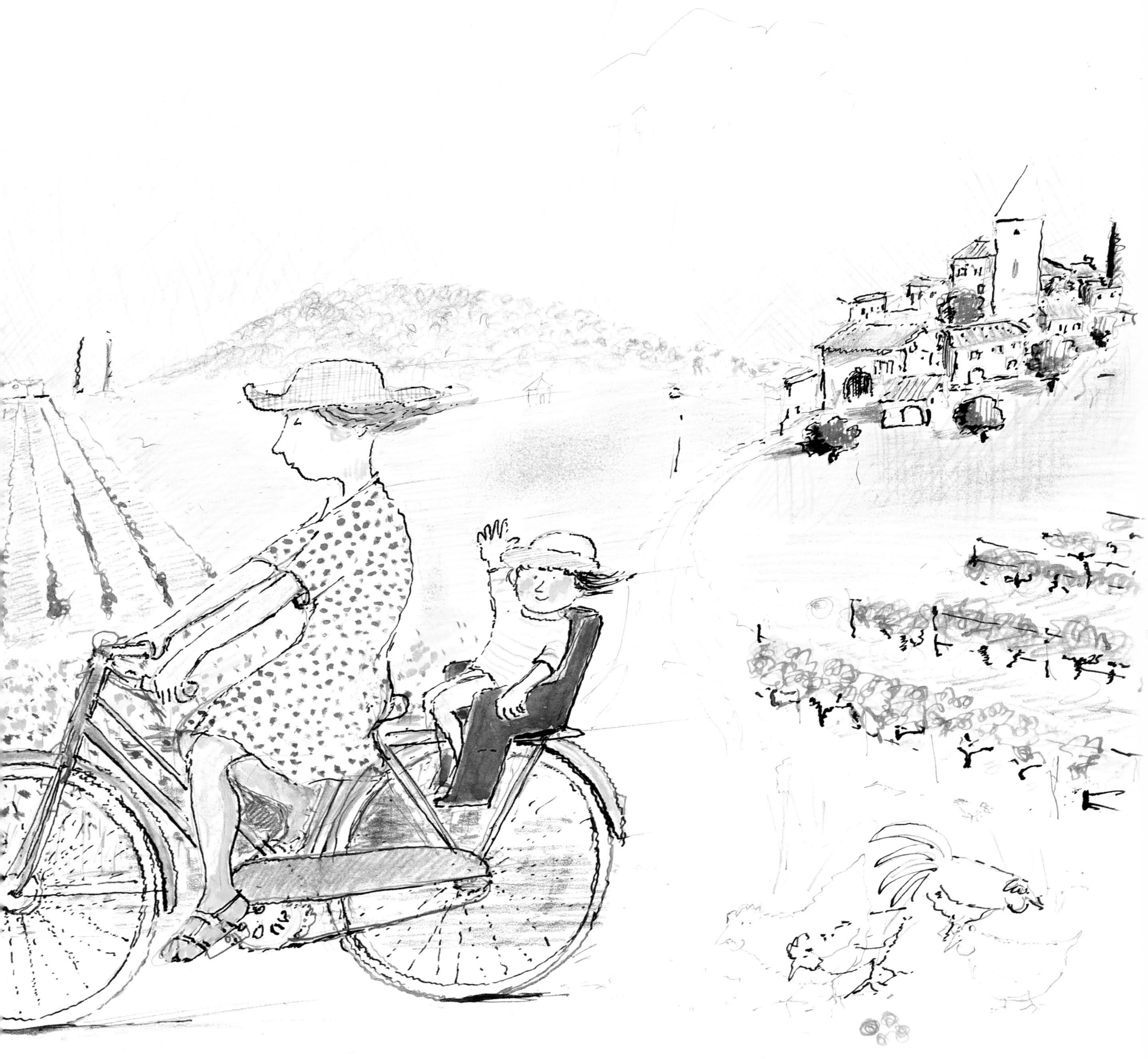

A notre cher Ami EDOUARD BEAUDU

MON LÉGIONNAIRE

Paroles de
Raymond ASSO

Musique de
Marguerite MONNOT

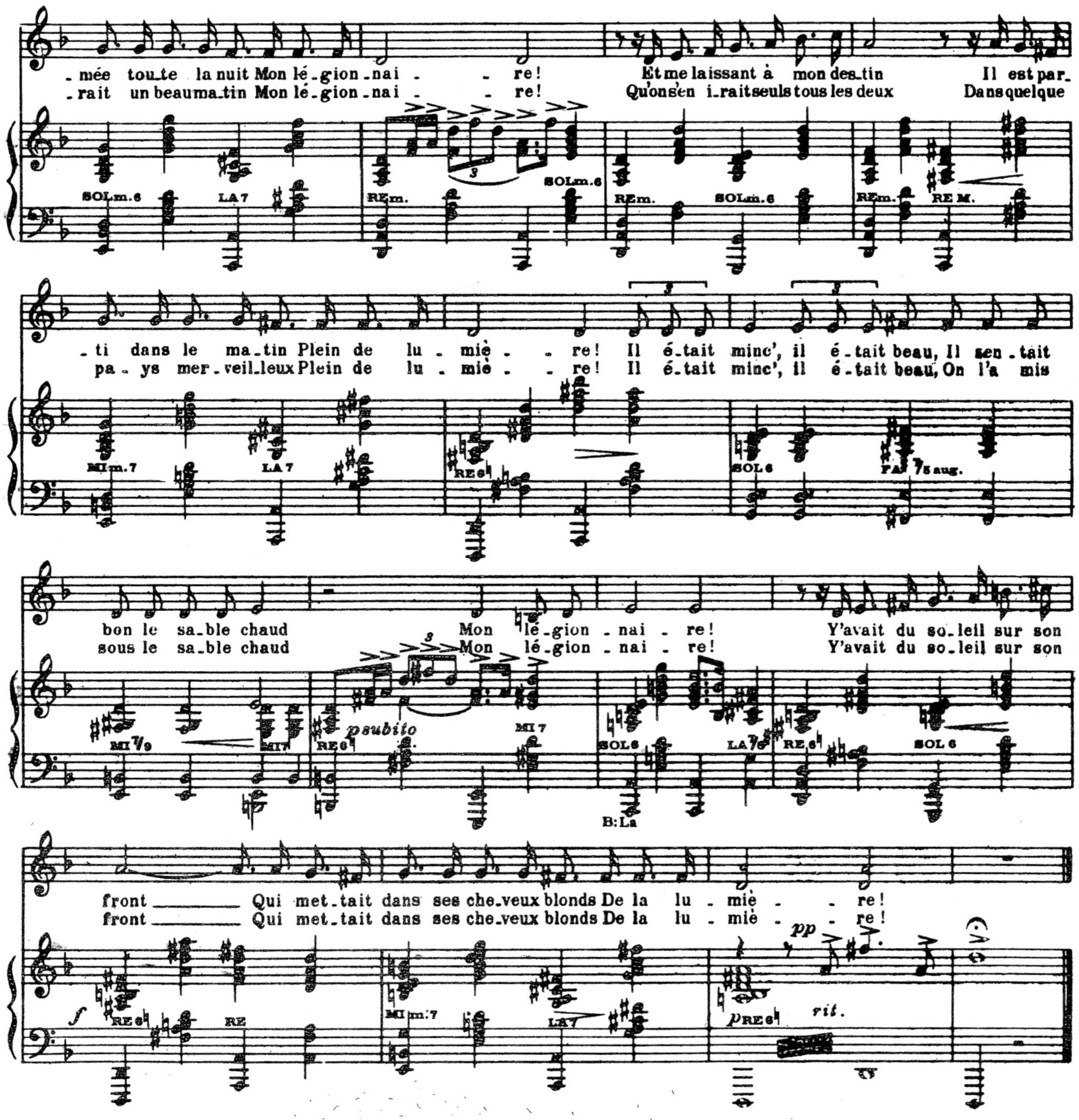

-mée tou-te la nuit Mon lé-gion-nai - - re! Et me laissant à mon des-tin Il est par-
-rait un beau ma-tin Mon lé-gion-nai - - re! Qu'on s'en i-rait seuls tous les deux Dans quelque
SOLm.6 LA 7 REm. SOLm.6 REm. SOLm.6 REm. RE M.
-ti dans le ma-tin Plein de lu-miè - - re! Il é-tait minc', il é-tait beau, Il sen-tait
pa-ys mer-veil-leux Plein de lu-miè - - re! Il é-tait minc', il é-tait beau, On l'a mis
MIm.7 LA 7 RE6 SOL6 FA 7/5 aug.
bon le sa-ble chaud Mon lé-gion-nai-re! Y'avait du so-leil sur son
sous le sa-ble chaud Mon lé-gion-nai-re! Y'avait du so-leil sur son
MI 7/9 MI7 RE6 psubito MI 7 SOL6 LA 7/6 RE6 SOL 6 B:La
front Qui met-tait dans ses che-veux blonds De la lu-miè - - re!
front Qui met-tait dans ses che-veux blonds De la lu-miè - - re!
f RE6 RE MIm.7 LA7 pp pRE6 rit.

DISQUES/PLATEN - EDITH PIAF (POLYDOR

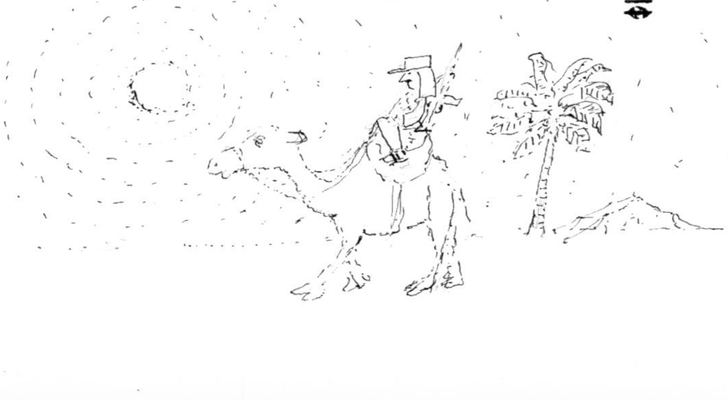

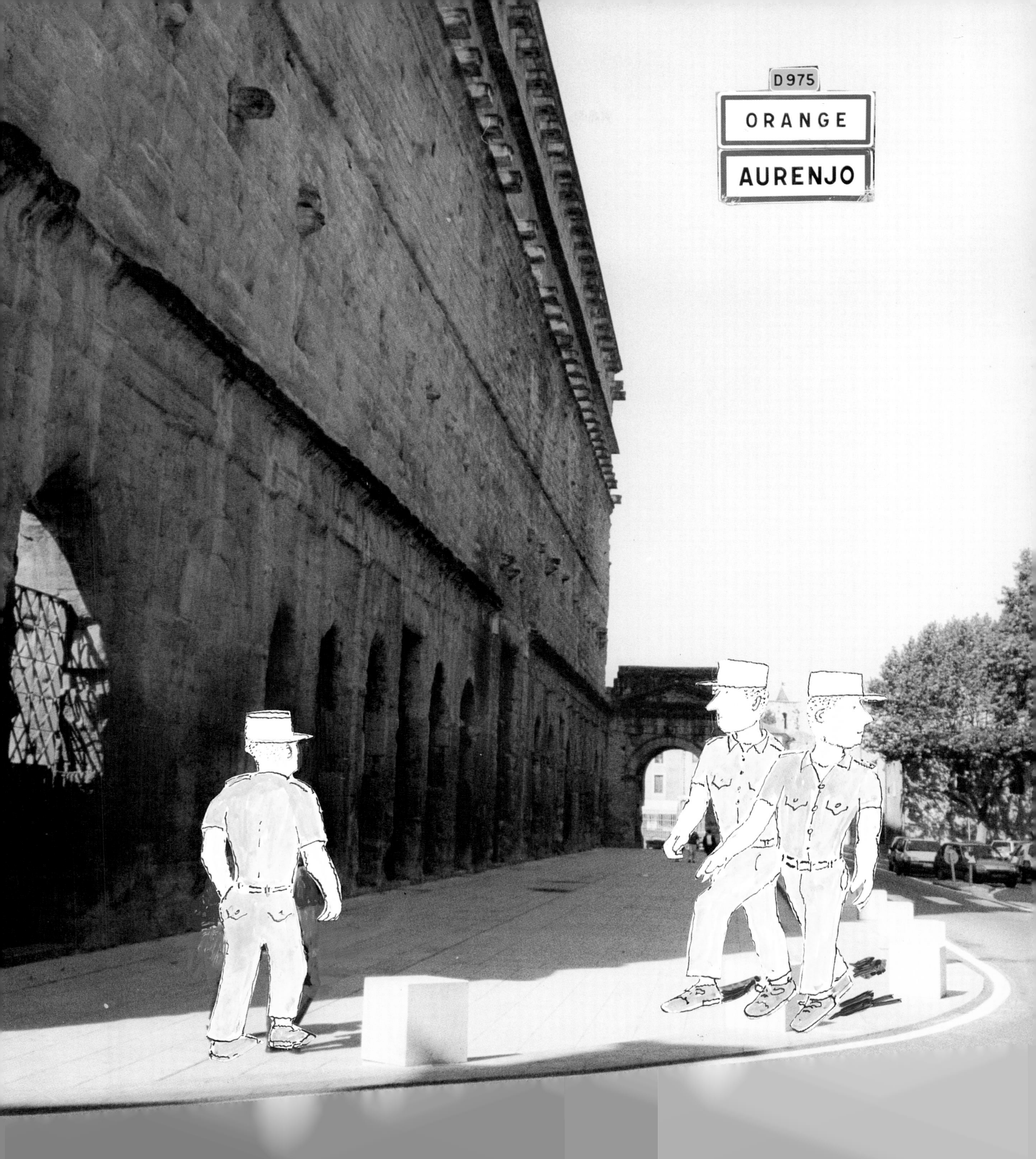
D975
ORANGE
AURENJO

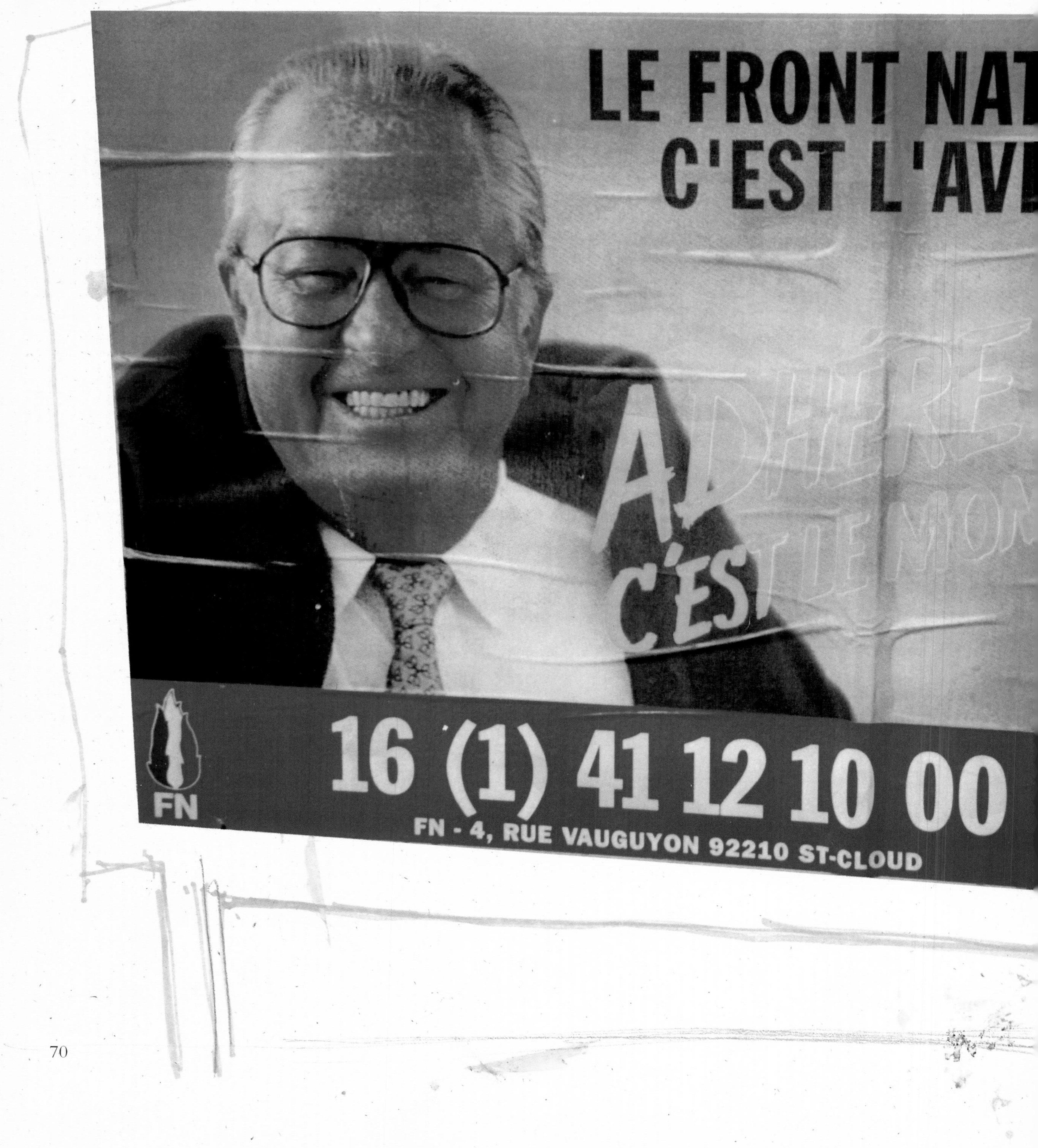
LE FRONT NAT
C'EST L'AVE
C'EST
FN
16 (1) 41 12 10 00
FN - 4, RUE VAUGUYON 92210 ST-CLOUD

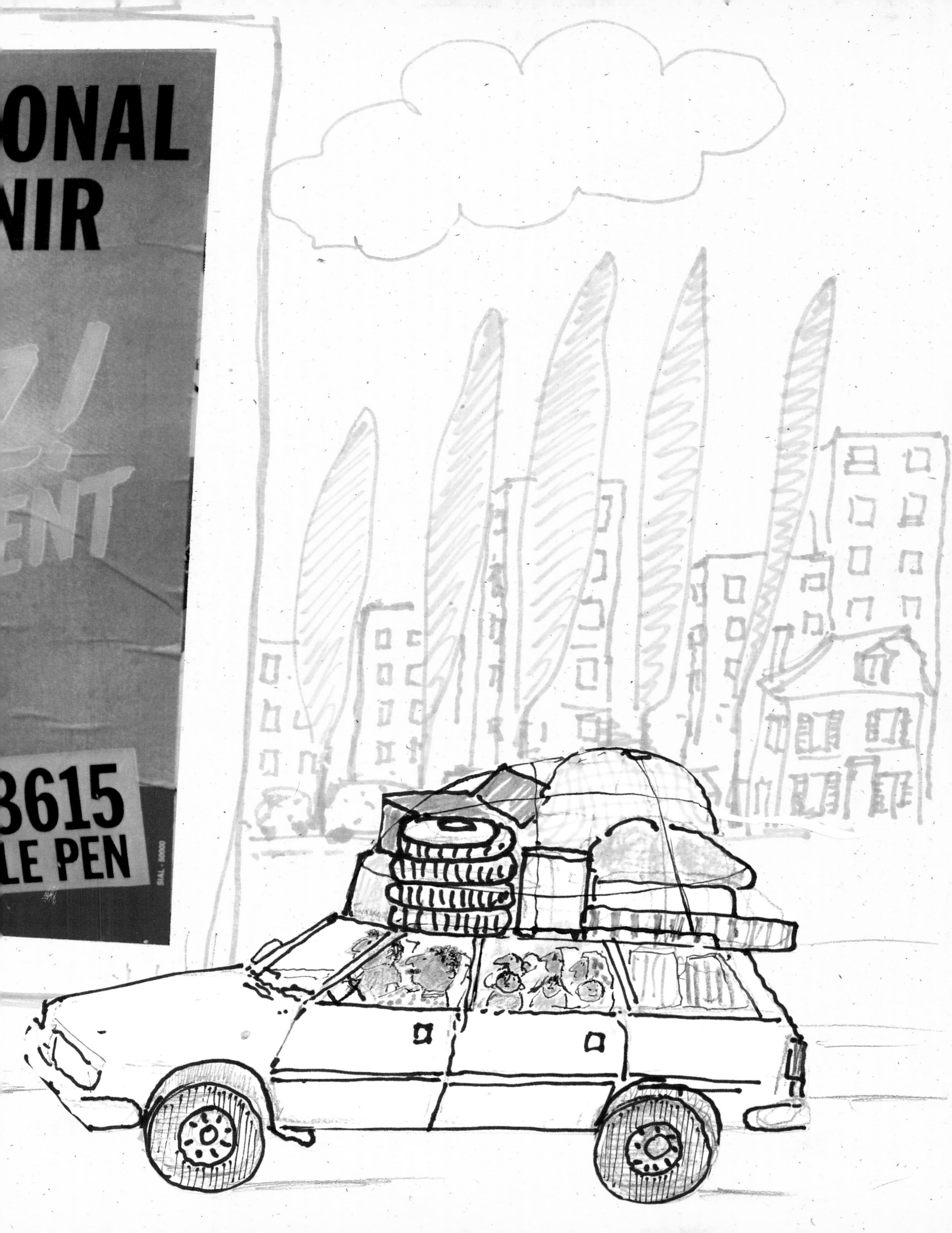
ONAL
NIR
ENT
3615
LE PEN

CNJA (Centre nationale des jeunes agriculteurs)

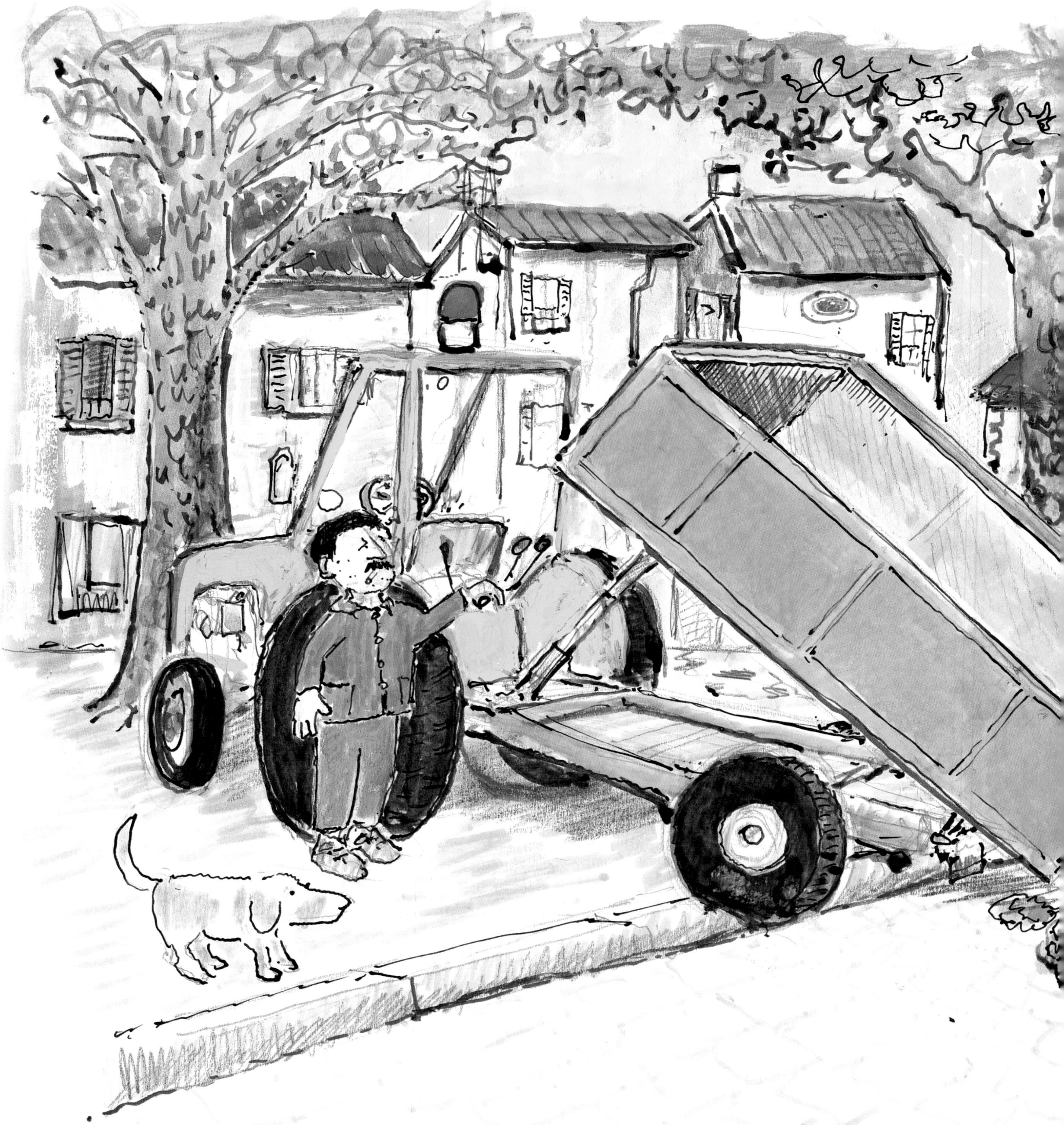

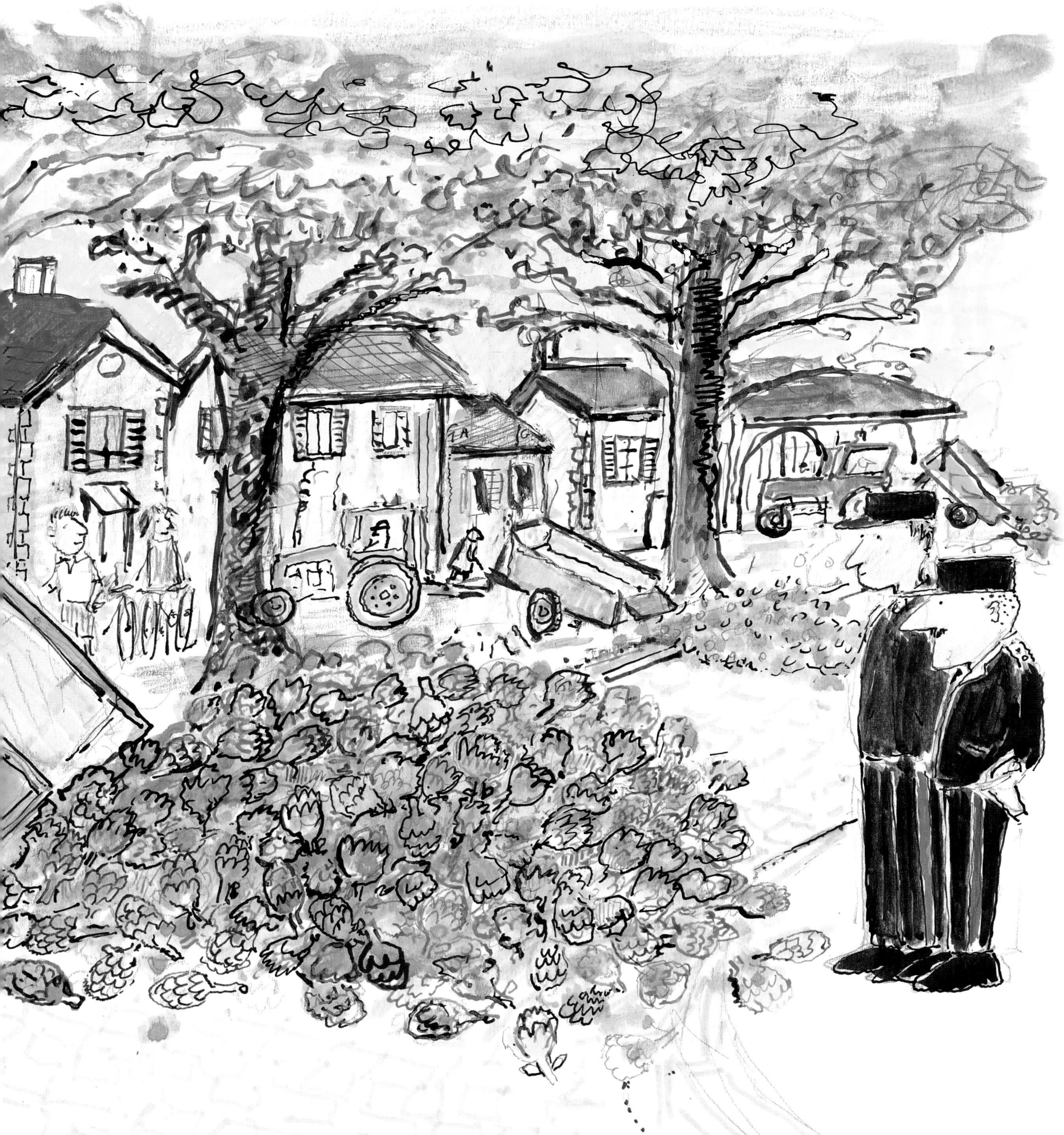

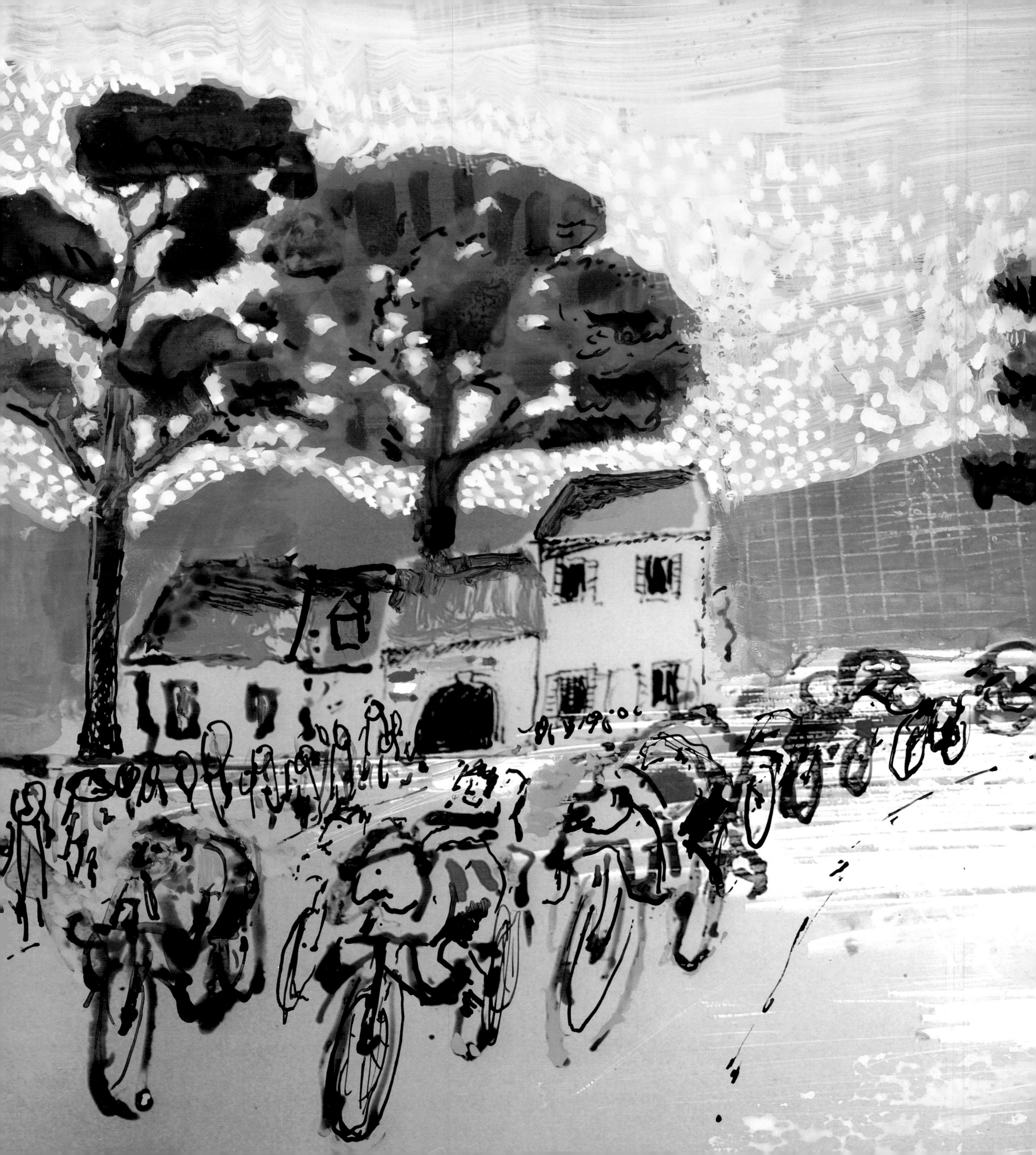

Tour de France

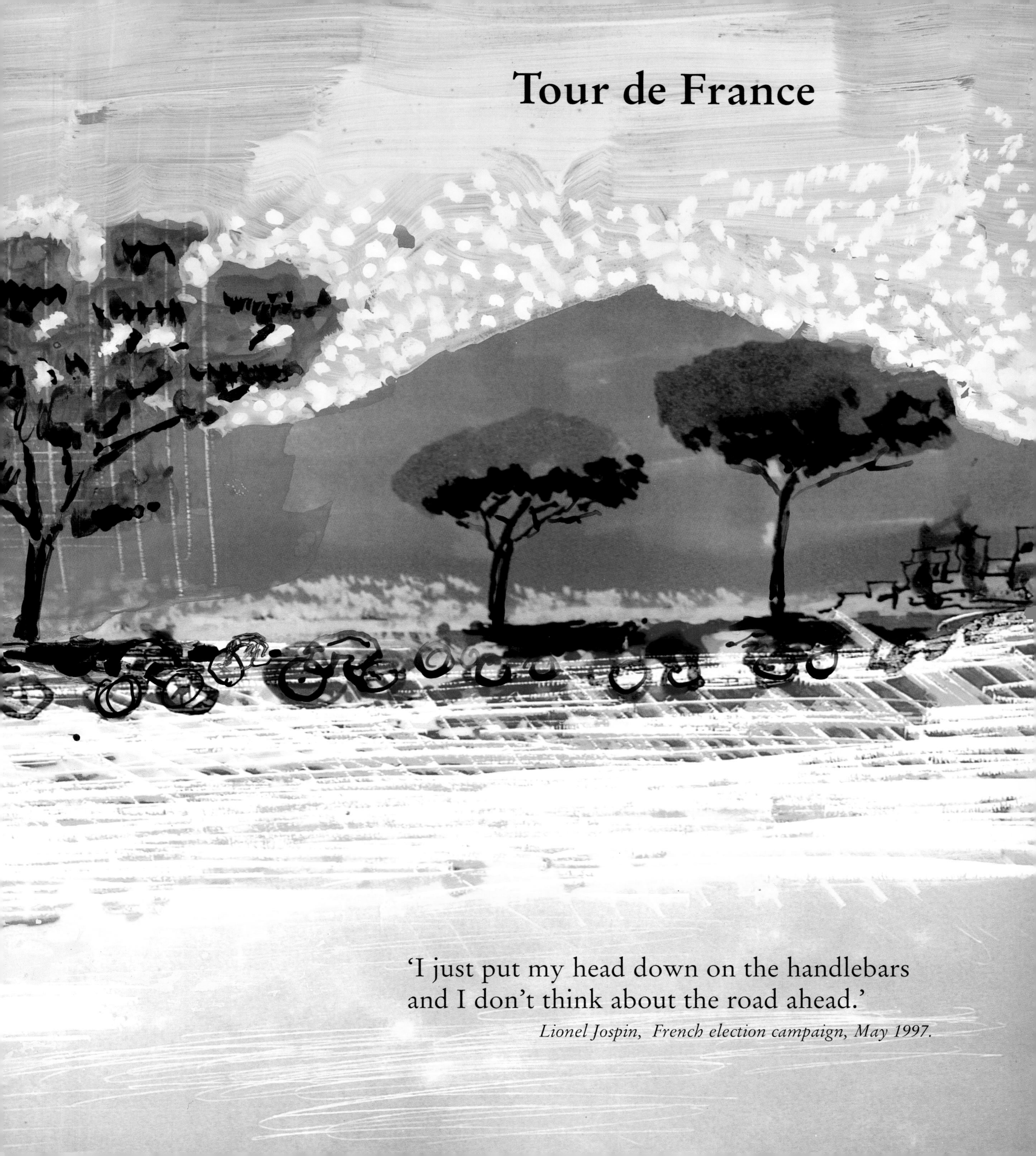

‘I just put my head down on the handlebars and I don’t think about the road ahead.’

Lionel Jospin, French election campaign, May 1997.

Jour de fête

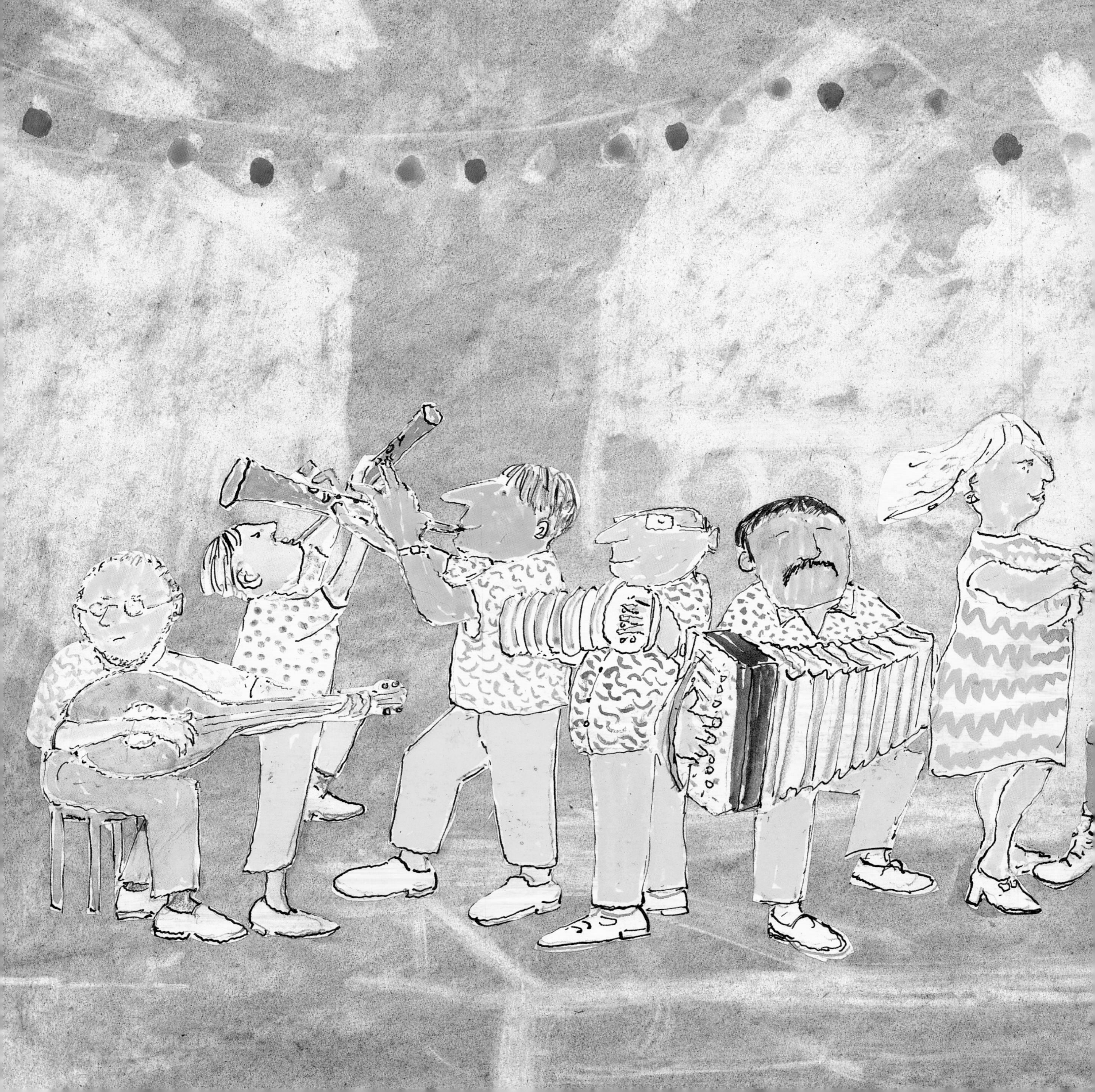

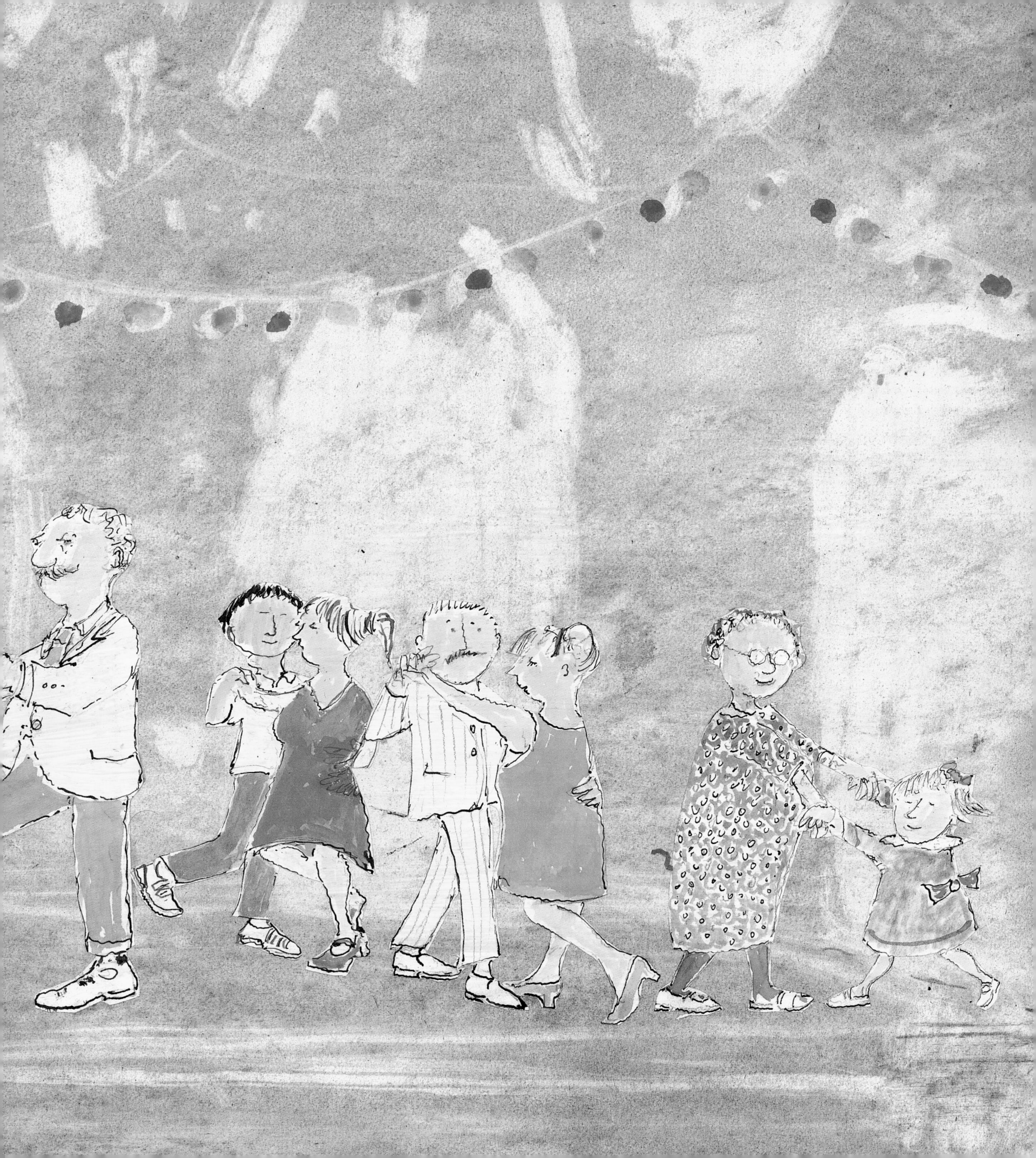

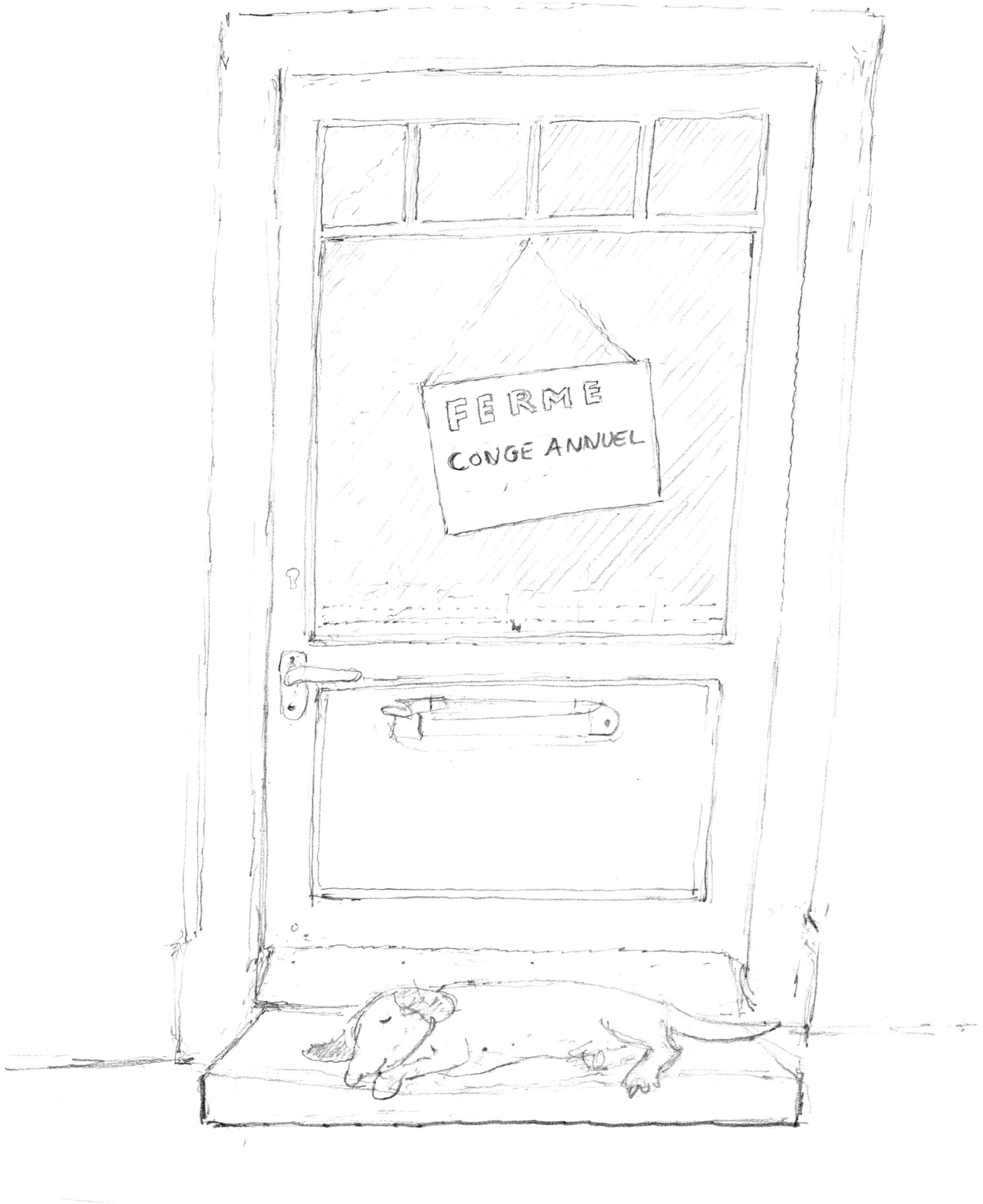
FERME
CONGE ANNUEL

Public Holidays

Traditionally August was the sole month for summer vacations, with many businesses closing entirely for the whole month. When a company closes down during the summer, all employees are obliged to take their vacation at the same time.

The government is now trying to encourage companies to stagger their employees' holidays throughout the summer, although this isn't popular with employees. Despite enticements and pleas from employers and the government, many French employees refuse to surrender their August annual holiday…

The only public holiday (*jours fériés*) that an employer in France is legally obliged to grant with pay is 1st May. However, most collective agreements include the following 11 public holidays:

Date	Holiday
1 January	New Year's Day
March or April	Easter Monday
1 May	Labour Day
8 May	Victory Day WWII/1945
May	Ascension Day - Thursday 40 days (6th Thursday) after Easter
May/June	Pentecost/Whitsuntide - 10 days (2nd Monday) after Ascension Day
14 July	Bastille Day/National Day
15 August	Assumption
1 November	All Saints' Day
11 November	Armistice Day
25 December	Christmas Day

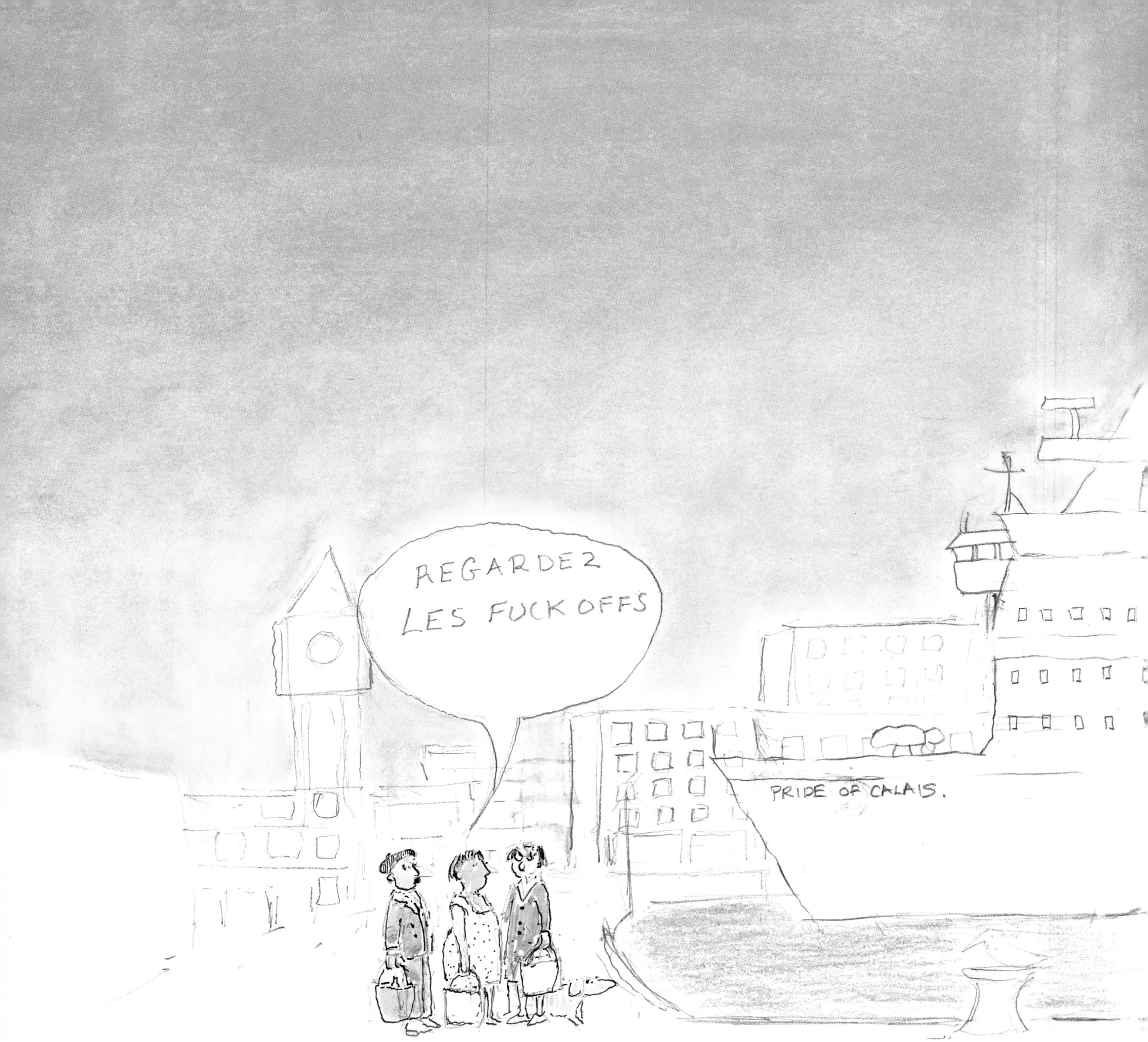
REGARDEZ
LES FUCK OFFS
PRIDE OF CALAIS.

In Calais the locals refer to the British tourists as 'Les Fuck Offs'

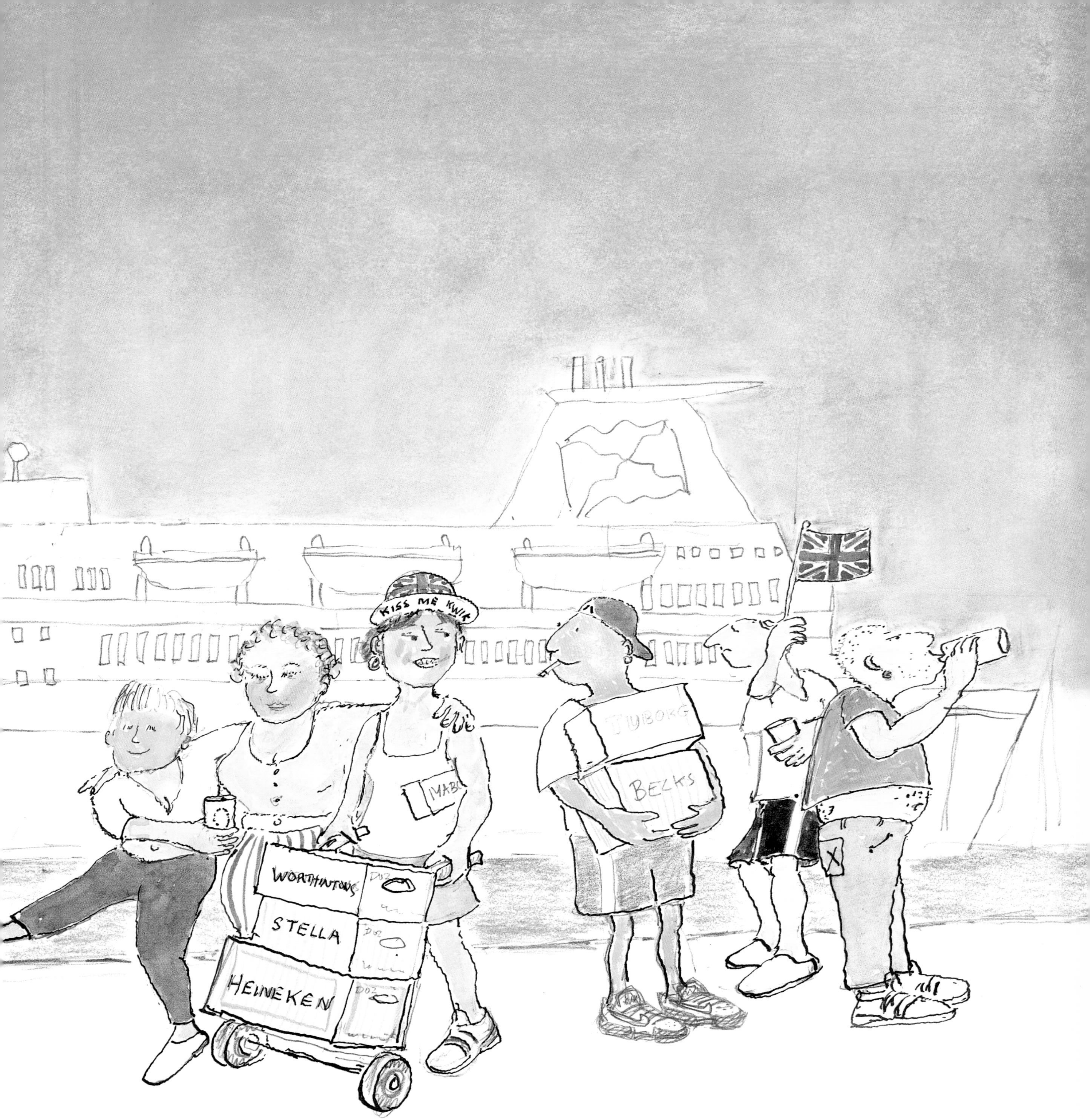
KISS ME KWIK
WORTHINTONS
STELLA
HEINEKEN
BECKS

BIENVENU AUX AUTOROUTES DE FRANCE

83

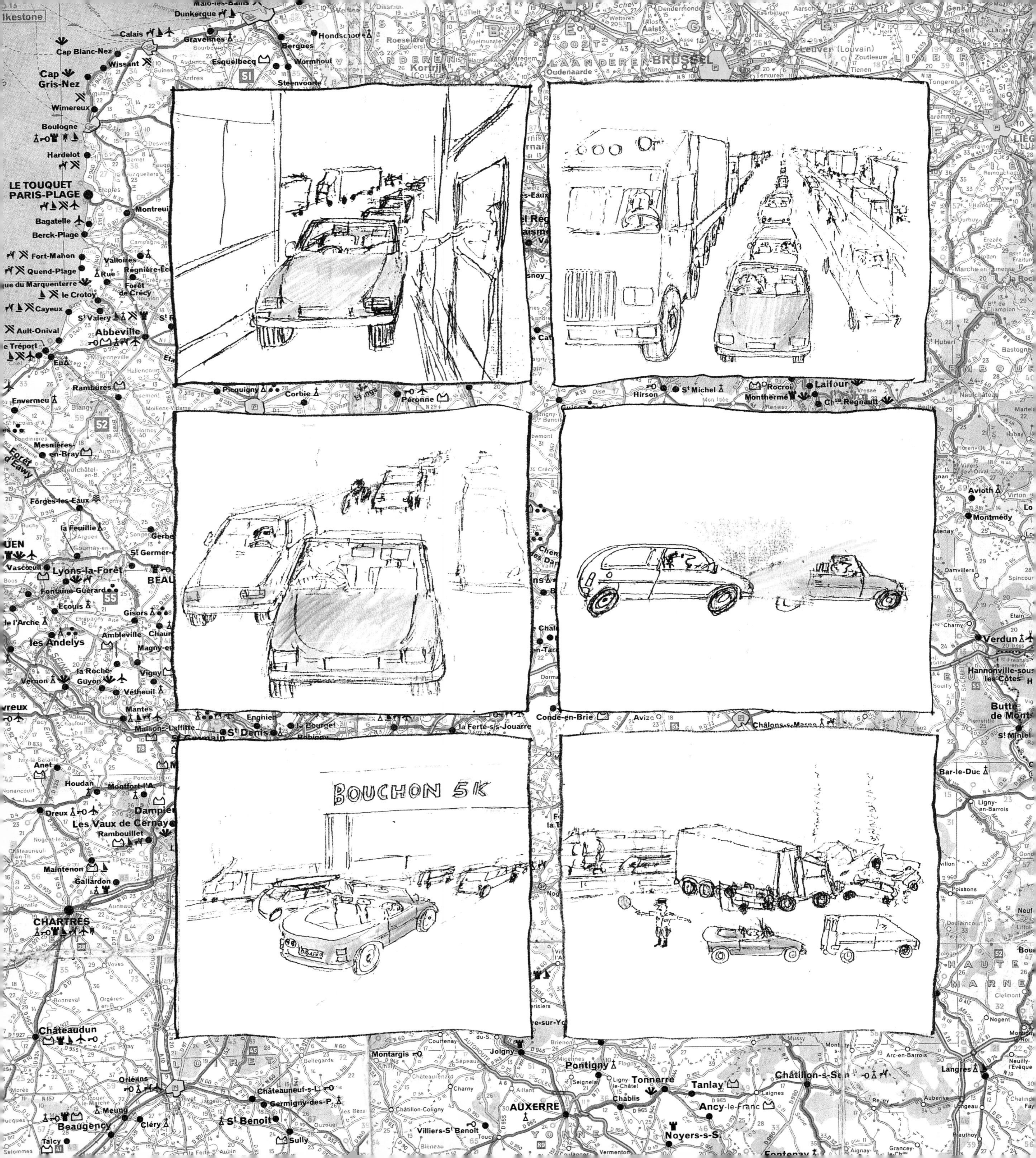
BOUCHON 5K
Dunkerque
Calais
Gravelines
Bergues
Hondschoote
Esquelbecq
Wormhout
Steenvoorde
Cap Blanc-Nez
Wissant
Cap Gris-Nez
Wimereux
Boulogne
Hardelot
LE TOUQUET PARIS-PLAGE
Montreuil
Bagatelle
Berck-Plage
Fort-Mahon
Quend-Plage
Rue
Valloires
Forêt de Crécy
le Crotoy
Cayeux
St Valery
Ault-Onival
Abbeville
le Tréport
Eu
Rambures
Envermeu
Mesnières-en-Bray
Forêt d'Eawy
Forges-les-Eaux
la Feuillie
Gerberoy
St Germer-de-Fly
Lyons-la-Forêt
Vascœuil
Fontaine-Guérard
Écouis
Gisors
Ambleville
les Andelys
Vernon
la Roche-Guyon
Vétheuil
Vigny
Mantes
Maisons-Laffitte
St Denis
le Bourget
Anet
Houdan
Montfort-l'A.
Dreux
Les Vaux de Cernay
Rambouillet
Maintenon
Gallardon
CHARTRES
Châteaudun
Orléans
Meung
Beaugency
Cléry
Talcy
Châteauneuf-s-L.
Germigny-des-P.
St Benoît
Sully
Montargis
Joigny
AUXERRE
Villiers-St Benoît
Pontigny
Tonnerre
Chablis
Tanlay
Ancy-le-Franc
Noyers-s-S.
Châtillon-s-Seine
Langres
Picquigny
Corbie
Péronne
Hirson
St Michel
Rocroi
Monthermé
Laifour
Chau Regnault
Condé-en-Brie
Avize
Châlons-s-Marne
la Ferté-s/s-Jouarre
BRUSSEL
Leuven (Louvain)
Kortrijk (Courtrai)
Roeselare
Oudenaarde
Aalst
Dendermonde
Hasselt
Genk
Verdun
Hannonville-sous-les Côtes
Butte de Montsec
St Mihiel
Bar-le-Duc
Avioth
Montmédy
Ligny-en-Barrois
Bastogne
St Hubert
Neufchâteau
HAUTE-MARNE

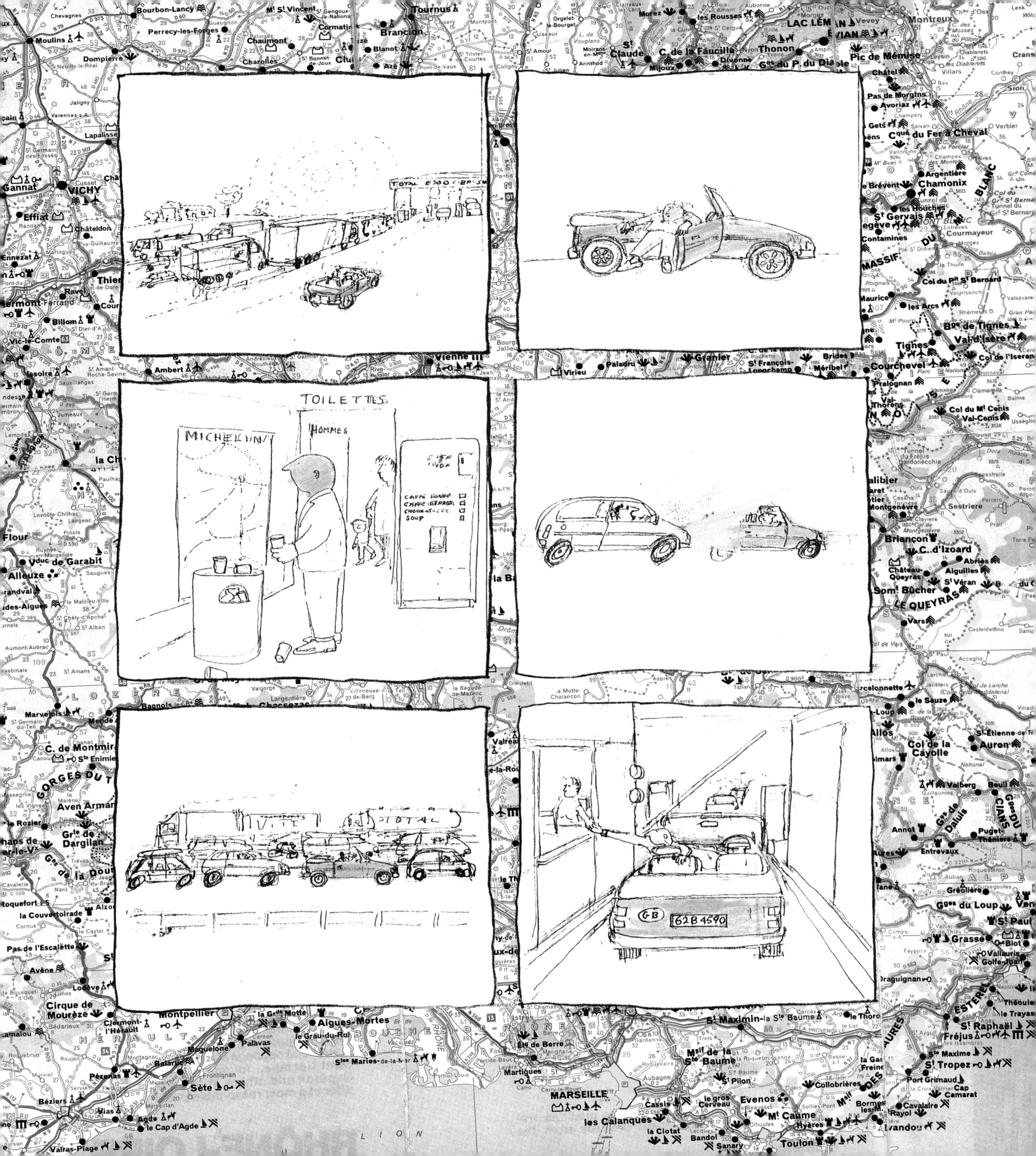
TOTAL ESSO BP
TOILETTES
HOMMES
MICHELIN
CAFFE LONGO
CHOCOLATIERE
SOUP
TOTAL
GB
62B 4590

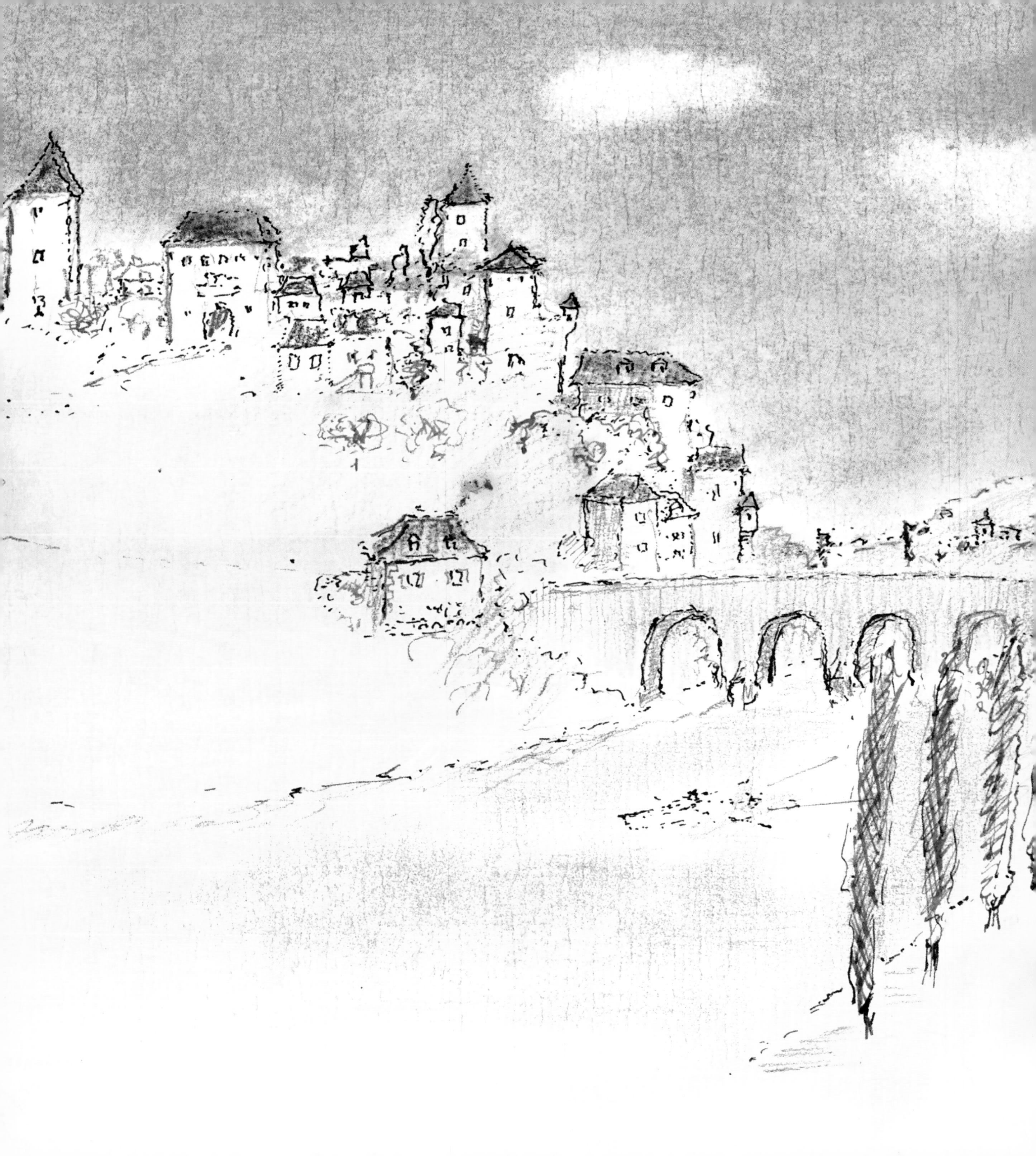

Dordogne

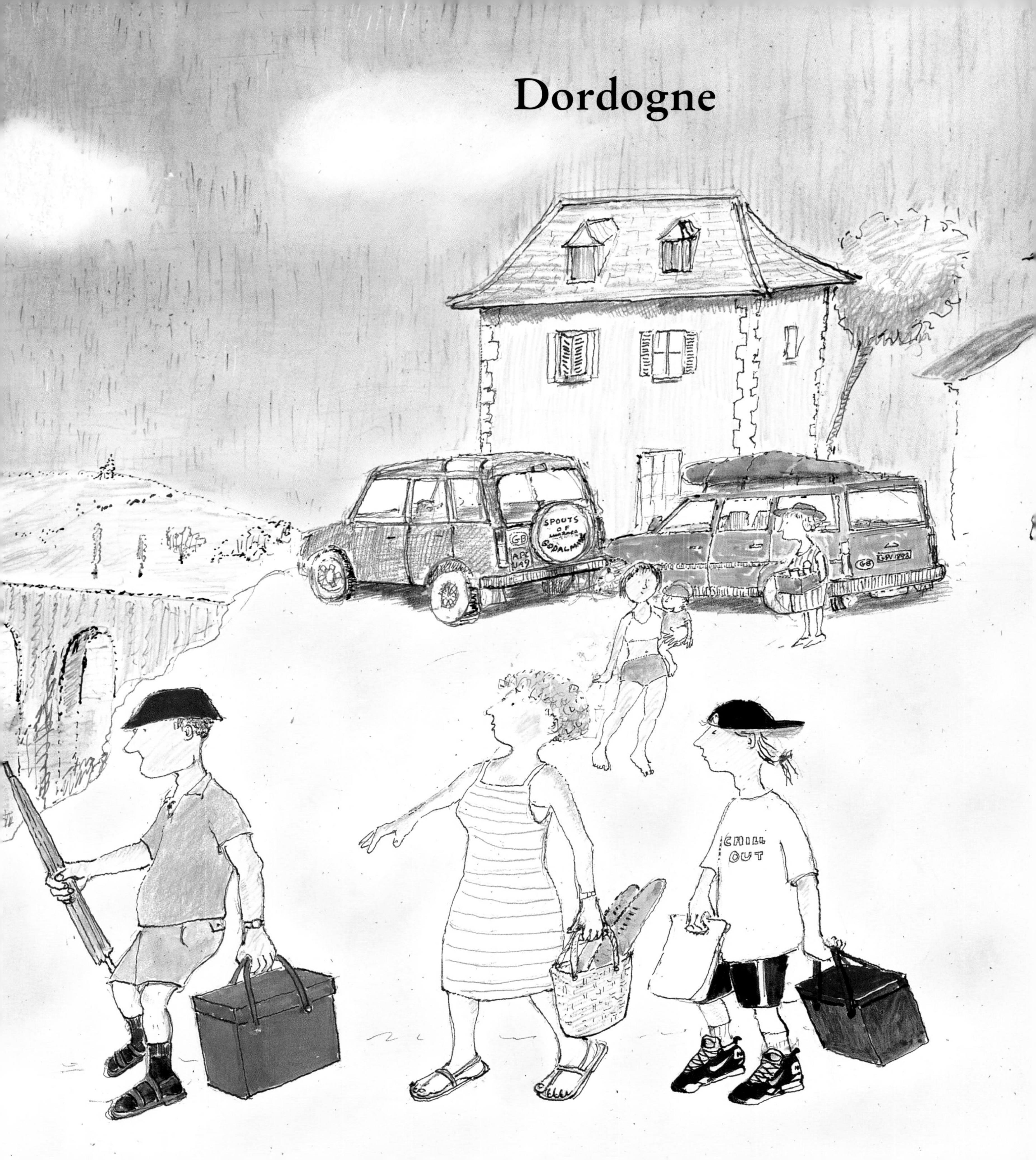
SPOUTS
OF
GB
CHILL
OUT

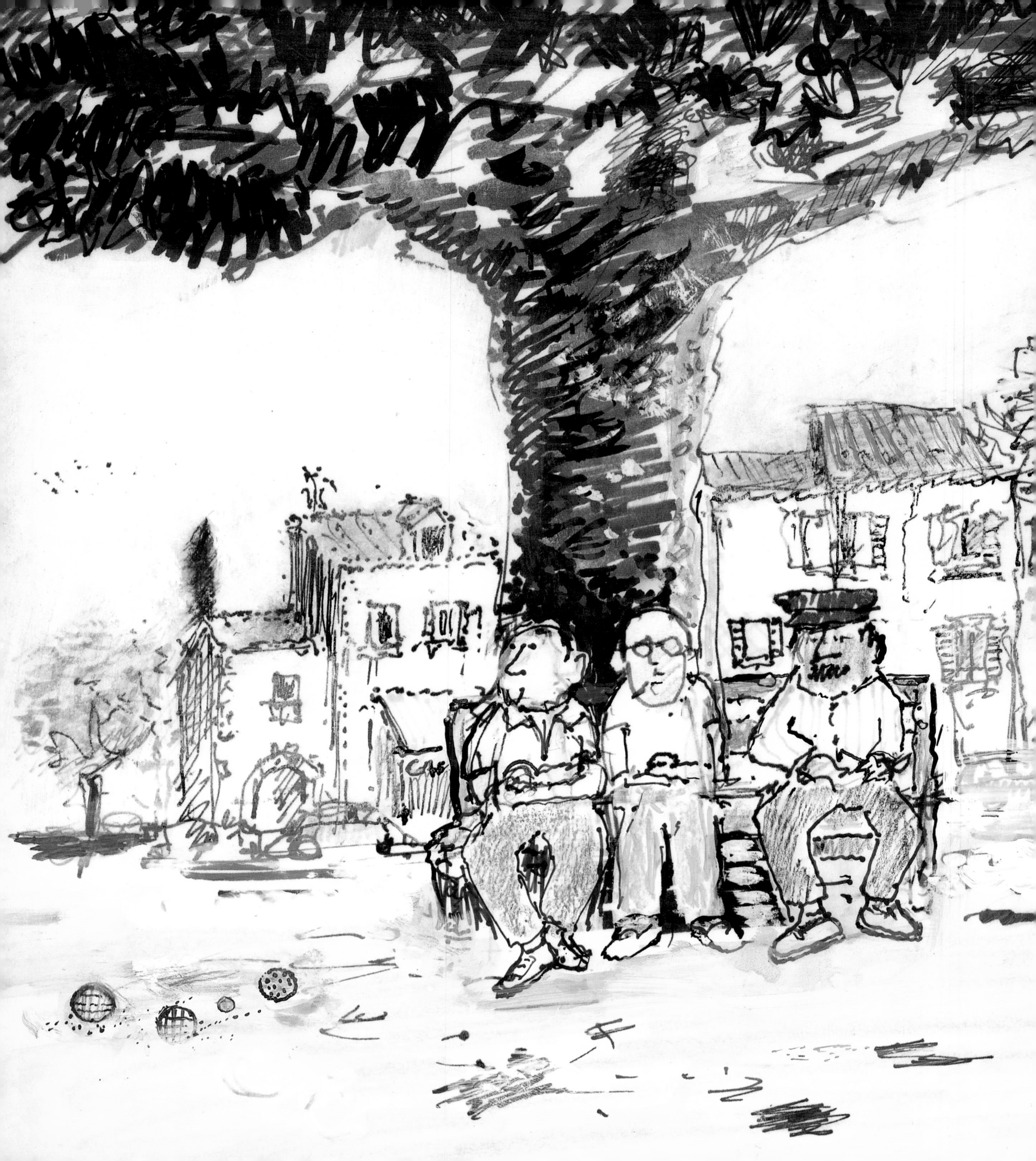

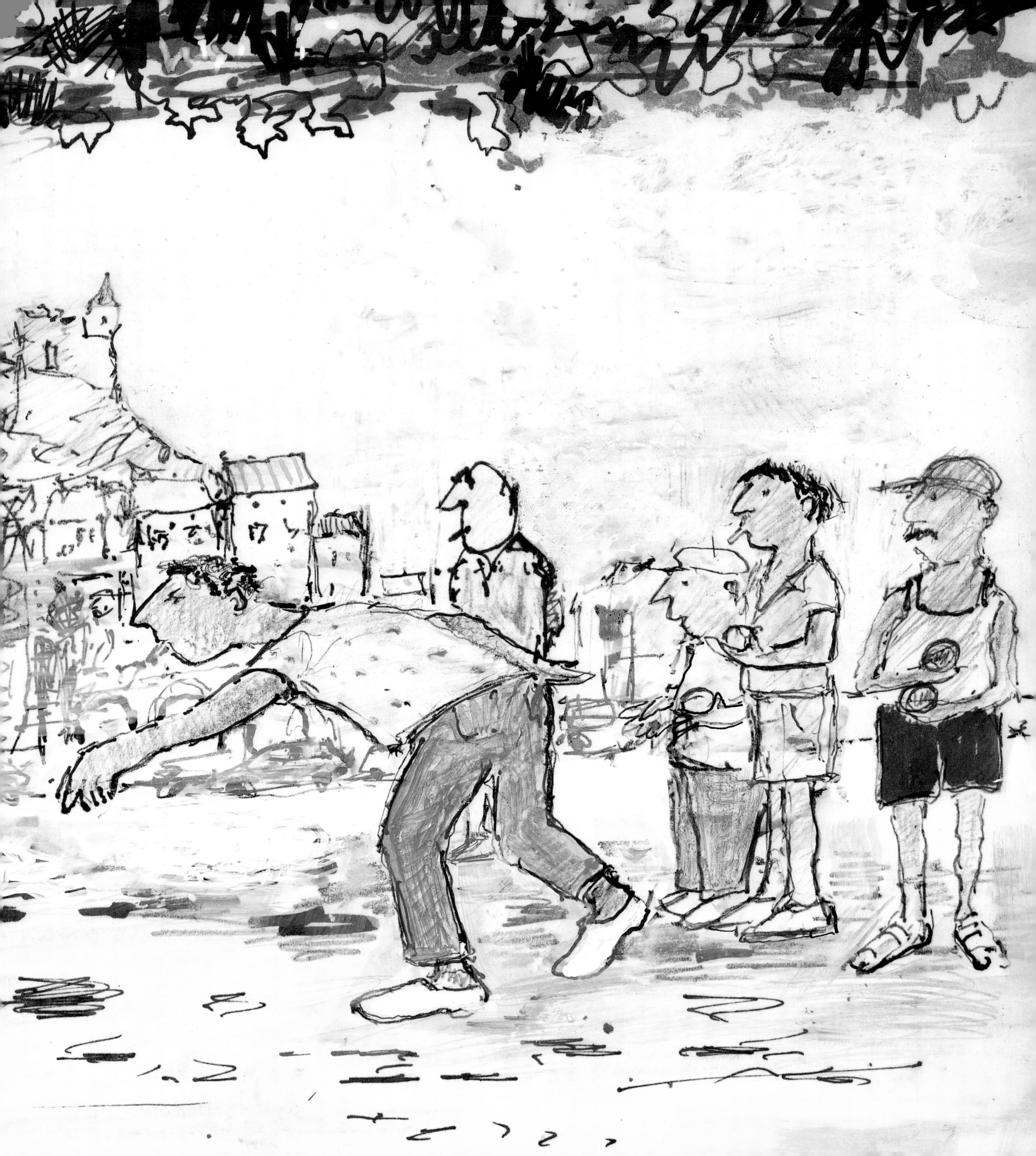

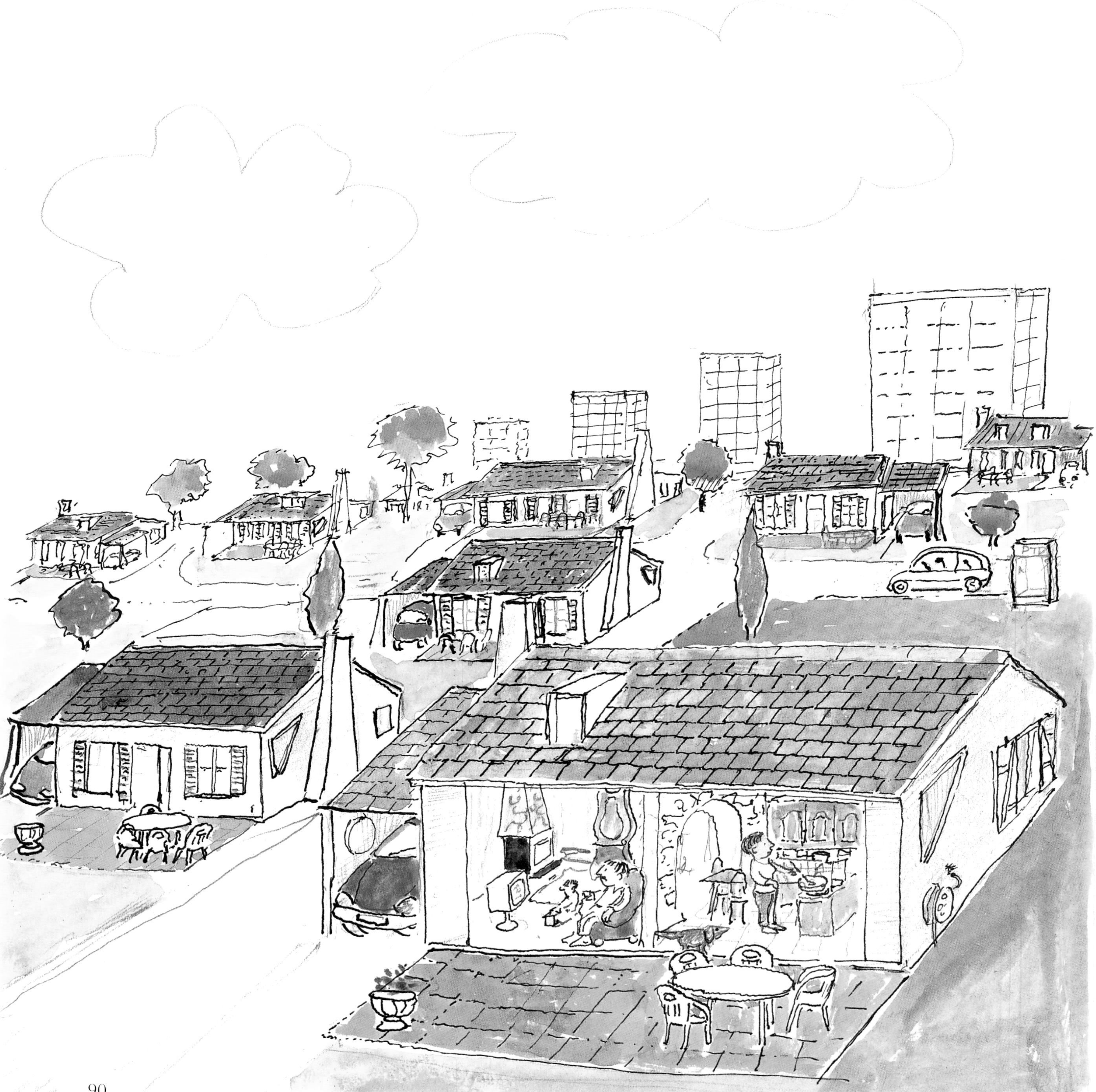

Le Camping

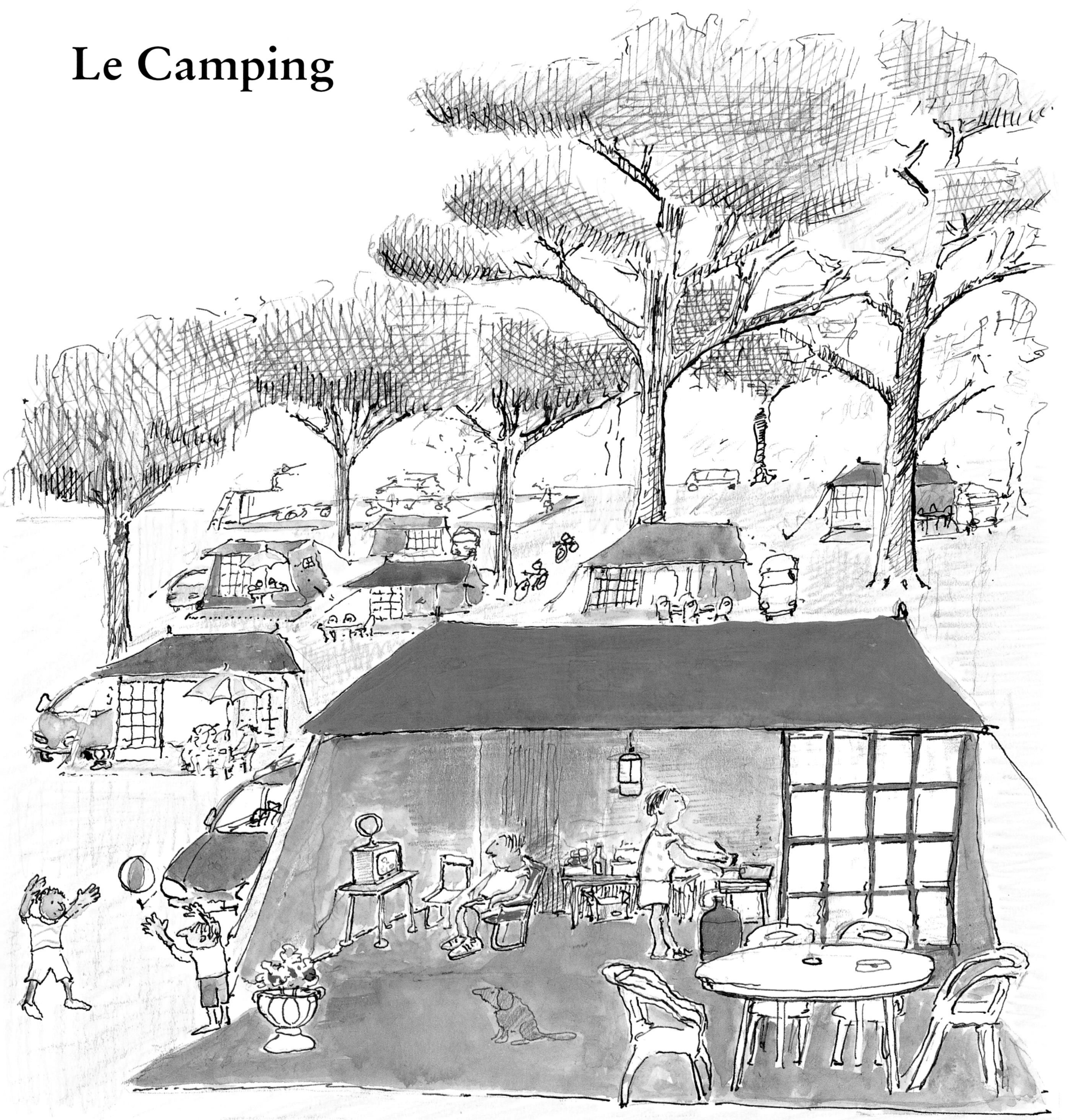

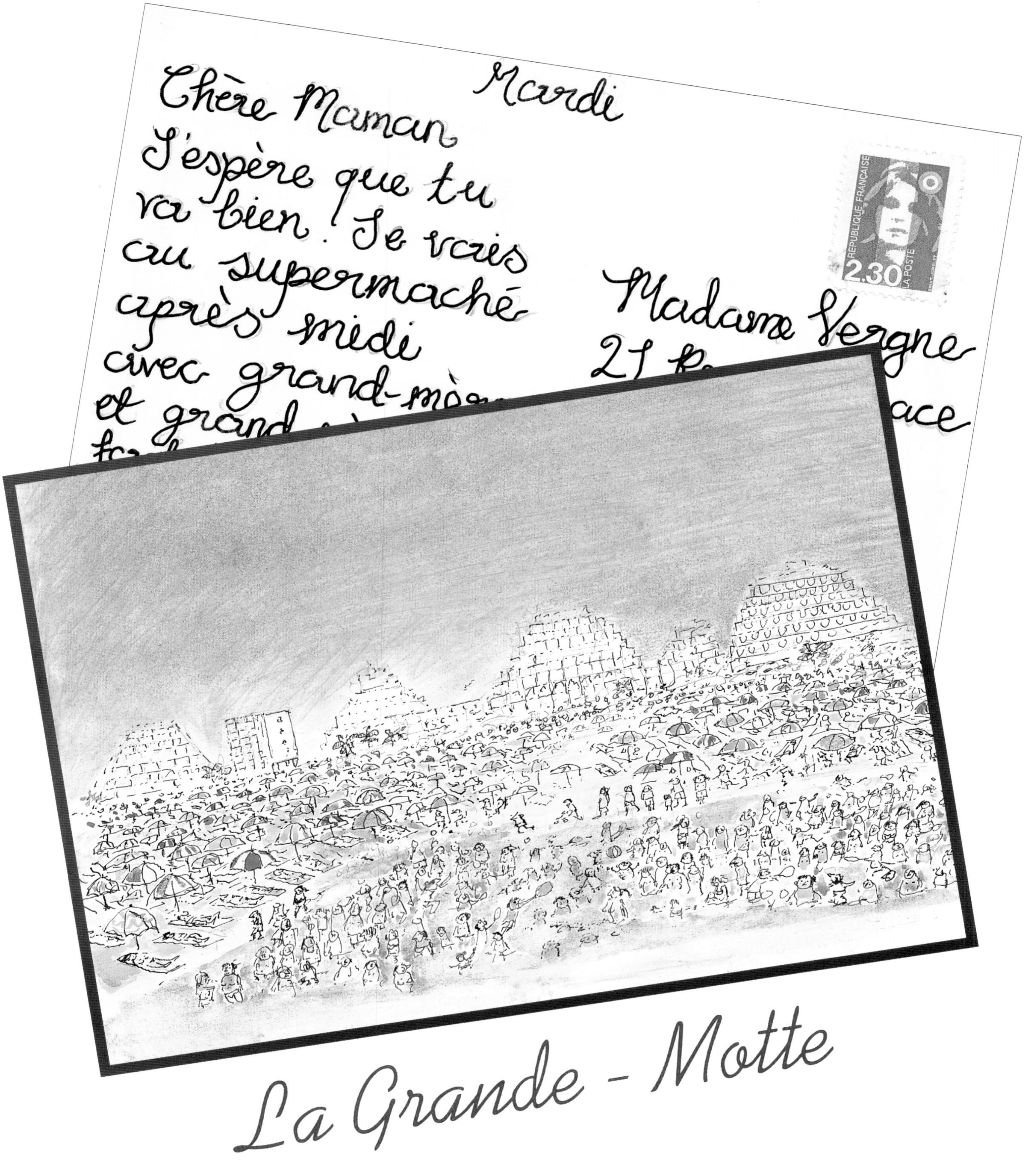

Mardi
Chère Maman
J'espère que tu
va bien! Je vais
au supermaché
après midi
avec grand-
Madame Vergne
RÉPUBLIQUE FRANÇAISE
LA POSTE
2,30
La Grande - Motte

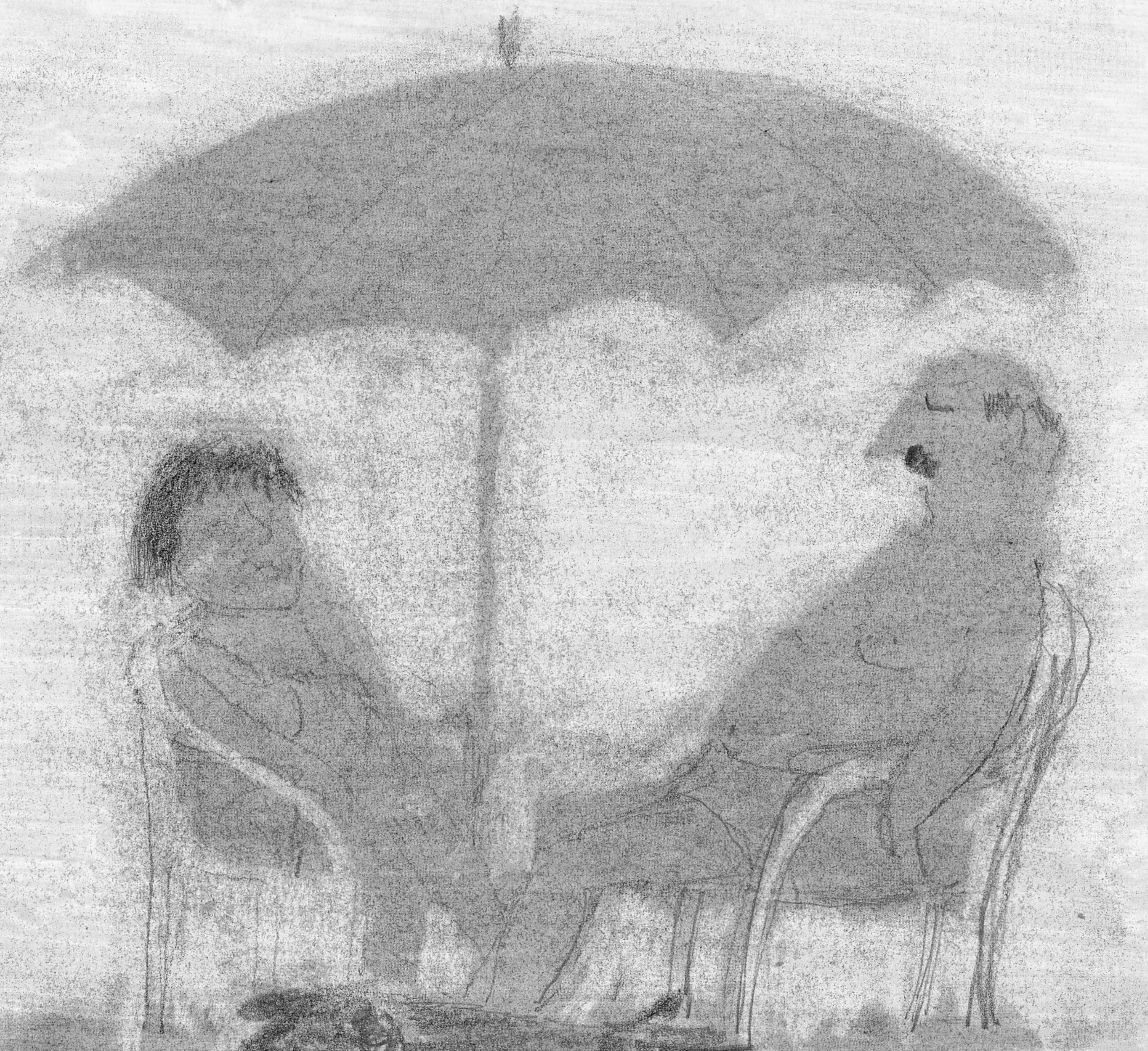

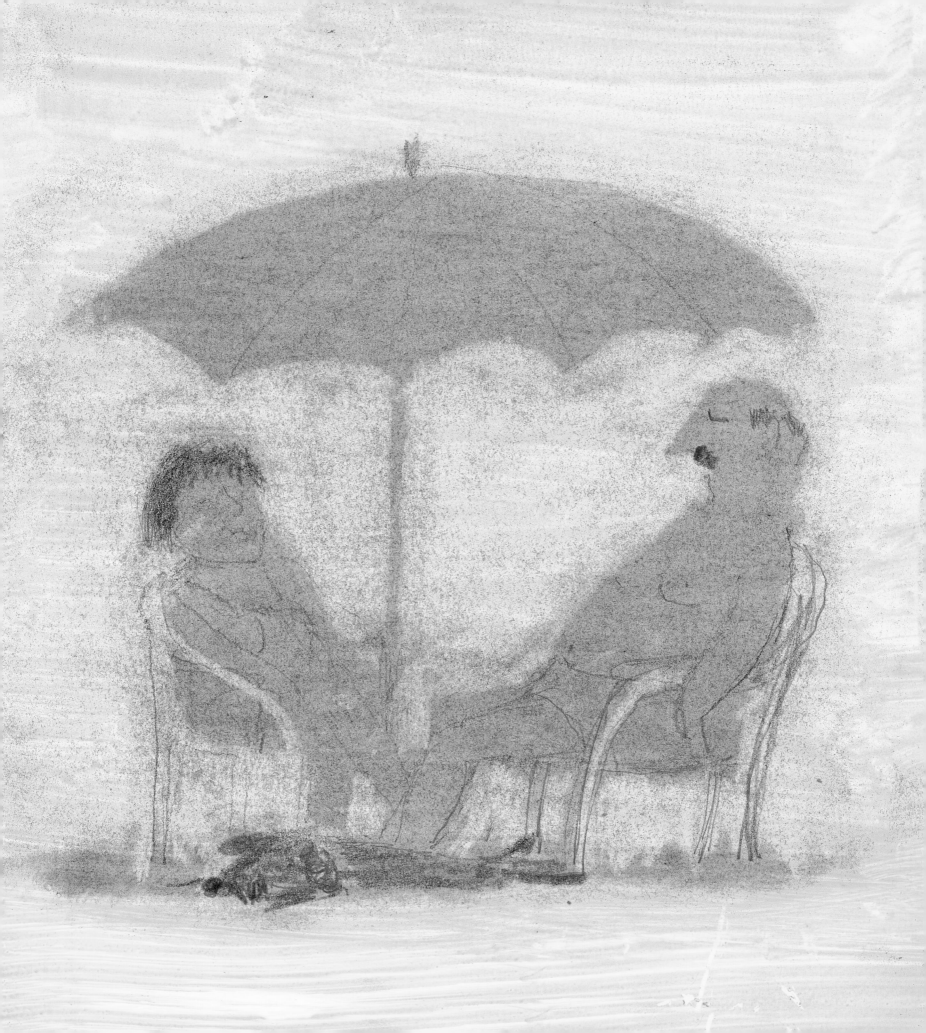

The French, too, might have decided that night to give up Verdun altogether, abandon the salient, and fall back to a more easily defensible line. But it was not to be: that midnight command of the defence of Verdun was given to General Pétain. He was determined not to allow the fortress to fall into German hands. 'Retake immediately any piece of land taken by him,' he insisted, and on the following day he issued the famous order: 'They shall not pass.'

In five months, more than twenty-three million shells were fired by the two contending armies at Verdun, on average more than a hundred shells a minute. Verdun itself remained in French hands, but the death toll there was 650,000 men. When added to that of the Somme, this made a five-month death toll of 960,459 men: almost a million. It was an average of more than 6,600 men killed every day, more than 277 every minute, nearly five men every second.

Martin Gilbert, *First World War*, 1994

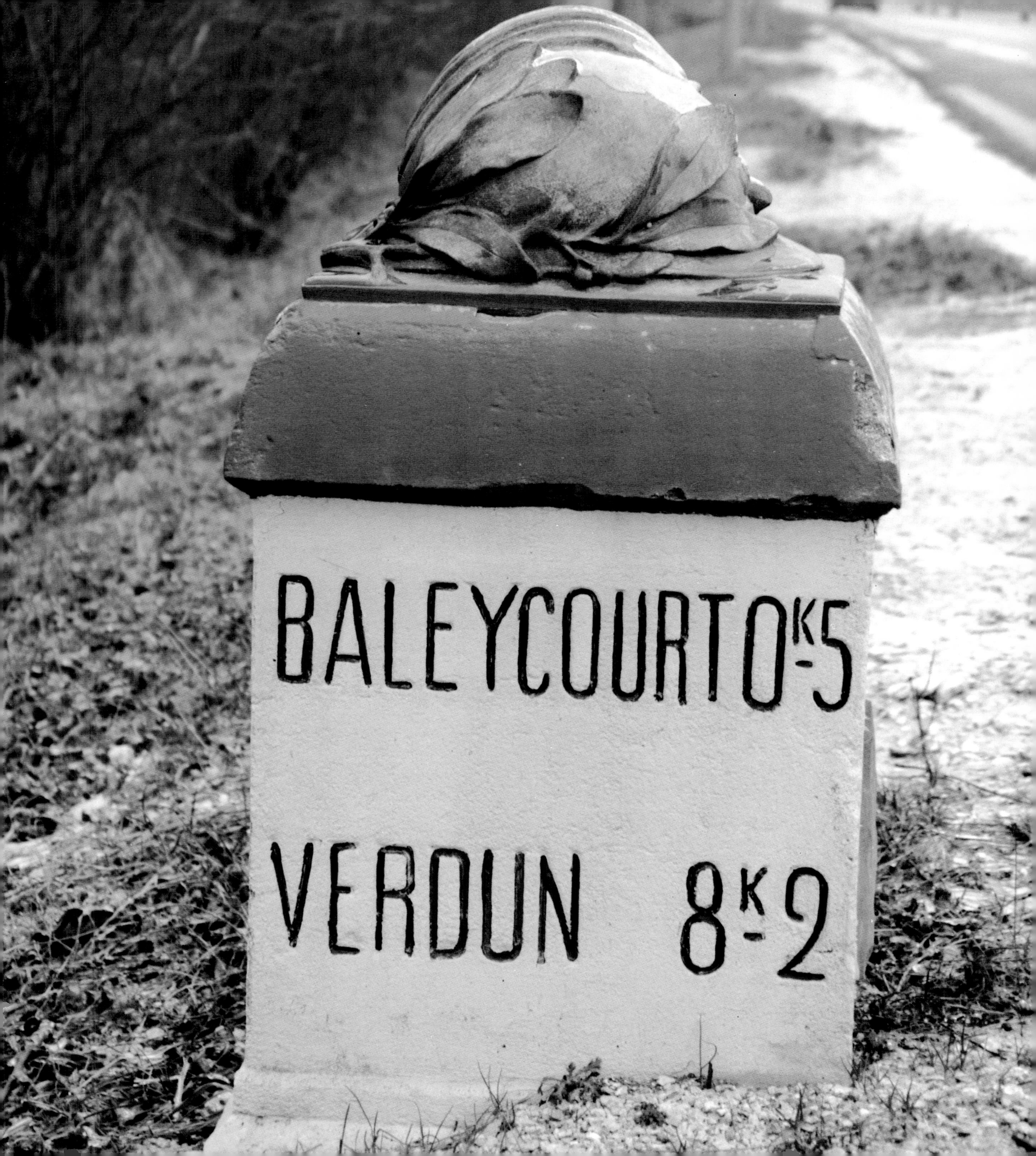
BALEYCOURT 0K5
VERDUN 8K2

Buvons un coup
Buvons en deux
À la santé des amoureux
À la santé du Roi de France
Et merde pour la Reine d'Angleterre
Qui nous a declaré la guerre

(Old French marriage toast still in use today)

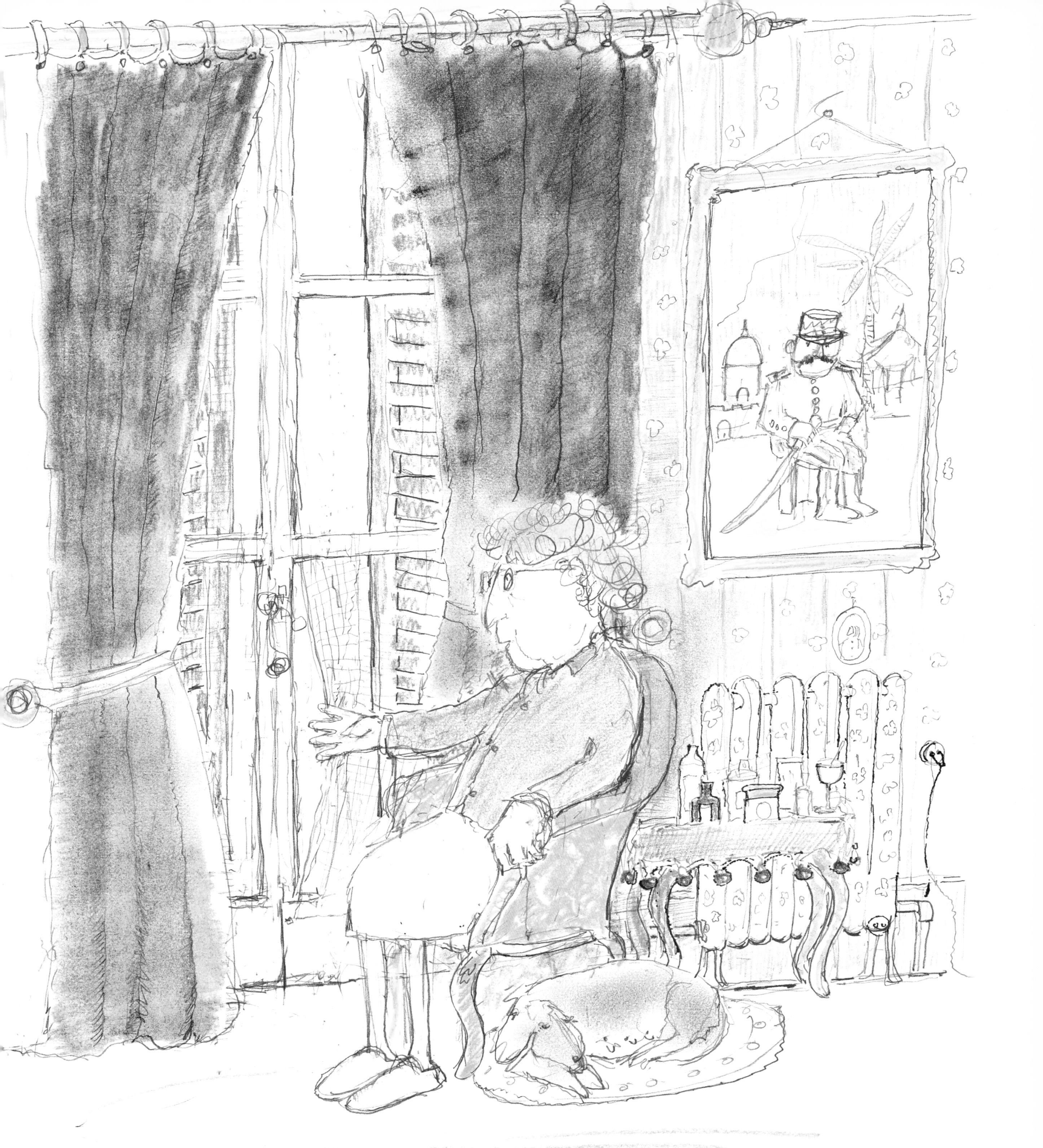

APPEL DU 18 JUIN 1940

TO ALL FRENCHMEN

France has lost a battle!

But France has not lost the war!

Makeshift governments may have capitulated, yielding to panic, forgetful of honour, delivering the nation up to slavery. Yet nothing is lost!

Nothing is lost, because this war is a world war. In the free universe, there are immense forces which have not yet been committed. One day, these forces will crush the enemy. When that day comes, France must have a part in the victory. Then will her liberty and her greatness be restored to her. That is my aim, my sole aim!

That is why I am calling on all Frenchmen, wherever they may be, to join with me in this battle, in this sacrifice and in this hope.

The life of our country is in danger.
Let us all fight to save her!

General de Gaulle,
Headquarters,
4 Carlton Gardens,
London SW1.

Les véritables Français parlent aux véritables Français

It has been my unhappy privilege to witness our three wars with the great and mighty Germany. I witnessed them in circumstances which enabled me at first to consider and to learn and, later on, to act.

I believe that this gives me the right to advise, to warn and to entreat my fellow-countrymen not to give way to their first impressions.

When we talk of cooperation and collaboration, these words, in some quarters and on some lips, might seem suspect. From the mouth of a man of honour, so wholly disinterested, who would truly ask for nothing more on this earth than a little rest in place of continual strife, such words cannot be seen in a suspicious light.

Cardinal BAUDRILLART
Rector of the Catholic Institute of France

Let me remind both the doubters and the stubbornly unyielding that when carried to excess, even the finest attitudes of pride and reserve may lose their force.

It is in all honour and in order to maintain the unity of France, a unity which has endured for ten centuries, within the conditions surrounding the creation of the new order in Europe that I embark today on the path of collaboration.

I speak to you today in the words of a commanding officer. Follow me: hold fast to your belief in the undying future of France.

Marshal PÉTAIN
Head of State

The atmosphere in which the talks took place was friendly. I might even say unexpectedly so, since it must not be forgotten that the war is not yet over.

If the French still look on Germany as their enemy, it is childish to ask for the release of prisoners of war.

If the people pay for the mistakes of their governments, they are also, by their efforts, the creators of recovery.

One page of World History has just turned, another virgin sheet lies before us on which to write as best we may, in a spirit of collaboration without which nothing anywhere in Europe can be achieved.

Georges SCAPINI
French Ambassador to Germany
Official declaration on his return from Berlin, November 1940

G MAZEYRIE Imprimeur Editeur PARIS

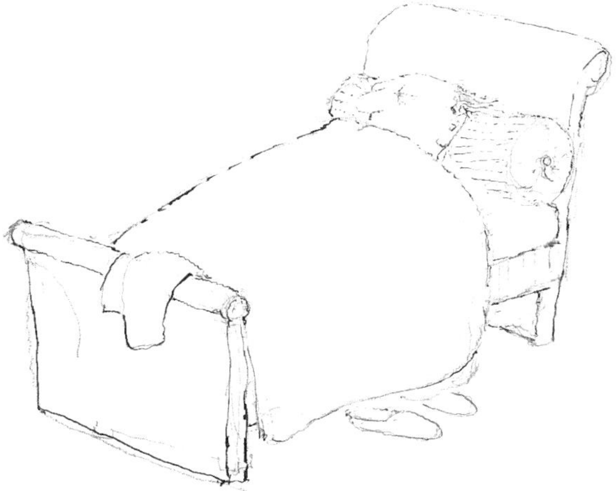

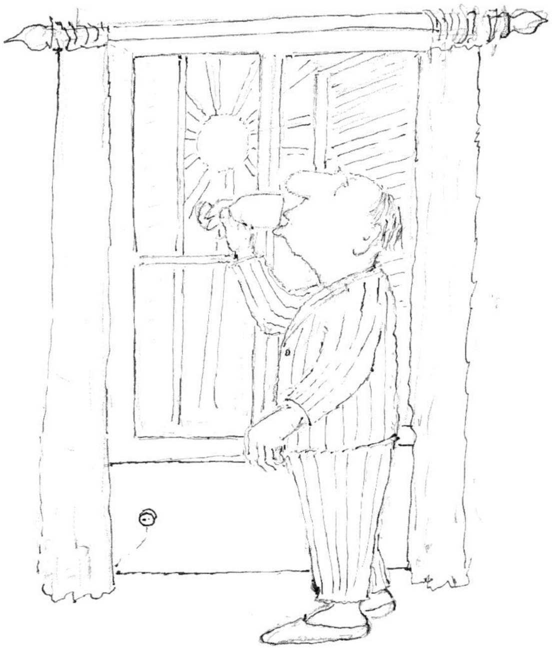

Petit Blanc

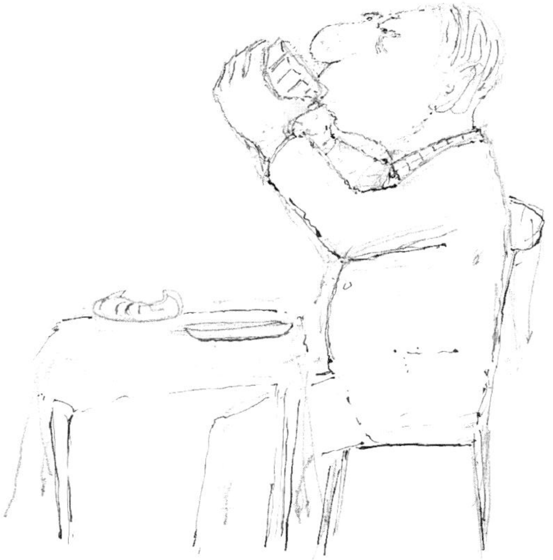

Café Calva

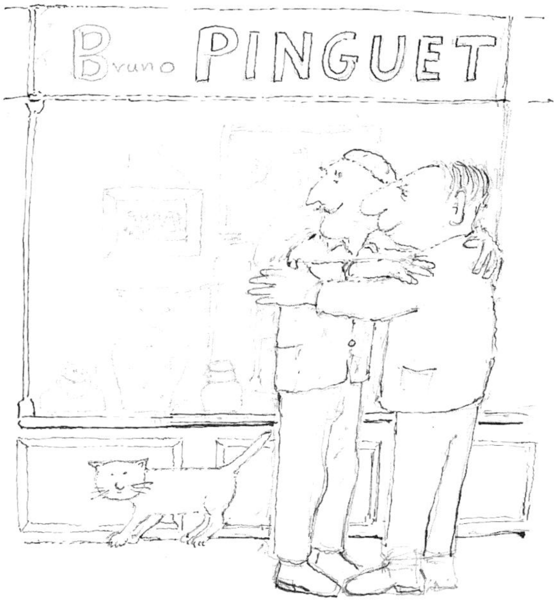
Bruno PINGUET

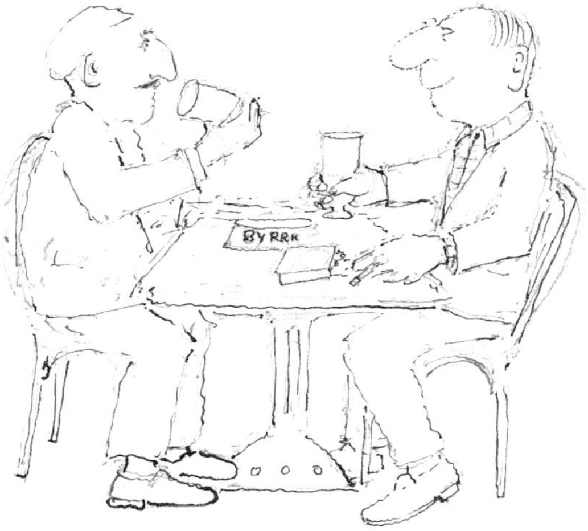

Bierre

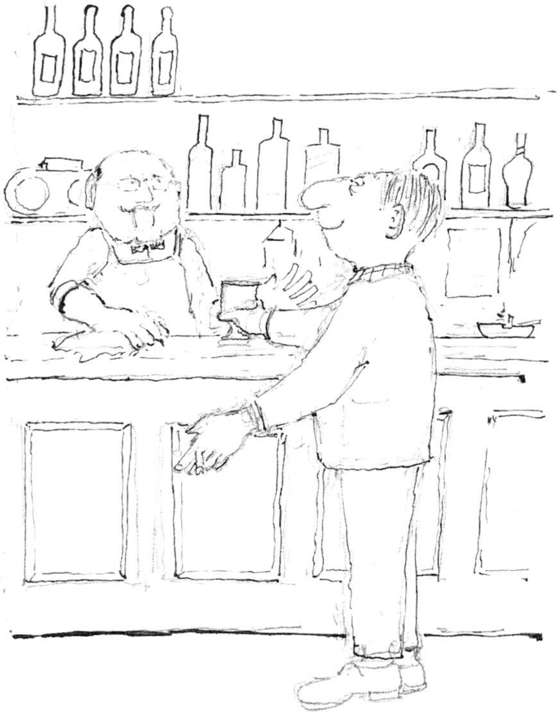

Pastis

Vin Rouge

Pastis

Vin Rouge

Cognac

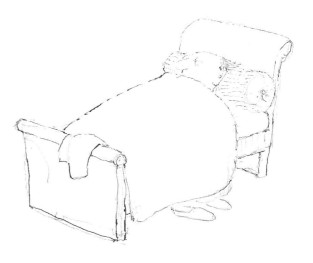

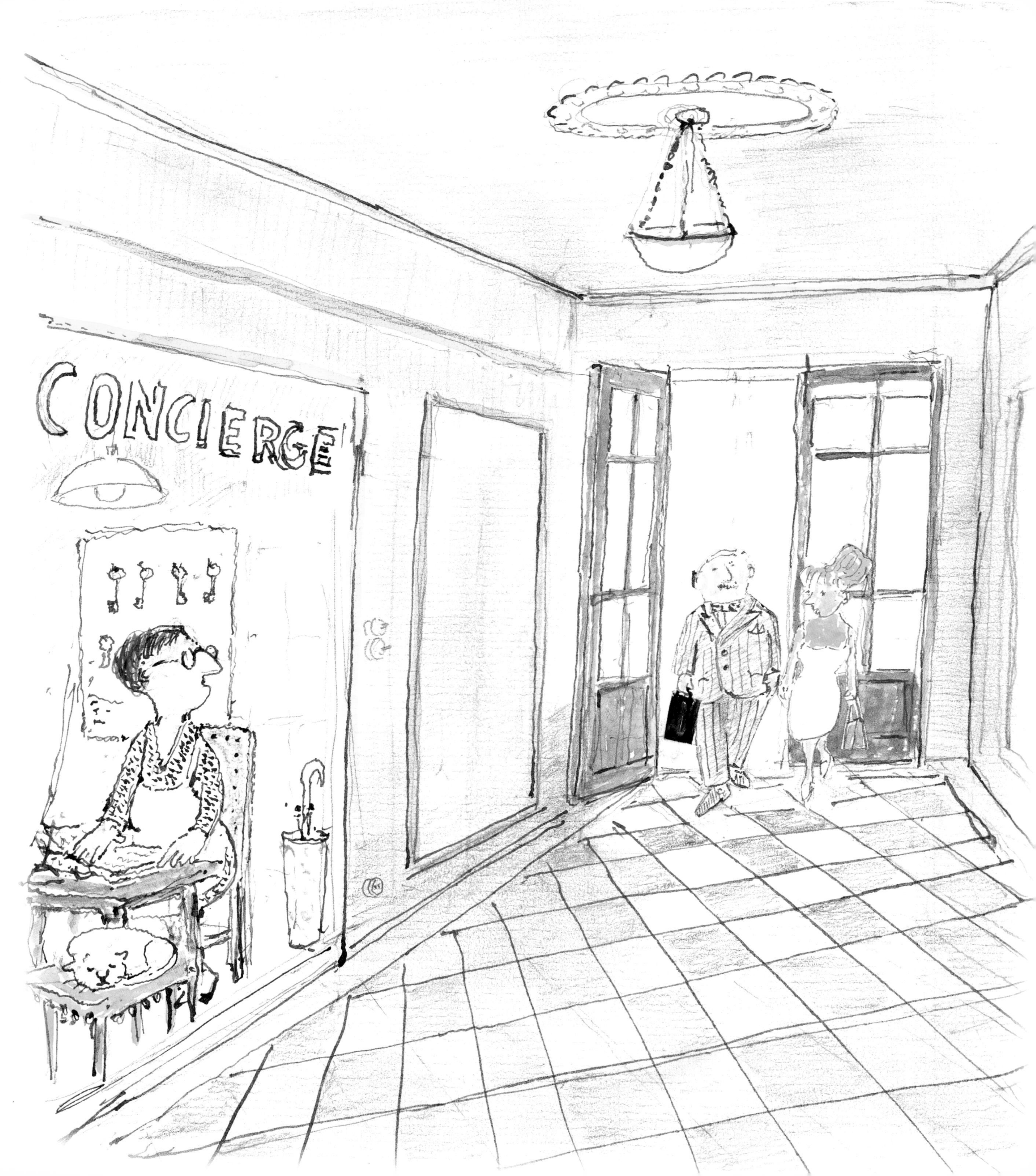
CONCIERGE

Guest/Concierge Relationships

The relationship between concierges and their guests is both a straightforward business relationship and one with complex psychological overtones. This is because the concierge, whom the guest hardly knows, is being entrusted with information and chores the guest considers highly personal. Concierges become the alter ego of their guests and must be able to function on their behalf. In order to do this, concierges become confidants and are privy to information that the guests do not always feel comfortable divulging. Concierges do their best work when they have enough information to know what their guests are attempting to do. The situation can be delicate, and it is the experience of working together repeatedly and successfully that enables both partners in the relationship to feel comfortable. How you, as a concierge, deal with this problem will make or break your reputation . . .

Discretion is of the essence. Concierges often know intimate details of their guests' lives. *Toute voire, rien dire* (see everything, say nothing) must be your motto. You will win the confidence of your guests by displaying respect for their privacy.

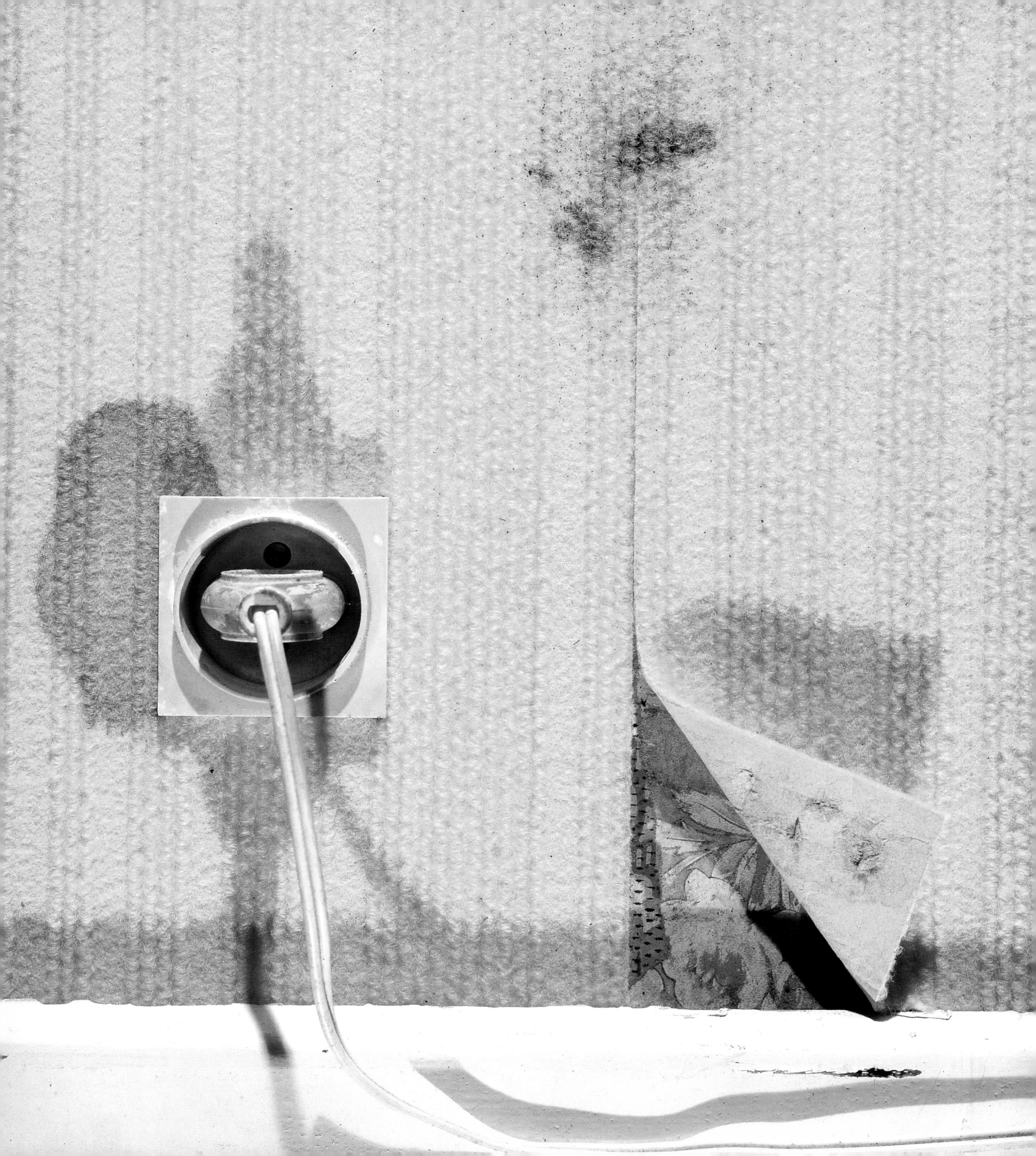

'It is difficult to describe the incredible range of materials, colours and subjects available today. Different styles are reproduced: damasks and Persian work, drapery and upholstery and toiles de Jouy. Modern designs are in strong colours or pale pastels, in cretonne or in leather, figured or varnished, or stencilled, with varied backgrounds, and plasticized. And this material can be used in so many pleasant ways, all over a wall or in panels, to create contrast or heighten a decorative effect. Finally, for a relatively low cost, wallpaper can change any family's decoration, in a word make walls live or, as Paul Valéry put it, make them sing.'

Pierre Morel, president of the Chambre Syndicale of French wallpaper makers

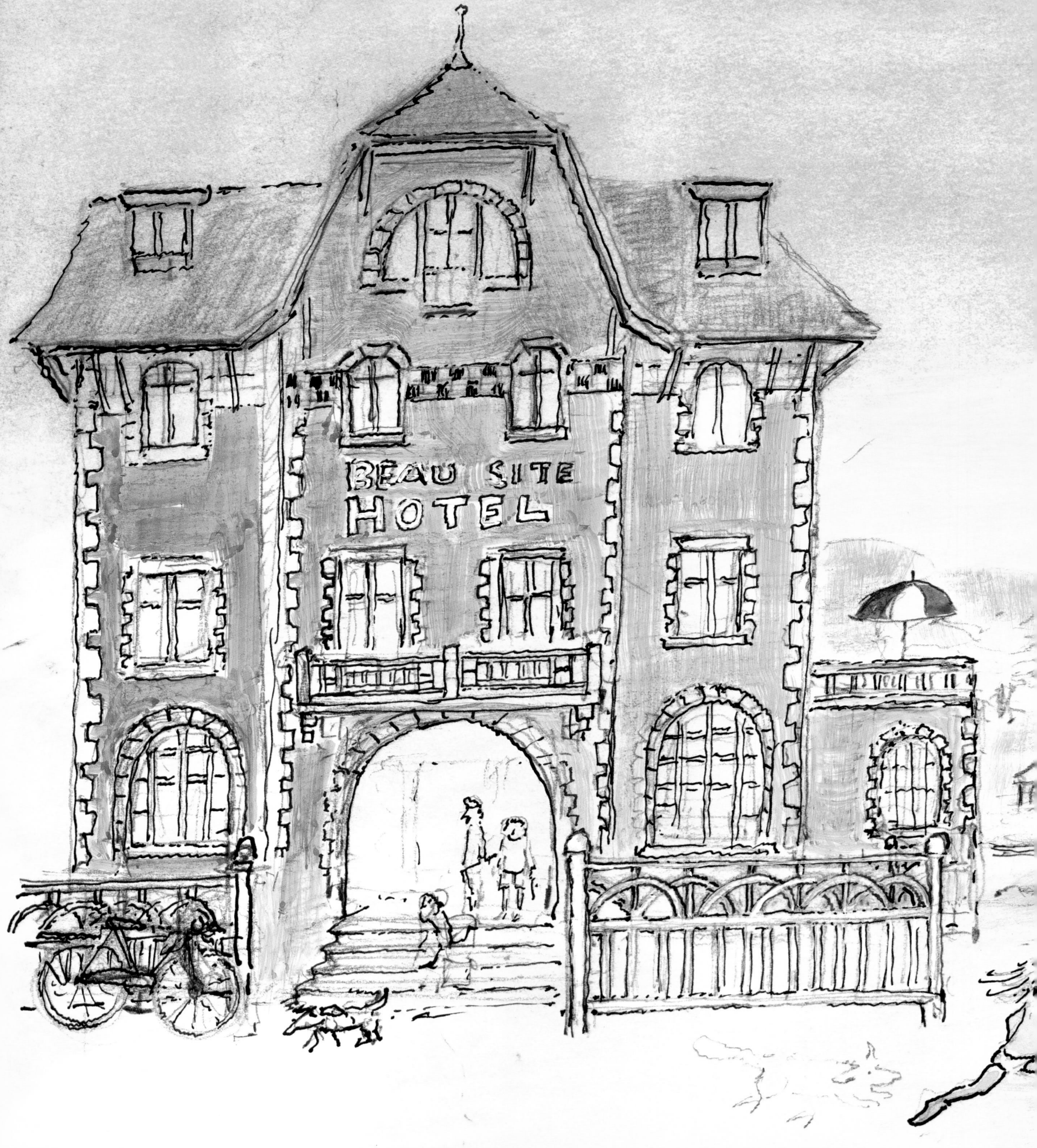
BEAU SITE
HOTEL

Côte de Granit Rose

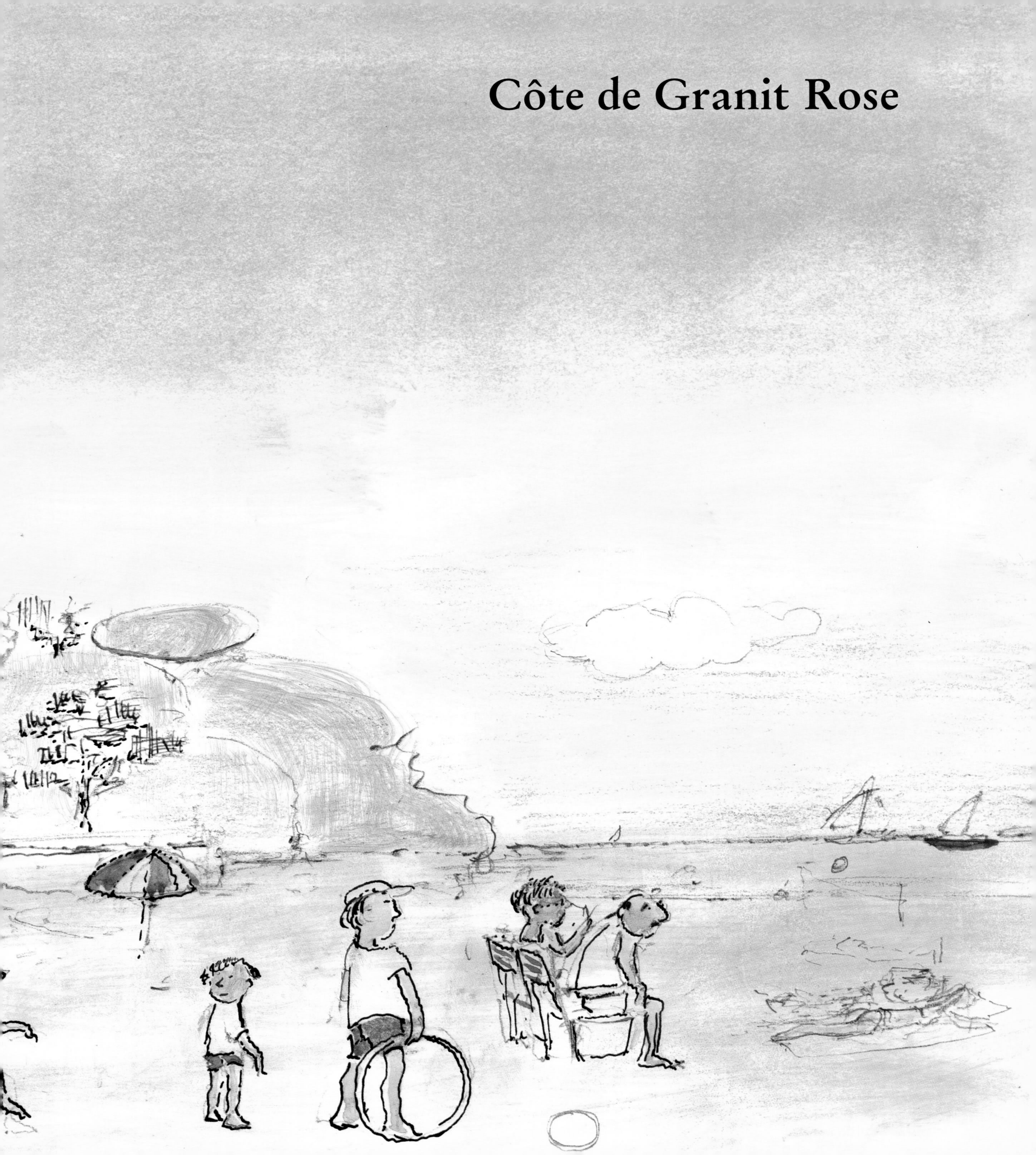

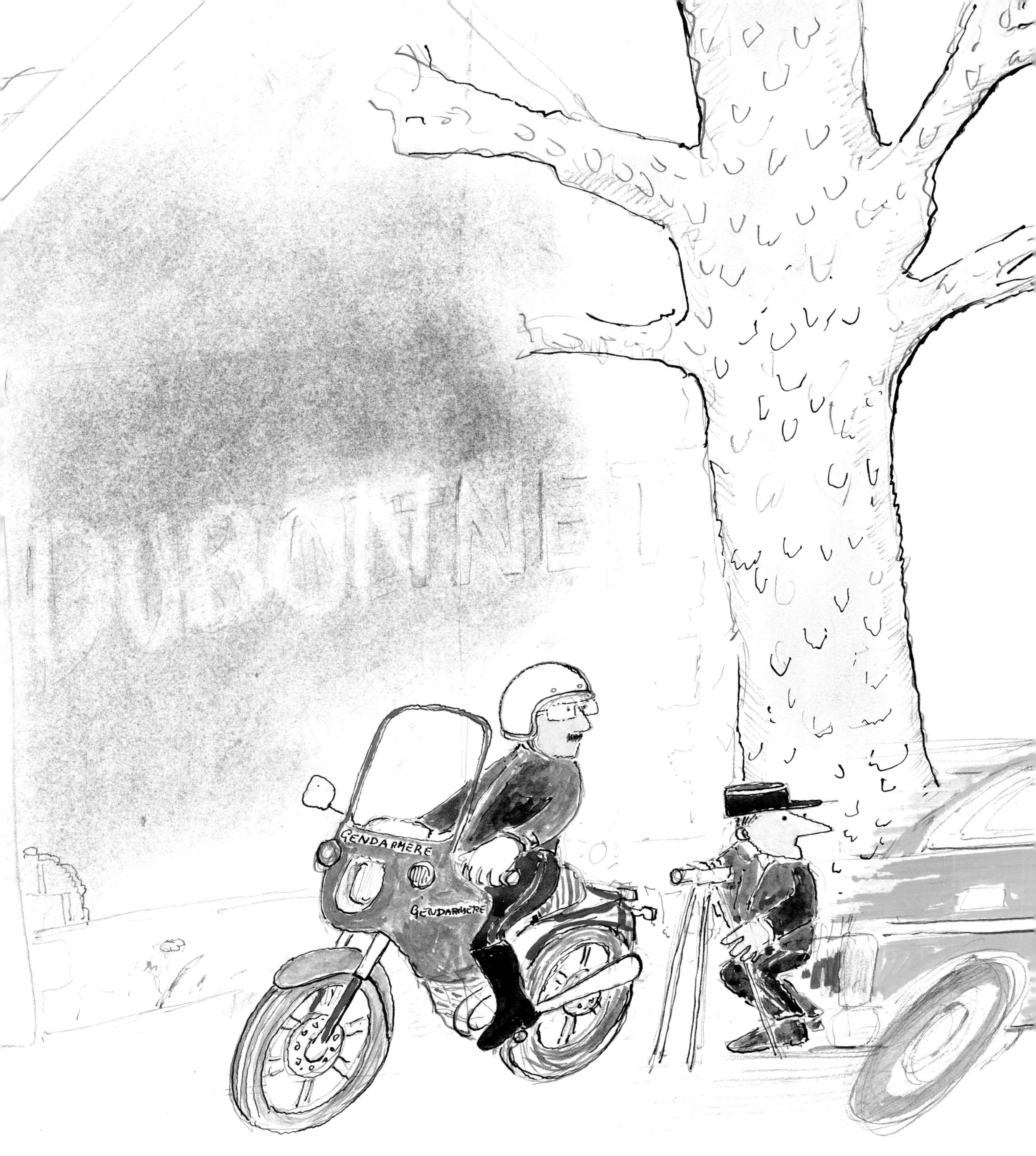
DUBONNET
GENDARMERE

NOTIFICATION D'ORDONNANCE PÉNALE

TRIBUNAL DE POLICE

TRIBUNAL DE POLICE
SQUARE BOURDET
21, Av. Auguste Renoir, CAGNES-S-MER

L
avec

R CAGNES-SUR-MER
RENOIR
5944

N° du parquet :

1138

N° du greffe :

1138

A Repercevoir

ÉTAT CIVIL

NOM (1) : PINGUET Bruno
Prénoms :
Profession : 19 avenue victor Hugo
Domicile : 84 ORANGE
(département) :

Date et lieu de naissance (Arrondt) : 7.2.43 à VILLEMONBLE SEINE
Filiation
Situat. fam^le. : enfant
Nat^té., Sit. mil^re.

INFRACTION

Nature : EXCES VITESSE 104 X 60
Date : 4.5.84 Lieu : CAGNES SURMER
Textes : R 10.1 ET R232.2 DU CR
N° d'Immatriculation : 8658 MD 07

RÉQUISITION

L'Officier du Ministère public requiert de condamner l'intéressé par ordonnance pénale, à une amende de 600 A 1200FRS francs, aux dépens, et de fixer la durée de la contrainte par corps au minimum.

Au Tribunal de Police, le 22 MAI 1984

L'officier du Ministère public

TRIBUNAL DE POLICE · MINISTÈRE PUBLIC · CAGNES-SUR-MER

3203470. 102.

ORDONNANCE PÉNALE

Vu les réquisitions du Ministère public, condamnons l'intéressé à une amende de 600 frs francs au paiement des frais indiqués ci-dessous et fixons la durée de la contrainte par corps au minimum.

Au Tribunal de Police, le 6/7/84
Le Président du Tribunal de Police,

Pour copie conforme :
Le Greffier en chef,

TRIBUNAL D'INSTANCE D'ANTIBES · GREFFE DE CAGNES-SUR-MER · (06)

Détail des condamnations

A Repercevoir

Amende	F	600
Frais	F	25
		625
TOTAL A PAYER		

15-82-52 (7801) - IMPRIMERIES ADMINISTRATIVES CENTRALES - 8, rue de Furstenberg, 75006 PARIS

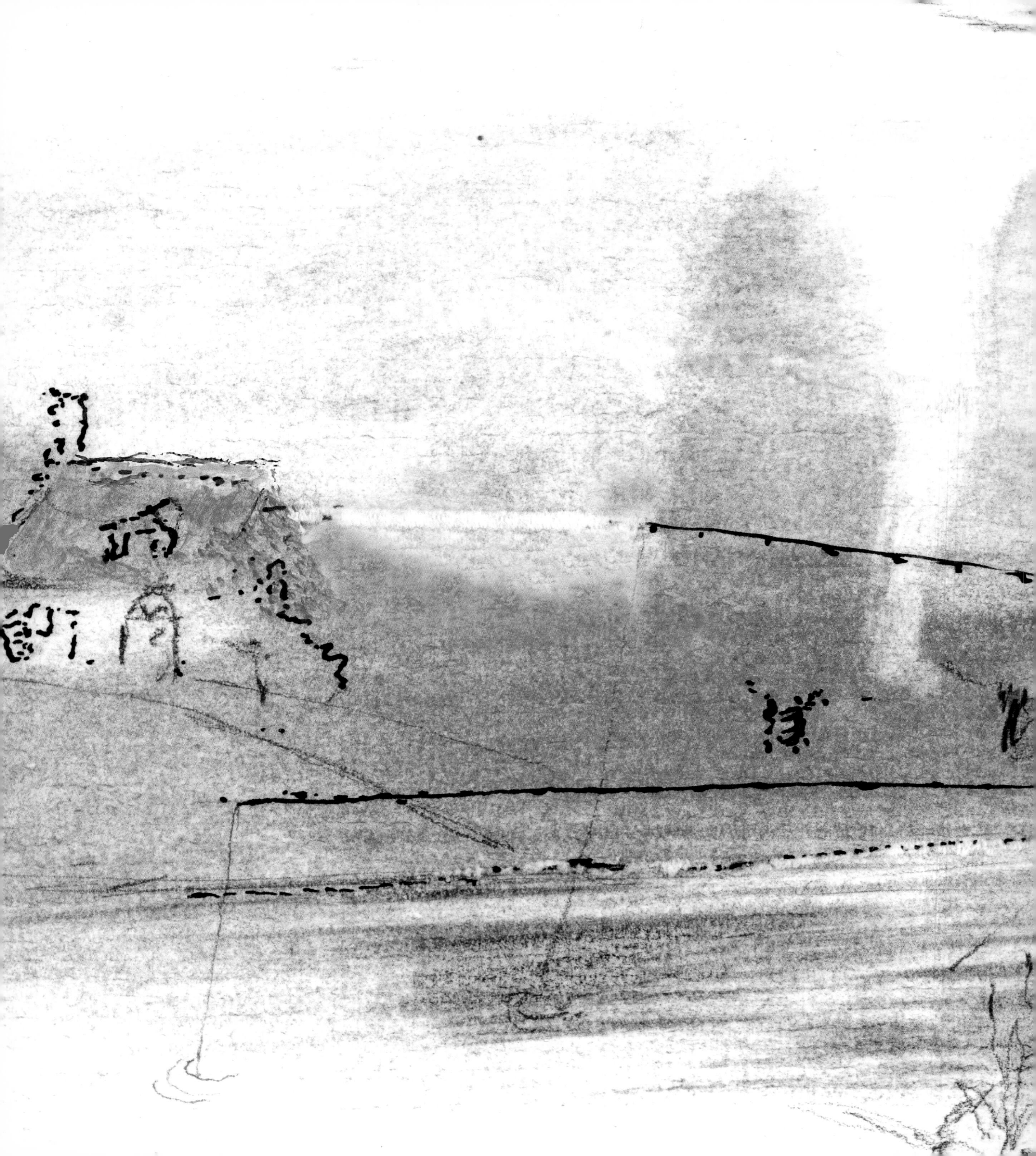

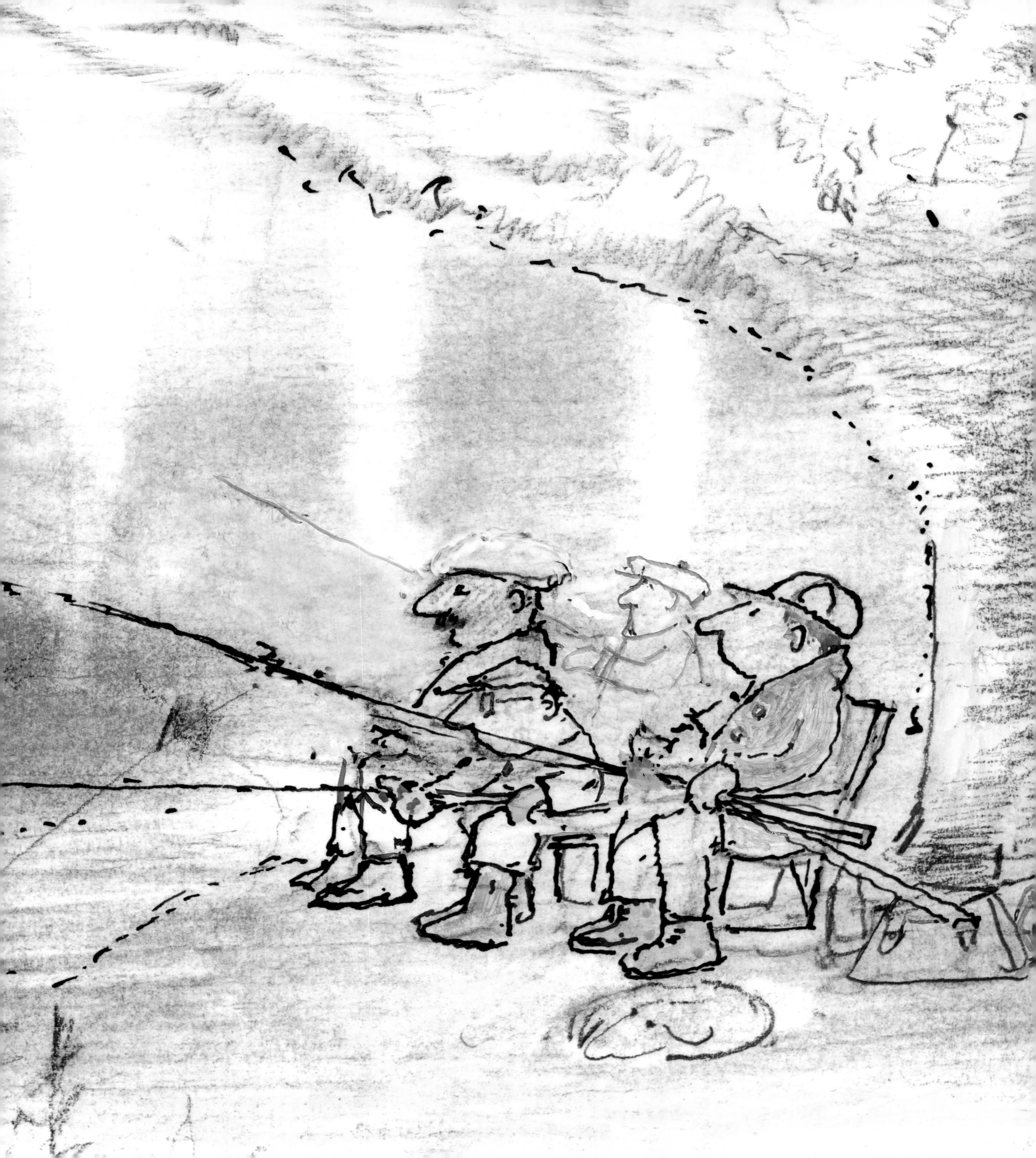

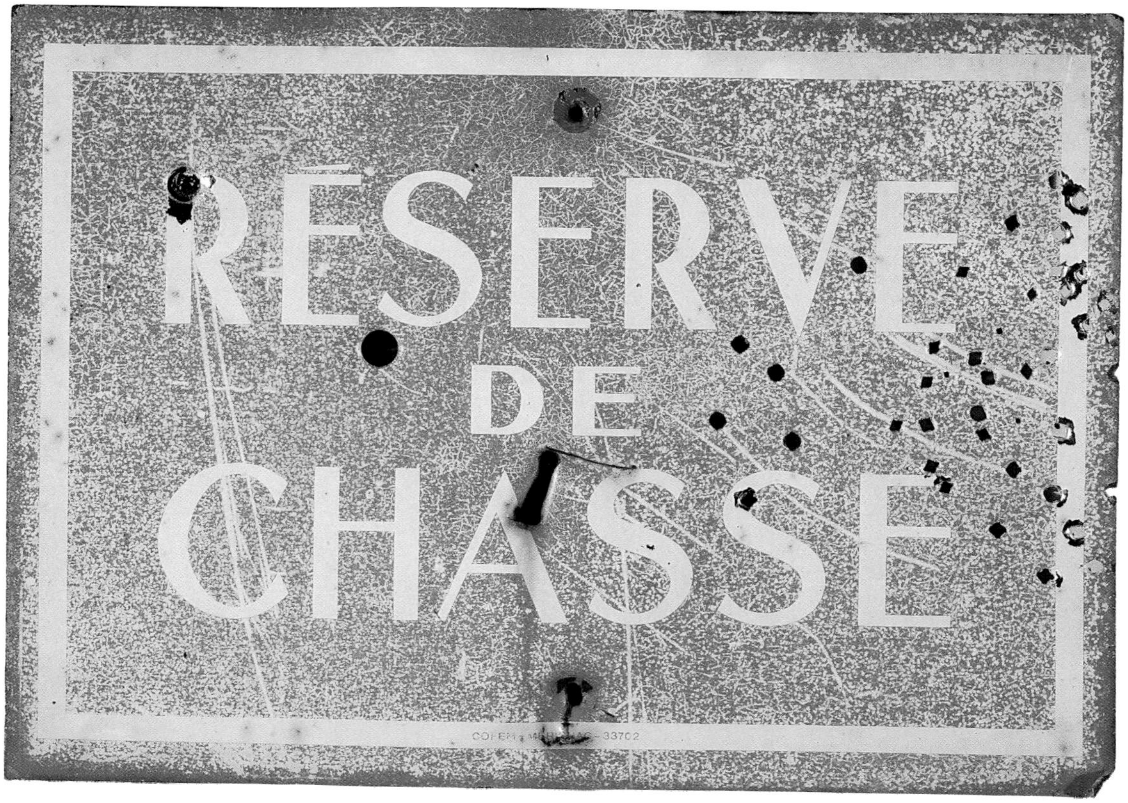
RÉSERVE
DE
CHASSE

Accidents: Number of accidents per year (**a**), killed (**k**), injured (**i**). *1965*: 190 a. (35 k./157 i.); *70*: 274 a. (52 k./250 i.); *75*: 281 a. (65 k./236 i.); *76* (compulsory licensing):236 a. (63 k./183 i.); *77*: 183 a. (45 k./139 i.); *80*: 125 a. (29 k./96 i.); *85*: 95 a. (26 k./67 i.); *87*: 64 a. (17 k./47 i.); *92*: 45 a. (21 k./27 i.); *93*: 54 a. (19 k./30 i.); *94*: 44 a. (15 k./30 i.); *95*: 43 a. (11 k./32 i.)

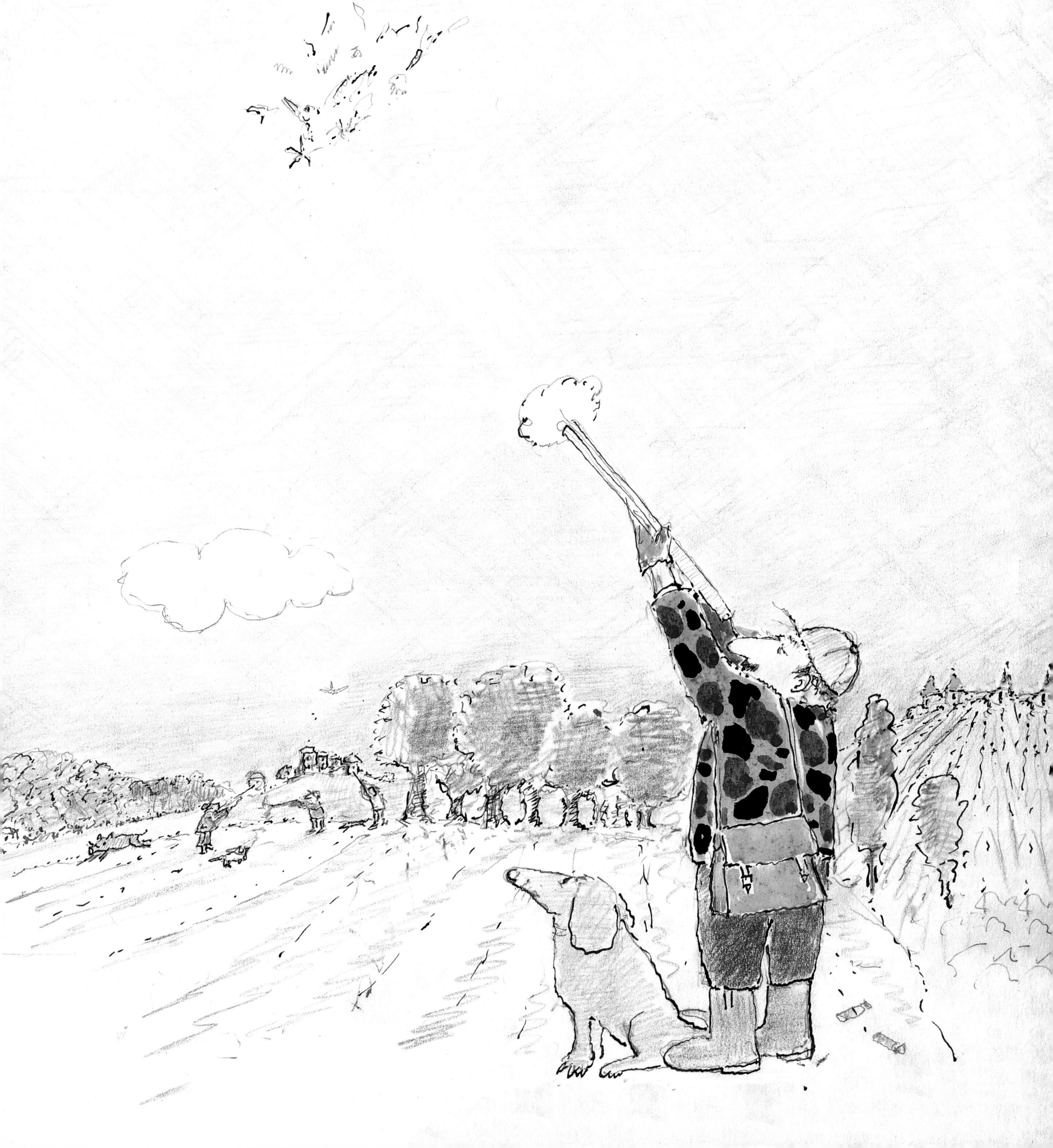

Aged colour with a soft fruit nose, gentle strawberry and marmite palate; some acidity in the dry finish.

❦

Complex and intense nose of spicy tropical fruit; full, balanced palate with an enjoyable, intense finish.

❦

Peach and melon nose with tart, apple-skin tones intruding on the palate. A crisp finish.

Crisp and clean melon and tropical-fruit nose with a lively acid zing on the palate.

❦

Fresh, creamy, citrus aroma; crisp, clean, lemony palate and a good, long-lasting, fresh finish.

❦

Full, rich, chocolatey Pinot fruit; palate dominated by rich, ripe, red-berry flavours. Elegant finish.

Pinot Noir showing more maturity; farmyard smell; vegetal with lovely damson fruit. Long, fragrant finish.

Creamy, dark fruit, biscuit nose with well balanced kiwi and passion fruit palate. A long, creamy finish

Pale colour, good underlying fruit beneath soft tannins, sweet cherries and gamey flavours. Complex structure.

Closed, creamy, green-fruit and honey nose. A long, balanced, tropical-fruit palate and pleasing finish.

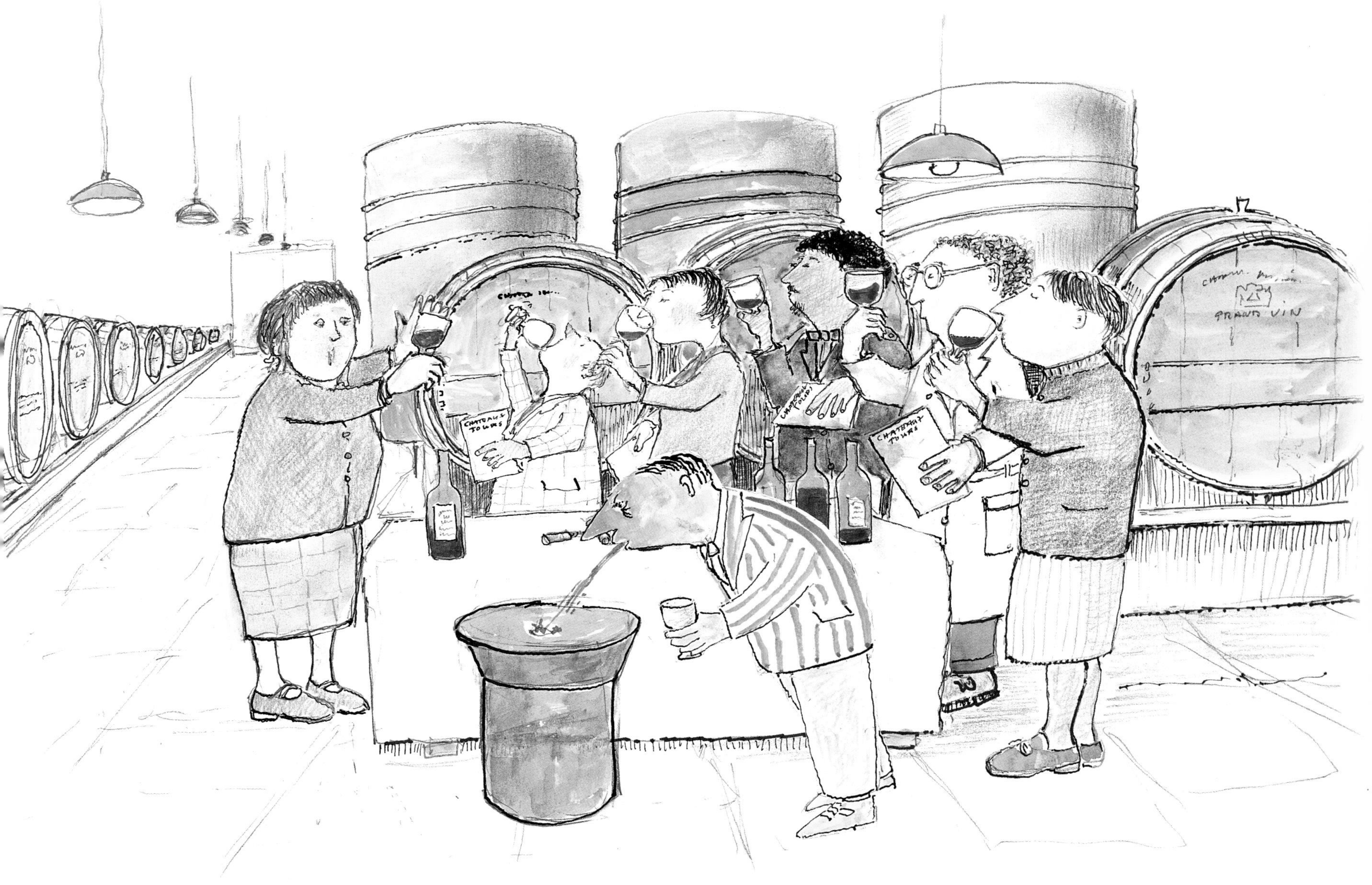

CGT (Confédération Générale du Travail)

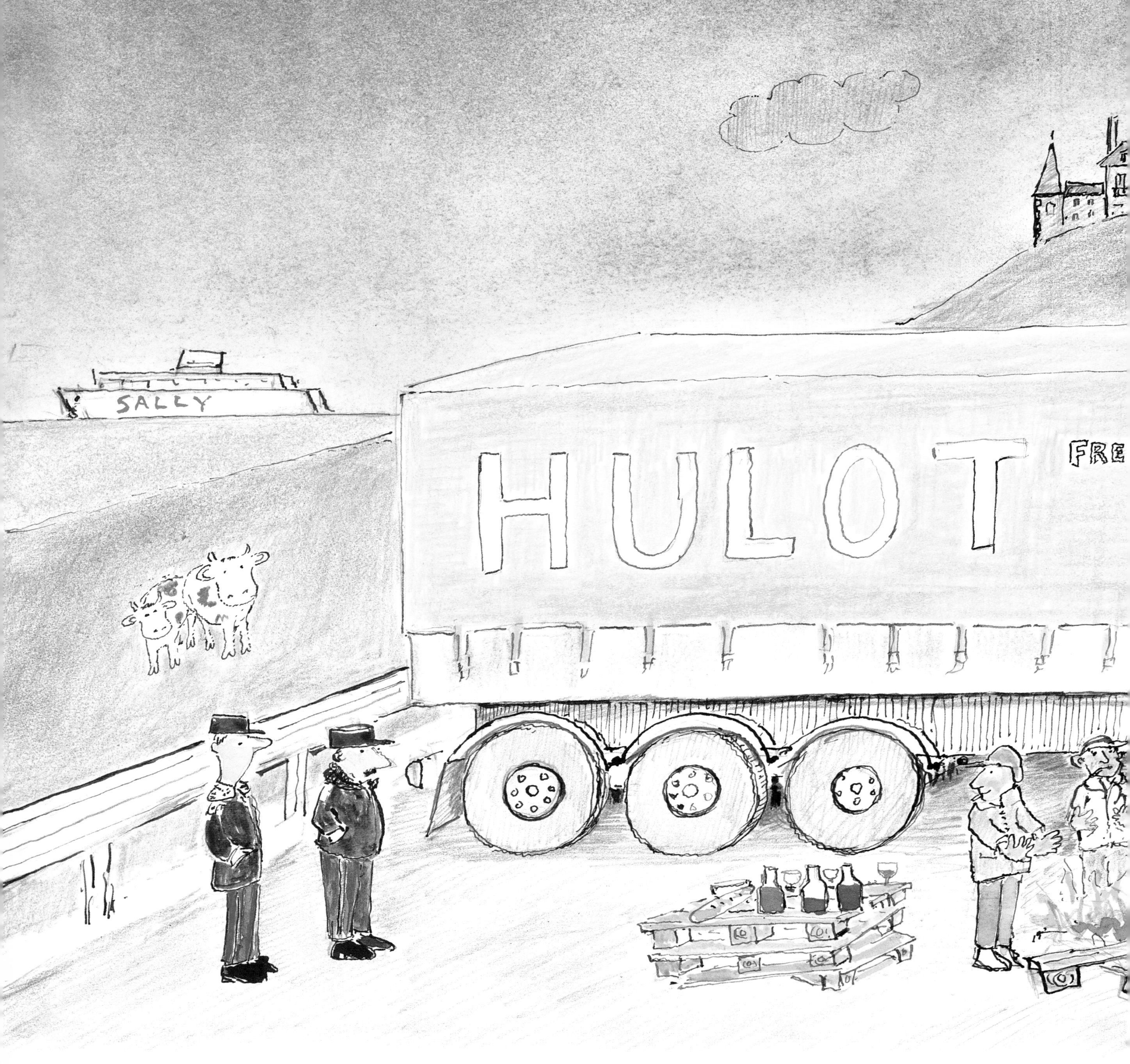
SALLY
HULOT
FRE

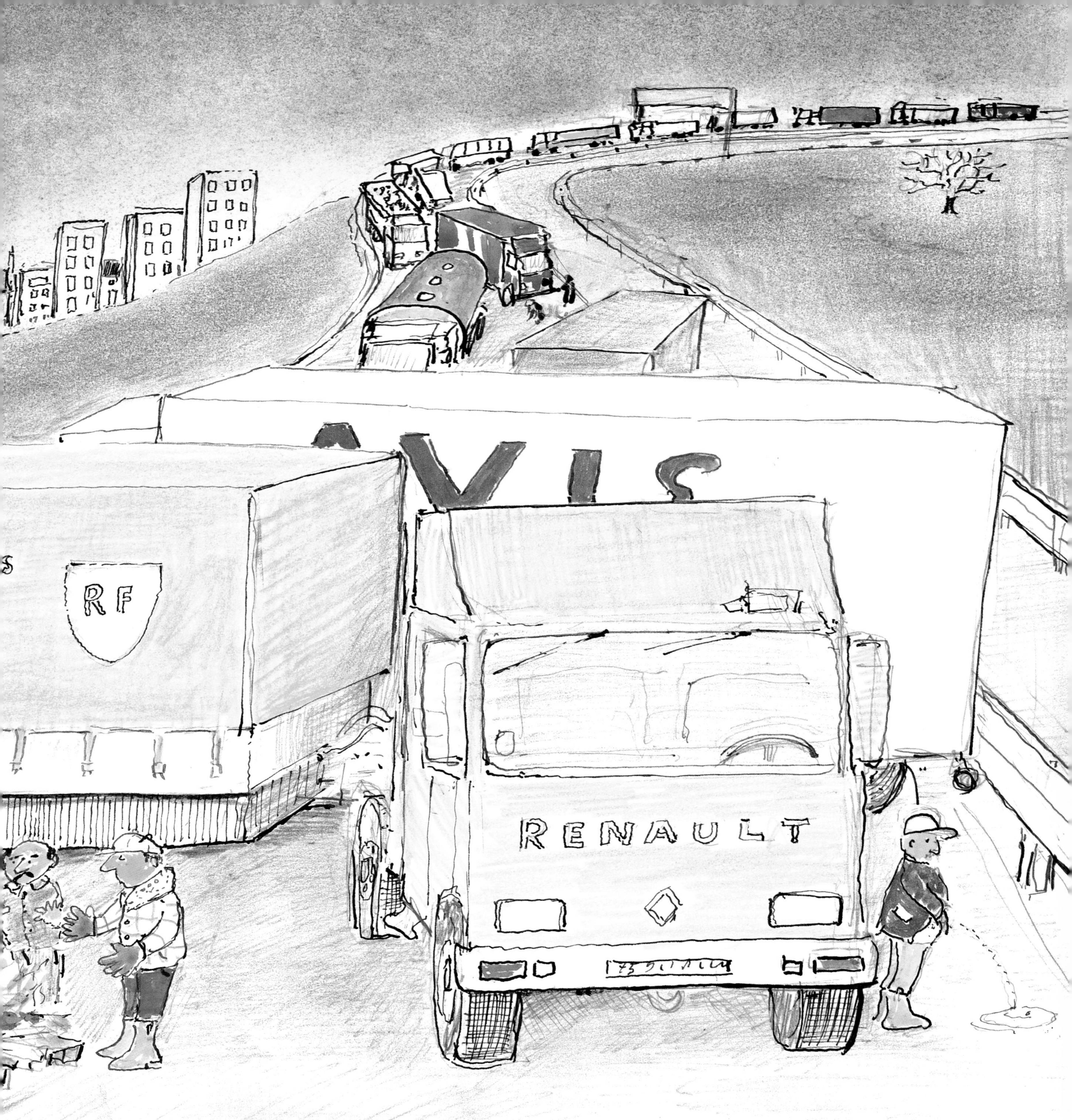
RF
RENAULT

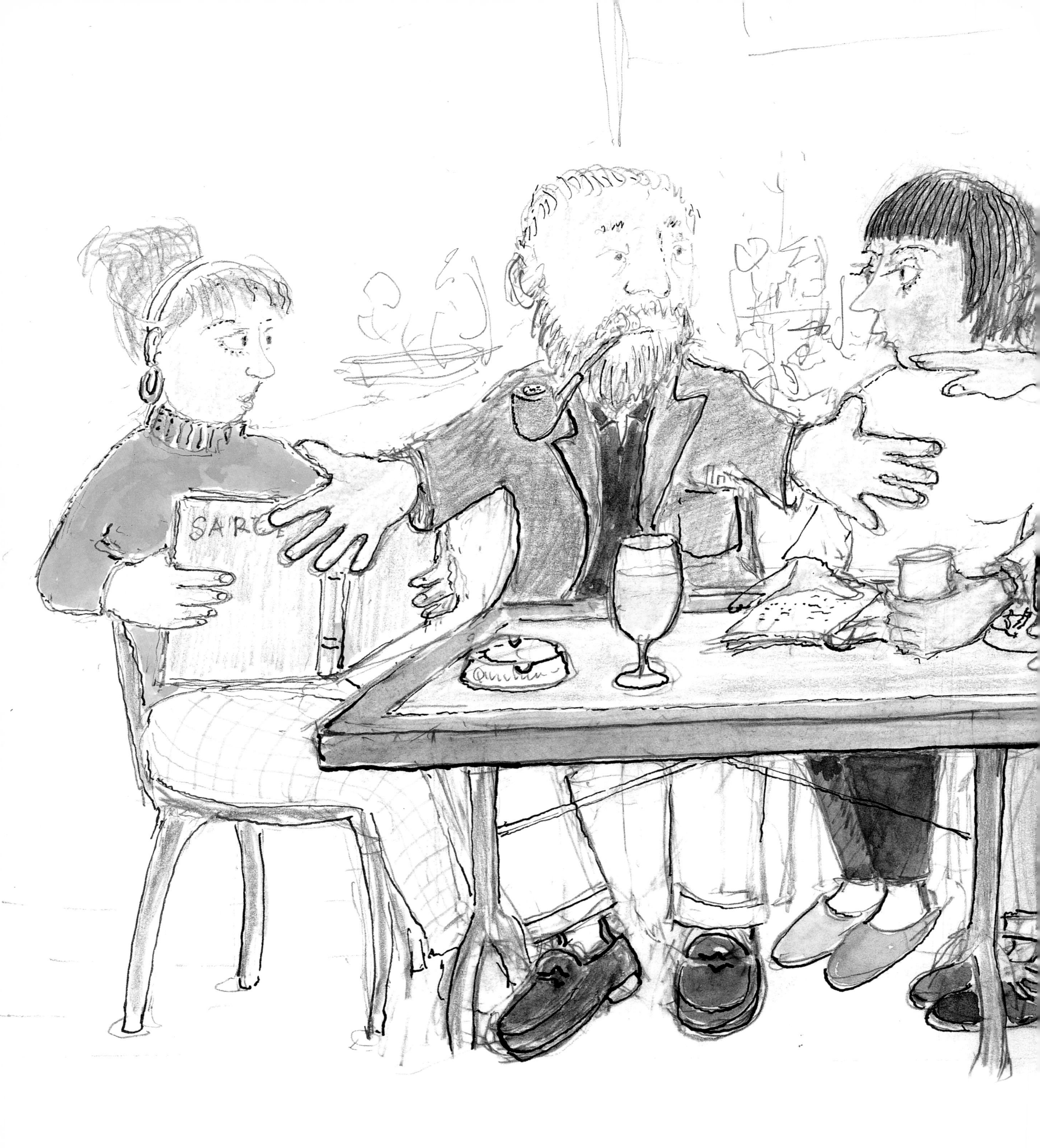

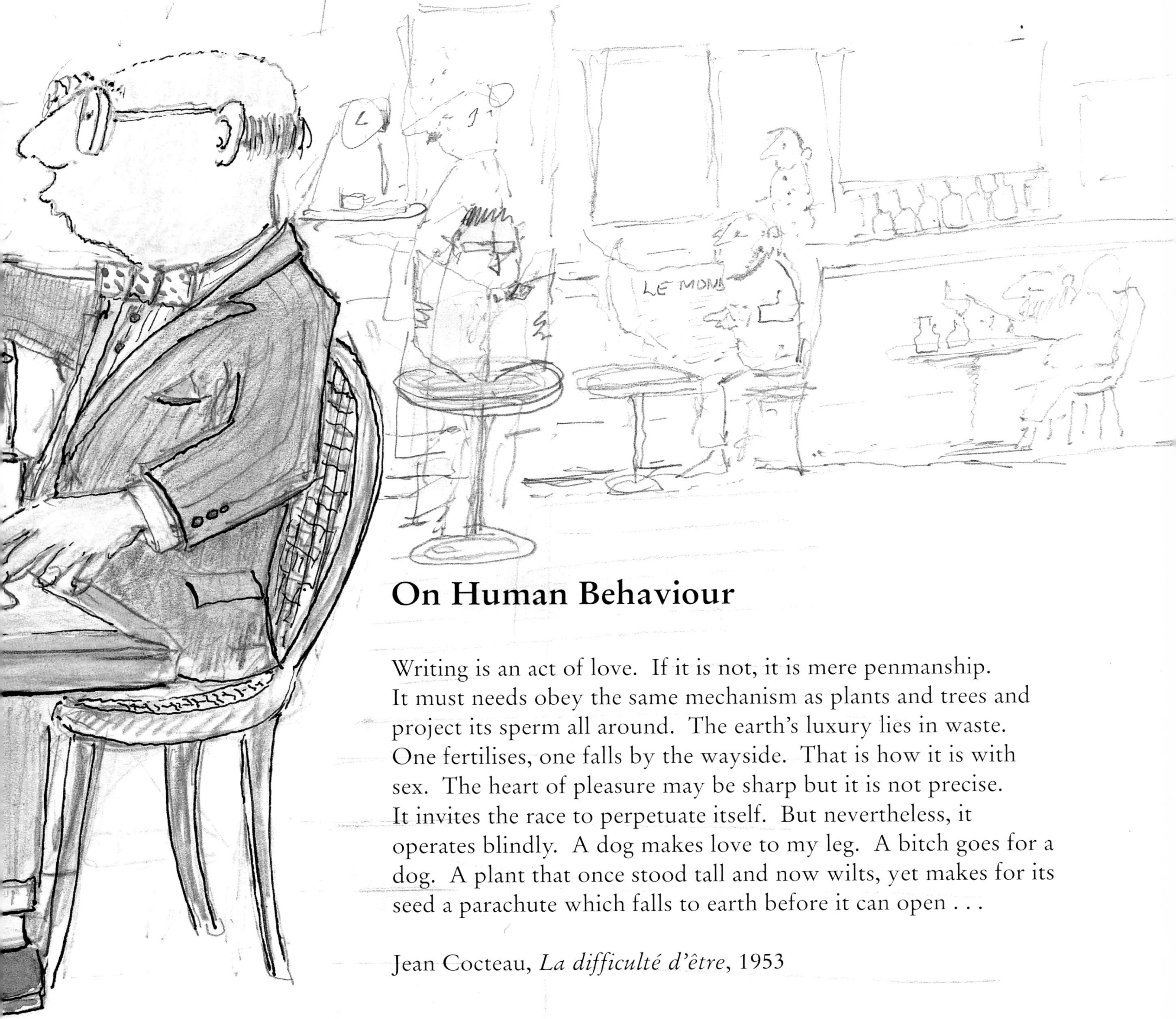
LE MON

On Human Behaviour

Writing is an act of love. If it is not, it is mere penmanship. It must needs obey the same mechanism as plants and trees and project its sperm all around. The earth's luxury lies in waste. One fertilises, one falls by the wayside. That is how it is with sex. The heart of pleasure may be sharp but it is not precise. It invites the race to perpetuate itself. But nevertheless, it operates blindly. A dog makes love to my leg. A bitch goes for a dog. A plant that once stood tall and now wilts, yet makes for its seed a parachute which falls to earth before it can open . . .

Jean Cocteau, *La difficulté d'être*, 1953

Jour des Morts, 2 November

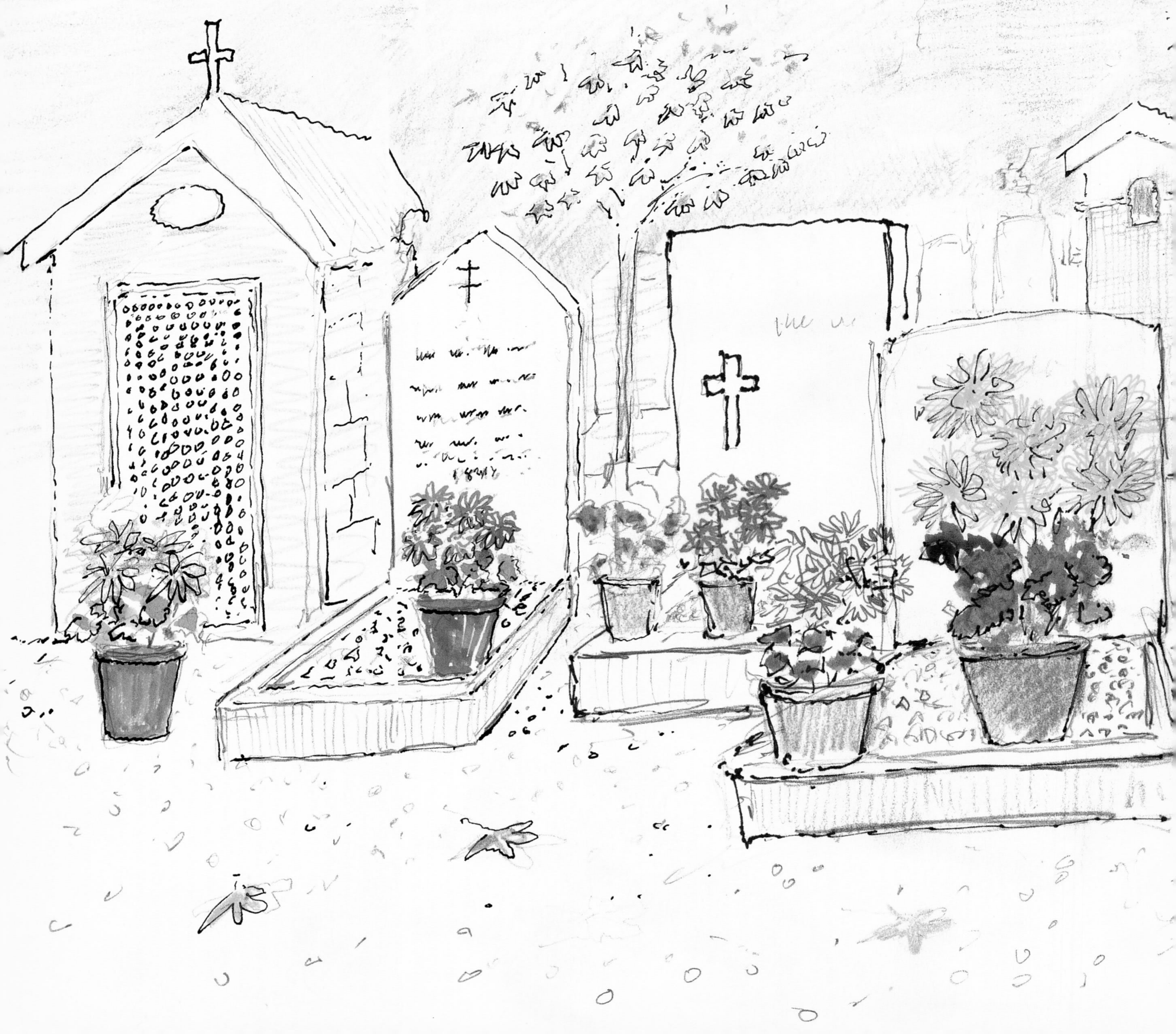

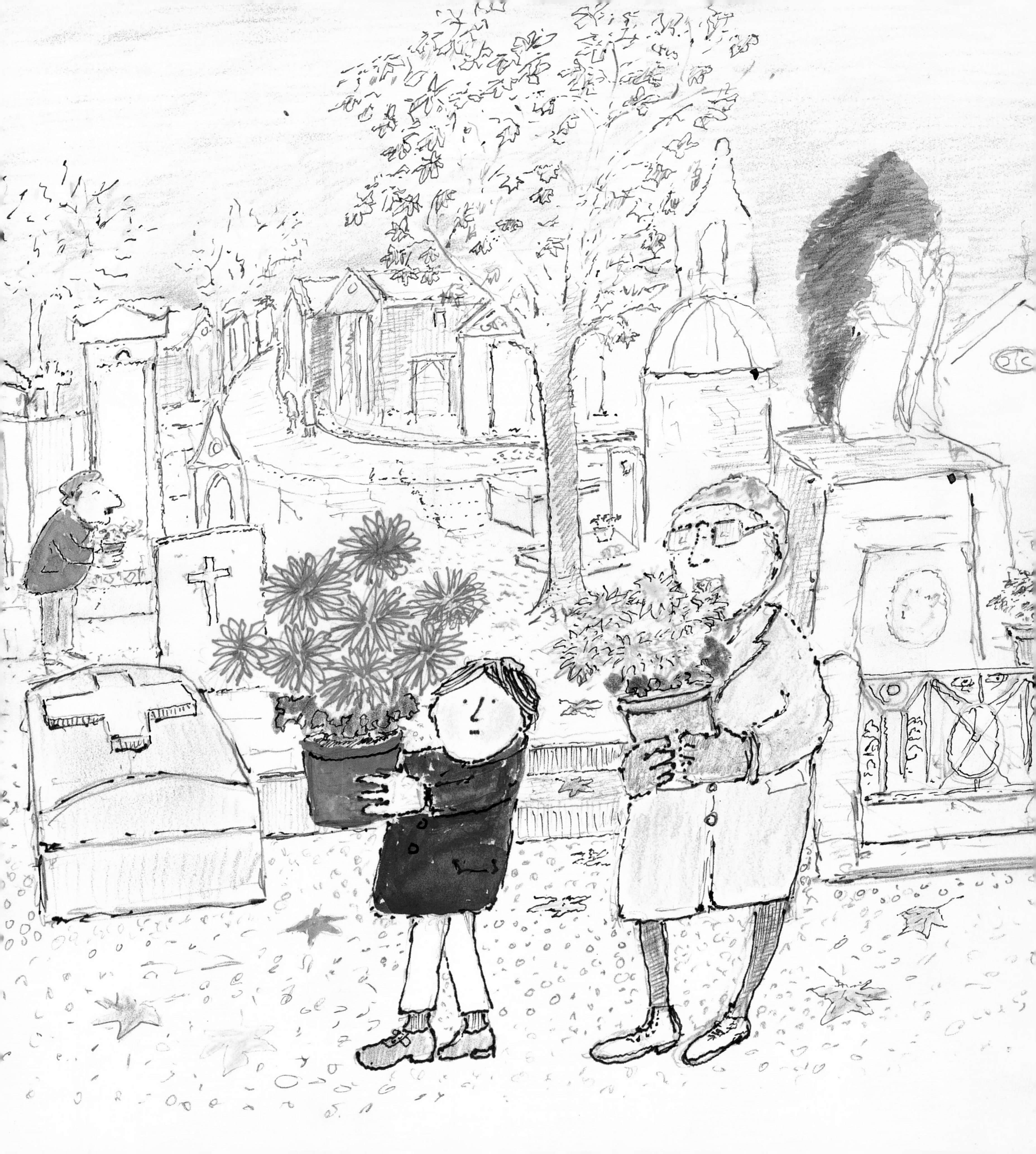

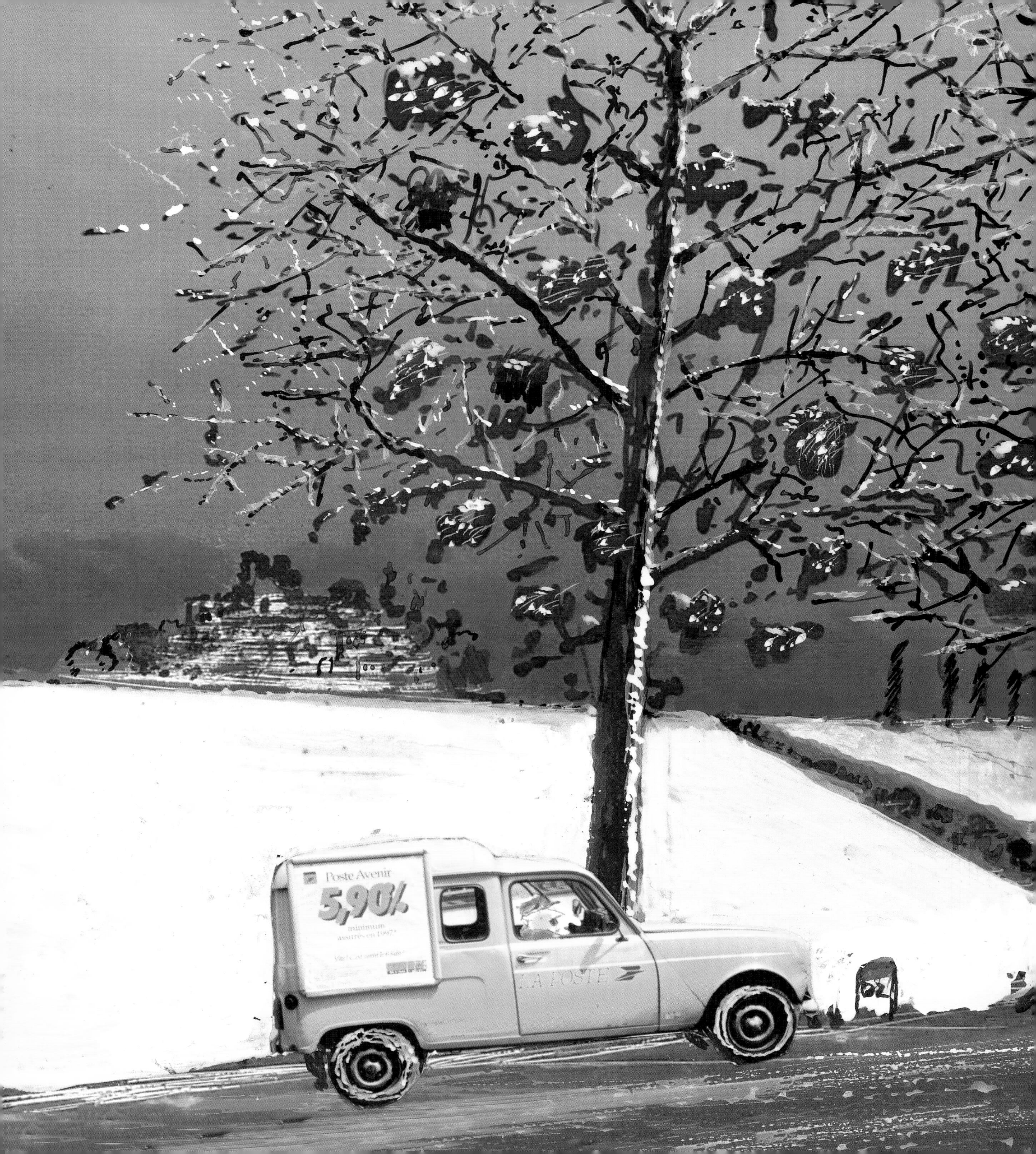
Poste Avenir
5,90%
minimum
assurés en 1997*
LA POSTE

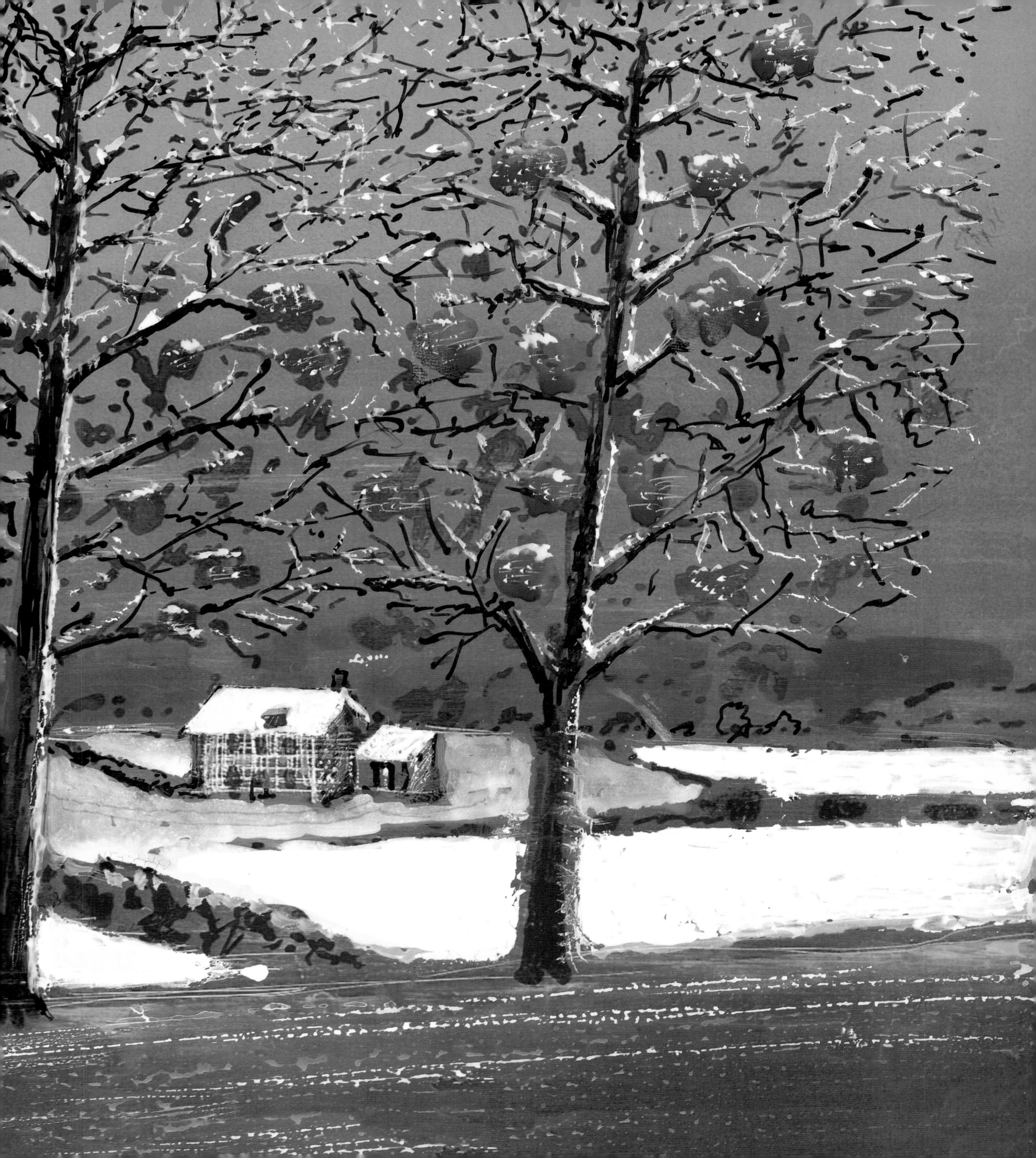

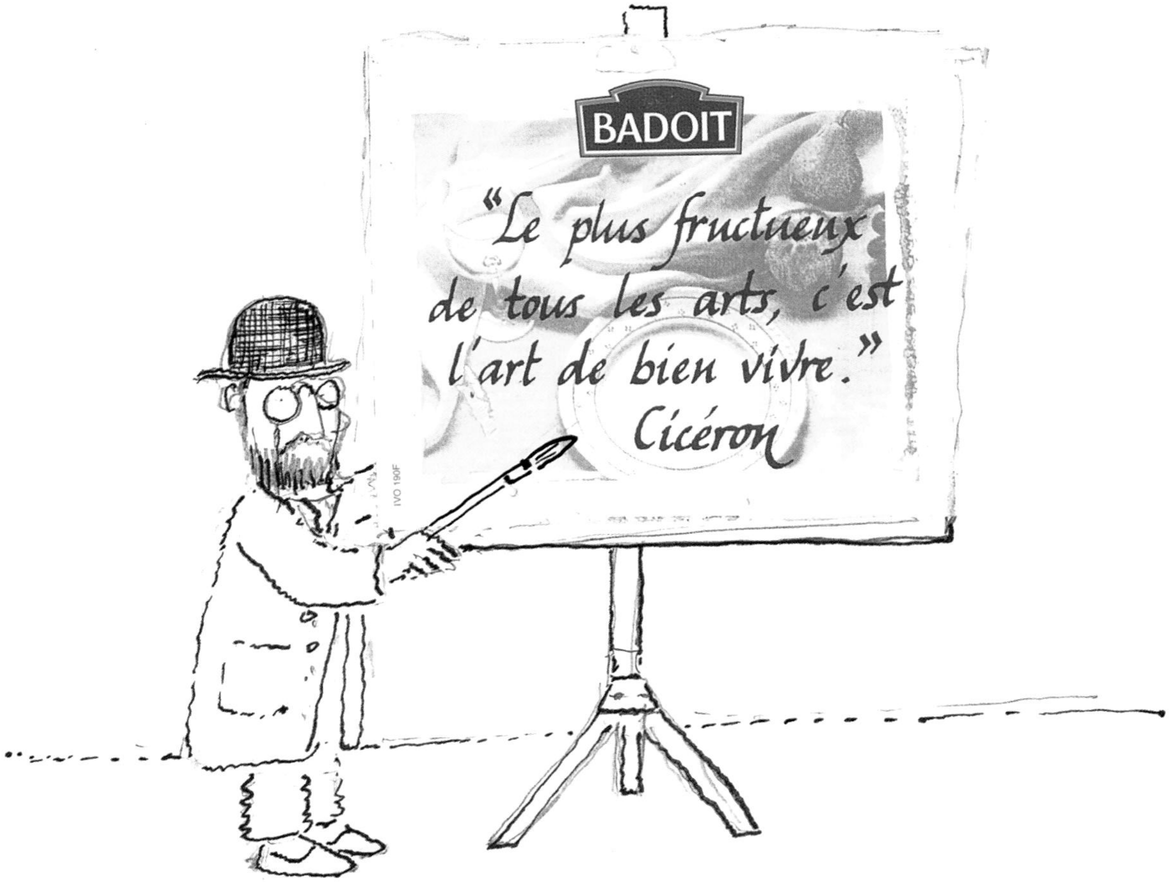
BADOIT
"Le plus fructueux de tous les arts, c'est l'art de bien vivre."
Cicéron

FIN

Acknowledgements & Sources

Page 5: Charles de Gaulle, quoted in Marcel Jullian, *De Gaulle: Pensées, Répliques et Anecdotes*, le cherche midi éditeur, 1994.

Page 6: A contemporary account by Mostrelet, quoted in N. H. Nicolas, *The History of the Battle of Agincourt*, 1827.

Page 14: From Joseph Wechsberg, *Blue Trout and Black Truffles*, Gollancz, 1953.

Page 18: From Brillat-Savarin's *The Physiology of Taste or Meditations on Transcendental Gastronomy*, Peter Davies, 1925.

Page 22: From *Larousse Gastronomique*, quoting Charles Gerard's *L'Ancienne Alsace à Table,* 1862.

Page 30: Frédéric Mistral (1830–1914) was a Provençal poet and founder of Le Félibrige, a mid-nineteenth-century movement for the revival of the Provençal language and culture. This poem was published in 1897.

Page 32: Annie Mignard, quoted in Jacques Wolgensinger, *La 2 CV: Nous Nous Sommes Tant Aimés*, Gallimard, 1995.

Page 39: From Roger-Henri Guerrand, *Les Lieux, Histoire des Commodités*, Editions La Découverte, 1985.

Page 46: *Under the Bridges of Paris* by J. Rodor and Vincent Sotto. Reproduced by kind permission of Editions Paul Beuscher and Editions Musicales Jaques Wolfsohn.

Page 66: Traditional nursery rhyme, from *La Livre des Enfants*, Hachette, 1877.

Page 68: *Mon Légionnaire,* words by Raymond Antoin Marie Roger Asso and music by Marguerite Angelie Monnot © 1937 S.E.M.I., Warner/Chappell Music Ltd., London W6 8BS. Reproduced by kind permission of I.M.P. Ltd.

Page 79: From David Hampshire, *Living and Working in France*, Survival Books, 1993.

Page 94: From Martin Gilbert, *First World War*, Weidenfeld & Nicolson, 1994. Reproduced by kind permission of the publisher and of A. P. Watt Ltd on behalf of Sir Martin Gilbert CBE.

Page 103: From McDowell Bryson and Adele Ziminski, *The Concierge*, John Wiley & Sons, 1938.

Page 105: Quoted in Françoise Teynac, Pierre Nolot and Jean-Denis Vivien, *Le Monde du Papier Peint*, 1981.

Page 112: From *QUID '98*, Editions Robert Laffont.

Page 116: From *Wine Magazine Pocket Buyer's Guide 1996-1997,* Dorling Kindersley, 1996.

Page 121: From Jean Cocteau, *La Difficulté d'être*, Editions du Rocher, 1953.

The Author and Publisher have made every effort to trace the holders of copyright in all extracts included in this book.
If, however, any query should arise, it should be addressed to the publisher.

Designed by Ian Craig with Dave Crook
Research by Rose Foot
Translations by Anne Carter

'The further off from England the nearer is to France ...'

Lewis Carroll, *Alice's Adventures in Wonderland*